A History of Psychology in Letters

A
HISTORY
OF
Psychology
IN
LETTERS

SECOND EDITION

LUDY T. BENJAMIN, JR.

Blackwell
Publishing

BLACKWELL PUBLISHING
350 Main Street, Malden, MA 02148-5020, USA
9600 Garsington Road, Oxford OX4 2DQ, UK
550 Swanston Street, Carlton, Victoria 3053, Australia

First edition published 1993 by Wm. C. Brown Communications, Inc.
Second edition published 2006 by Blackwell Publishing Ltd

1   2006

Library of Congress Cataloging-in-Publication Data

Benjamin, Ludy T., 1945–
A history of psychology in letters / Ludy T. Benjamin, Jr. — 2nd ed.
p.   cm.
Includes bibliographical references and index.
ISBN-13: 978-1-4051-2611-3 (hard cover   :   alk. paper)
ISBN-10: 1-4051-2611-6 (hard cover   :   alk. paper)
ISBN-13: 978-1-4051-2612-0 (pbk.   :   alk. paper)
ISBN-10: 1-4051-2612-4 (pbk.   :   alk. paper)   1. Psychology — History.
2. Psychologists — Correspondence.   I. Title.

BF95.B44 2005
150'.9 — dc22
2005015448

A catalogue record for this title is available from the British Library.

Set in Palatino 10/12^1/$_2$
by SNP Best-set Typesetter Ltd., Hong Kong

For further information on
Blackwell Publishing, visit our website:
www.blackwellpublishing.com

Contents

Preface

This is a book of journeys, a book that will allow you to travel in time and place, peering into the lives, indeed the very souls, of individuals who were important for the development of psychology. You will read their letters, letters that express the gamut of human emotions – happiness, fear, love, anxiety, sadness – letters filled with hope and others with expectations of doom, and letters expressing new ideas and invoking intellectual debates that shaped psychology.

Your travels in this book will take you to Holland in the 1600s to read the letters philosopher John Locke was writing to his cousin, offering his advice on the raising of children. You will be in England in the nineteenth century, reading the letters of philosopher John Stuart Mill on the subjection of women and of naturalist Charles Darwin on the nature of species change. You will join an American graduate student in Leipzig, Germany in the 1880s where he was working in the first psychology laboratory and writing home to his mother and father about his experiences. You will read the letters of philosopher and psychologist William James and thus become involved in séances in the home of a famous Boston medium in the 1880s as she tries to make contact with the spirits of the dead. In nearby Cambridge, Massachusetts you will learn of Mary Whiton Calkins's struggles as a woman to gain access to psychology courses and a doctoral degree at Harvard University. You will be in Vienna and Zurich in 1909 as Sigmund Freud and Carl Jung write to one another about their upcoming trip to the United States, a new and much anticipated experience for both. You will experience some of the horrors of Nazi Germany in the 1930s as Adolf Hitler comes to power. And you will be in New York City on May 17, 1954 for the jubilation experienced by African-American Kenneth Clark when he learns of the Supreme Court's decision to declare school segregation unconstitutional, a decision based, in part, on his psychological research.

The stories in this book are often stories of great drama as revealed through the medium of correspondence. Letters are personal documents, private missives, often intended only for the eyes of the letter's recipient. The most powerful human dramas are perhaps best revealed in the often private thoughts expressed in letters. Historians understand that, and they understand the obligations they have as scholars to treat such personal documents with respect.

The letters reprinted in this book exist because someone had the foresight to preserve them. Typically they are part of some archival collection, made available to scholars for their research. Indeed, they are the raw data of historians. They are what historians use to make sense of the printed record. In the language of a cognitive psychologist, letters can provide the deep structure that makes sense of the surface structure, that is, that gives real meaning to what we know. Such is the richness of letters.

The idea for this book grew out of my undergraduate and graduate courses on the history of psychology, courses I have been teaching for more than 35 years. Almost from the beginning of my teaching, I have used letters of individuals, famous in the history of psychology, to supplement my lectures: letters from Sigmund Freud describing the evolution of his ideas on psychoanalysis, letters from Harry Kirke Wolfe describing his frustrations with establishing his psychology laboratory at the end of the nineteenth century, and letters from Christine Ladd-Franklin as she sought to gain access to an all-male psychology club where she might present some of her research on experimental psychology.

As it became apparent that students liked this kind of material, I added more of it to my courses. I even began using it in my introductory psychology course as a supplement to lectures on conditioning, personality theory, the psychology of gender, and social psychology. Students greatly enjoy these letters and have consistently rated them among the most favorable aspects of my courses. Consequently, this book is intended to make this kind of material readily available to students and instructors. As students, you should find the content of this book easy to read, inherently very interesting, and helpful in your understanding of the development of the discipline of psychology. In the process you will learn some world history and some American history, as these letters are imbedded in the broader historical context of which they are a part.

This book is not a comprehensive history of psychology. It could be used as a stand-alone text in a history of psychology course but would be more valuable reinforced with other reading, such as a history of psychology textbook or original source reading by the individuals treated in this book. This book is also very appropriate for senior capstone courses, honors introductory psychology courses, or graduate pro-seminar courses where the objective is to expose students broadly to multiple areas of psychology. Moreover, this book is appropriate as a supplement to a textbook in introductory psychology courses. See Tables 1 and 2 for a suggested matching of the chapters of this book with those commonly found in texts in the history of psychology and in introductory psychology.

As in the first edition, individuals were selected for this book in order to cover a broad spectrum of psychology both with regard to time period and subfield of psychology. Inclusion does not imply that these persons were the *most* significant figures in psychology. Although that criterion is followed where possible, some

Table 1 Using This Book for a History of Psychology Course

History of Psychology Textbook Chapter		*Corresponding Chapter in This Book*
Historiography	1	Reading Other People's Mail
Empiricism	2	John Locke
	4	John Stuart Mill
Evolution/Functionalist Antecedents	3	Charles Darwin
Wundtian Psychology	5	James McKeen Cattell
Beginnings of American Psychology	6	Harry Kirke Wolfe
	9	Mary Whiton Calkins
Structuralism	10	Edward B. Titchener
Functionalism	5	James McKeen Cattell
	7	William James
	8	Hugo Münsterberg
Behaviorism	12	John B. Watson
Psychoanalysis	11	Sigmund Freud and Carl Jung
Gestalt Psychology	13	Koffka, Köhler, and Lewin
Neobehaviorism	15	B. F. Skinner
Applied Psychology	8	Hugo Münsterberg
	14	Society for the Psychological Study of Social Issues
Psychology in the Post-Schools Era	14	Society for the Psychological Study of Social Issues
	16	Kenneth B. Clark

significant figures were excluded because no letters exist for them, or because it was not possible to secure permission for publication of their letters. Others were excluded because the content too closely paralleled other letters in the collection.

Where possible, only letters have been used. However, in several cases a few journal or notebook entries have been used to supplement the letters. The letters and journal entries in seven of these chapters are now in print, although in four chapters they represent letters that were scattered across several published sources and have been integrated here for our purposes. The inclusion of these letters in this book reflects the permission of literary heirs and publishers as noted in the acknowledgments. For eight chapters, the letters are previously unpublished (except in four cases in the earlier edition of this book). These have been taken from several archival collections, and are reprinted here with permission.

Five of the chapters are new for this edition. One of those – the opening chapter – is a treatment of some of the issues of historiography, that is, the theories and methods of doing history. It is meant to give you a richer understanding of how historians do their work. There are new chapters on the work of Hugo

Table 2 Using This Book for an Introductory Psychology Course

Introductory Psychology Textbook Chapter		Corresponding Chapter in This Book
Introduction (history,	5	Cattell in Leipzig
approaches, methods)	6	Struggles for Laboratories
	10	Titchener's Experimentalists
	12	Behaviorism
	11	Psychoanalysis
	13	Gestalt Psychology
Biological Psychology	3	Darwin and Evolution
Sensation and Perception	7	James and Psychical Research
Learning	12	Watson's Behaviorism
	15	Skinner's Aircrib
Cognition	5	Cattell in Leipzig
	7	James and Psychical Research
	13	Gestalt Psychology
Development	2	Locke as Child Psychologist
	12	Watson's Behaviorism
	15	Skinner's Aircrib
Gender (Sex Roles, Sex Differences)	4	Mill and the Subjection of Women
	9	Calkins' Quest for Graduate Education
	10	Titchener's Experimentalists
Personality	11	Psychoanalysis
Abnormal Psychology and Treatment	11	Psychoanalysis
Social Psychology	13	Founding of SPSSI
	16	Clark and *Brown v. Board*
Forensic Psychology	8	Hugo Münsterberg
	16	Clark and *Brown v. Board*

Münsterberg in applying psychology to the profession of law (forensic psychology) and Kenneth B. Clark on the use of psychological research to battle prejudice and discrimination. Although there were chapters on John B. Watson and B. F. Skinner in the first edition, those chapters are virtually new in this edition. The Skinner chapter contains all new letters, and the Watson chapter uses only a few letters from the first edition. All of the other chapters have been rewritten, some of them extensively so, because of the availability of additional letters, because of the existence of new scholarship since the first edition was published, and because of feedback users of the first edition have given me.

Each chapter typically features the letters of a single individual, although there are several exceptions. The letters for each chapter were selected according to a particular theme, for example, William James's involvement in psychical research, Charles Darwin's delay in publishing his *Origin of Species*, James McKeen Cattell's work as a graduate student in the earliest psychology laboratory in the 1880s, and B. F. Skinner's use of his science to create a better crib for his infant daughter.

Each chapter begins with a brief essay intended to set the stage for the letters. Then the letters are presented in sequence, usually chronologically, with brief footnotes where needed. *The footnotes are important to understanding the meaning of the letters and should be read as part of the text.* The letters are followed by an epilogue, new to this edition, that typically completes the story. Finally, each chapter ends with an annotated list of suggested readings that adds explanation to the chapter's content and serves as a guide to sources of further information for interested readers.

When a book finally emerges from the typed pages of the author, bound in its shiny cover, it exists because of the efforts of many people. I express my gratitude for the very helpful assistance of the staff at Blackwell Publishing, whose talents turned my manuscript into an actual book: Sarah Coleman, Joanna Pyke, Rhonda Pearce, Desirée Zicko, and Ellie Keating. I am especially grateful to my editor, Chris Cardone, whose confidence in me and my ideas for this book have made for a productive and very pleasant working relationship. I also thank Michael Sokal, David Baker, Julie Vargas, and Darryl Bruce who made suggestions to improve several of the chapters in this book. Robin Cautin, Donald Dewsbury, Raymond Fancher, and Kathy Milar reviewed the entire manuscript. They deserve much credit and none of the blame for this final product. I greatly appreciate the scholarship and sense of history they brought to the task. I thank my undergraduate and graduate students of many years whose comments and questions have shaped the content and structure of this book. There are many individuals, libraries, archives, and publishers who allowed me to reprint letters and photographs in this book, and to them I express my considerable appreciation. Finally, I thank my wife, Priscilla, who has worked with me for more than 40 years, and who brings her talents as librarian and educator to all of my writing projects.

To the readers of this book, I confess that as a historian of psychology, some of my most enjoyable professional experiences have occurred in archives reading the personal correspondence of individuals whose ideas shaped my discipline and my world. I hope you enjoy something of that feeling in your reading of the letters in this book. And I hope that you will be stimulated to go beyond the brief stories presented here to learn more about these subjects.

Ludy T. Benjamin, Jr.

Credits

The following sources are credited for granting permission to reprint the letters, photographs, and other copyrighted materials used in this book.

Chapter 2: Letters in the public domain from Rand, B. (Ed.) (1927). *The Correspondence of John Locke and Edward Clarke*. London: Oxford University Press. Photo: Courtesy of the National Library of Medicine.

Chapter 3: Letters reprinted from Burkhardt, F., & Smith, S. (Eds.) (1987, 1991). *The Correspondence of Charles Darwin*, Vols. 3 and 7. New York: Cambridge University Press. Reprinted with the permission of Cambridge University Press. Photo: Courtesy of the Archives of the History of American Psychology, University of Akron.

Chapter 4: Mill letters in the public domain are from Elliot, H. S. R. (Ed.) (1910). *The Letters of John Stuart Mill* (2 vols.). New York: Longmans Green. The Mill–Taylor letters are from Hayek, F. A. (1951). *John Stuart Mill and Harriet Taylor: Their Friendship and Subsequent Marriage*. Chicago: University of Chicago Press. By permission of Bruce Caldwell, General Editor of the Collected Works of F. A. Hayek. Photo of Mill is courtesy of the National Library of Medicine; photo of Taylor is courtesy of the British Library of Political and Economic Sciences.

Chapter 5: Cattell letters are from Sokal, M. M. (Ed.) (1981). *An Education in Psychology: James McKeen Cattell's Journal and Letters from Germany and England, 1880–1888*. Cambridge, MA: MIT Press. Permission granted by M. M. Sokal and MIT Press. Cattell photo courtesy of the Library of Congress; Wundt photo courtesy of the Archives of the History of American Psychology, University of Akron.

Chapter 6: Wolfe letters are from the Harry Kirke Wolfe Papers at the Archives of the History of American Psychology, University of Akron. Permission granted by Harry Kirke Wolfe II in 1991 for all subsequent editions. Photo courtesy of the Archives of the History of American Psychology.

Chapter 7: James letters in the public domain from James, H. (Ed.) (1920). *The Letters of William James* (2 vols.). Boston: Atlantic Monthly Press. Photo: Courtesy of the Archives of the History of American Psychology, University of Akron.

Chapter 8: Letters are from the Hugo Münsterberg Papers in Boston Public Library/Rare Books Department. Reprinted by courtesy of the Trustees of the Boston Public Library. Photo courtesy of the Archives of the History of American Psychology, University of Akron.

Chapter 9: Calkins letters reprinted courtesy of the Wellesley College Archives, Wilma R. Slaight, Archivist. Photo is courtesy of Wellesley College Archives, photo by Partridge.

Chapter 10: Titchener letters are from the Edward Bradford Titchener Papers, #14-23-545. Reprinted by permission of the Division of Rare Books and Manuscript Collections, Cornell University Library. Experimentalists photo and Ladd-Franklin photo are courtesy of the Archives of the History of American Psychology, University of Akron.

Chapter 11: Jung letters to his wife are from Jung, C. G. (1961). *Memories, Dreams, Reflections*. New York: Random House. Permissions granted by Marissa Brunetti, Permissions Manager, Random House, Inc., 1992 for all subsequent editions. Freud–Jung letters are from McGuire, W. (Ed.) (1974). *The Freud/Jung Letters*. Princeton: Princeton University Press. Permission granted by Princeton University Press. Photo courtesy of the Archives of the History of American Psychology, University of Akron.

Chapter 12: Letters from Robert Yerkes are part of the Yerkes Papers at Yale University and are reprinted with permission of the Manuscripts and Archives Department of the Yale University Library. The Watson letters are reprinted by permission of James Scott Watson, grandson of John B. Watson. Photo courtesy of the Archives of the History of American Psychology, University of Akron.

Chapter 13: Wolfgang Köhler letters are reprinted by permission of the American Philosophical Society. Molly Harrower–Kurt Koffka letters are from Harrower, M. (1983). *Kurt Koffka: An Unwitting Self-Portrait*. Gainesville: University Presses of Florida. Permission granted by Molly Harrower in 1991 for all subsequent editions. Kurt Lewin letter is reprinted with permission of his daughter, Miriam Lewin. It was previously published as Everything within me rebels: A letter from Kurt Lewin to Wolfgang Köhler, 1933. *Journal of Social Issues*, 1987, 42 (4), 39–47. Photos courtesy of the Archives of the History of American Psychology, University of Akron.

Chapter 14: Letters from the Society for the Psychological Study of Social Issues (SPSSI) are reprinted with permission of the Archives of the History of American Psychology, University of Akron, David Baker, Director. Krech photo courtesy of the Archives of the History of American Psychology, University of Akron. Stagner photo courtesy of his daughter, Rhea Stagner Das.

Chapter 15: B. F. Skinner letters from the Harvard University Archives are reprinted by permission of Julie Skinner Vargas and the B. F. Skinner Foundation. Photo of Skinner courtesy of the Archives of the History of American

Psychology, University of Akron. Photo of Eve and Debbie Skinner and the baby tender courtesy of the B. F. Skinner Foundation.

Chapter 16: Kenneth B. Clark letters are part of the Kenneth Bancroft Clark Papers in the Library of Congress collections and are in the public domain. Photo courtesy of the Library of Congress.

CHAPTER

Reading Other People's Mail: The Joys of Historical Research

Historians are archival addicts. They do much of their work in archives because archives contain the raw data that historians need to do their research. Historians relish those opportunities – all too rare, it seems – to sit at a table in an archive, poring over the yellowed and fragile papers of important individuals, long dead, whose personal papers have been preserved to allow subsequent generations to examine their lives and times, to know their stories.

There are the letters of Zelda Fitzgerald that tell of her tumultuous life with famed novelist F. Scott Fitzgerald. There are the letters of former Supreme Court justice, Thurgood Marshall, that describe his strategy as a young attorney to end school desegregation in the American South in the landmark case that became known as *Brown v. Board of Education*. There are the journals and letters of Charles Darwin that tell of his five-year voyage around the world on *HMS Beagle* and his subsequent use of the experiences and observations from that historic voyage to construct his theory of evolution by natural selection.

There are literally thousands of collections of letters of individuals, most of them famous, but some not. And in those historically significant collections are millions of stories waiting to be told. Michael Hill (1993) has described the joys of archival research in this way:

> Archival work appears bookish and commonplace to the uninitiated, but this mundane simplicity is deceptive. It bears repeating that events and materials in archives are not always what they seem on the surface. There are perpetual surprises, intrigues, and apprehensions . . . Suffice it to say that it is a rare treat to visit an archive, to hold in one's hand the priceless and irreplaceable documents

Note: Portions of this chapter were adapted from a chapter on historiography in Benjamin (1997).

of our unfolding human drama. Each new box of archival material presents opportunities for discovery as well as obligations to treat the subjects of your . . . research with candor, theoretical sophistication, and a sense of fair play. Each archival visit is a journey into an unknown realm that rewards its visitors with challenging puzzles and unexpected revelations. (pp. 6–7)

"Surprise, intrigue, apprehension, puzzles, and discovery" – those are characteristics of detective work, and historical research is very much about detective work. A historian begins the search for information in a handful of likely locations. That work leads to other searches which lead to still others. Some searches provide valuable information; others turn out to be dead ends. And most searches point the historian to other sources that might be useful. The search is ended when all the leads have been followed, when there seems no place else to look. Then, if there is sufficient information, the story can be told.

Sometimes this historical detective work leads to an unexpected discovery. Consider this example from historian Gloria Urch who was researching the records in a county historical society when she discovered Rachel Harris, who she describes as perhaps the only African-American nurse during the US Civil War era. Urch wrote:

I was looking for something else when I found her photo . . . I held it for a moment and studied it . . . I put her photo aside and continued my research. A few minutes later the photo – which I thought I had placed securely on the shelf above me – fell into my lap, and those same eyes were gazing up into mine again. Before I left that day I made a copy of Rachel's photo and obituary and tucked it away. (cited in Hill, 1993, p. 81)

And because of that photo falling into Gloria Urch's lap, we now know about the life and career of a very interesting person, previously lost to history.

A Secret Society of Psychologists

I have an accidental discovery of my own to describe. I was sitting in the reading room of an archives at the University of Akron one afternoon in 1975, reading the personal correspondence of a psychologist I was researching. On my worktable was a gray cardboard box, made of acid-free material so as to better preserve the unique and valuable documents within. I reached into the box to withdraw a file folder of interest, but when I took it out, I realized that I had withdrawn a second folder, one I had not intended to read. I started to put it back, but the index tab on the folder caught my eye. It read "P.R.T.," and I wondered what those initials stood for. So I opened the folder – a very thin folder with only four one-page letters inside – and I began to read.

The first thing I noticed was the names on the letters, that is, who wrote them and to whom they were addressed. They were well-known psychologists, individuals who had distinguished themselves as among the best in their field, although that could not be said of them in the late 1930s when they wrote the letters in that folder. The second thing I noticed was that none of the letters indicated what the initials PRT stood for, although it was mentioned in all of the letters. Even so, there was enough content in the letters that I had a guess about the PRT – it was some kind of a secret psychological society. Secret societies are always of interest to historians, so I decided to see what I could learn about the PRT.

I began by asking some colleagues who were senior to me in the field of psychology if they had ever heard of an organization called the PRT. No one had. Well that made sense; it was, after all, a secret society. Certainly the psychologists whose names were in the PRT folder should know about it, and some of them were still alive. So I wrote to several of them. In return I received a couple of lengthy letters reminiscing about their attendance at the annual meetings of a group that called itself the Psychological Round Table, or PRT. It was indeed a secret organization, begun in 1936 by six experimental psychologists who were in their late twenties to early thirties. The organizers decided to invite about 30 other young psychologists to a weekend meeting in December.

There were some unusual aspects to this group. They did not consider themselves an organization, and they did not call those who attended members. They were, instead, invitees. They were there by invitation only from the organizing group which called itself the "secret six," and the invitations were issued anew each year. One could not be certain that he would be invited back. "He" is the right pronoun here because the invitees were all males; females were excluded. Further, no invitee could attend once he had reached his fortieth birthday. It was to be a group of young, male experimental psychologists who would meet once each year to discuss the research they were doing or planning.

My correspondents gave me the names of other psychologists they recalled from the meetings, again names that were well known to me, names of the leading researchers in the fields of perception, learning, biopsychology, motivation, and so forth. I wrote to many of those individuals as well who gave me other names and other information about PRT, and I expanded my correspondence network to contain each new set of names. One of these correspondents made an interesting observation in his letter to me. He said that from the language of my letter it appeared that I believed the PRT was a society of the past, whereas it was still an active, albeit secret society.

Most of the people I contacted were pleased to help me in my search for information about the PRT, especially about the early years of the group. They sent me audiotapes, long letters describing their experiences at the meetings, and some individuals even scheduled interviews with me. Yet there were a few who were not encouraging. One psychologist wrote that he saw no purpose in my research and that I should leave the PRT alone and move on to other topics. By that time, however, I knew a great deal about the PRT and about the crucial role it had played in the careers of many of the young psychologists who had attended those meetings. There was too much substance and too much intrigue to just walk away from the story.

I decided that I would focus my research on the PRT from its founding in 1936 through its first 15 years, that is, to around 1951. I chose that narrow time frame because I was most interested in understanding why and how the society started and how it functioned in its earliest years. I knew too that by cutting off my research in 1951 I would not be writing about anyone who might be a member of the contemporary group or even a member in recent years. Over the next year I continued my correspondence and visited a few former PRTers for interviews. I also attended the PRT meeting in Philadelphia in 1976, the fortieth anniversary of the society.

The phone call inviting me to attend the meeting came out of the blue. The caller identified himself and said that he was a member of the current secret six. He said that the group had heard of my research and decided, because it was their fortieth anniversary, to invite me to their meeting to tell them something about the origins of the society. He also told me that not all those of the secret six were in favor of my being invited, and that there would be people at the meeting who might talk to me about not publishing the results of my work. It also was made clear to me that I was a special one-time invitee.

The meeting was an interesting experience. No one was rude to me, although a few thought I should delay publication for a few years. My most salient observation was how similar the structure and purpose of the meeting in 1976 was to the accounts I had been given of the meetings in the late 1930s. The major difference was that women were now invited.

In its first 40 years, the PRT was a virtual *Who's Who* of experimental psychologists, many of whom went on to be elected to the prestigious National Academy of Sciences. For many of the PRTers, the annual meetings of this group were crucial for shaping the research they did. The sheer intellectual talent in the room during the research discussions resulted in studies that were far better designed and more meaningful than they had been in their original form. It was arguably among the most important psychological groups in shaping the course of experimental psychology in the United States in the twentieth century, and at a personal level, it was hugely important for the careers of the young psychologists who had the good fortune to participate (for histories of the PRT, see Benjamin, 1977; Hardcastle, 2000).

My research on the PRT proved to be fascinating work. In the course of it, I was able to correspond and meet with some of the most influential experimental psychologists of the day. The article that was published about the PRT not only informed many psychologists about an important society that they knew nothing about, but it allowed them to understand the influential role such a group could play in the history of American psychology.

The Nature of Archives

Archives are special places. They house collections of unique materials, usually unpublished documents that do not exist anywhere else in the world. Archives may contain the papers of large corporations, like the Coca-Cola Company, or organizations, like the National Association for the Advancement of Colored People (NAACP) or the American Psychological Society, or more commonly, the papers of individuals such as inventors Thomas Edison and Alexander Graham Bell; Susan B. Anthony, one of the founders of the women's suffrage movement; American poet Walt Whitman; anthropologist Margaret Mead; physicist Robert Oppenheimer, who headed the team that developed the atomic bomb; and Gregory Pincus, who developed the birth-control pill. These are among the thousands of collections of personal papers housed in archives, collections that are referred to as **manuscript collections**.

Manuscript collections also exist for many famous psychologists such as William James and B. F. Skinner (at Harvard University), G. Stanley Hall (at Clark University), Mary Whiton Calkins (at Wellesley College), James McKeen Cattell (at the Library of Congress), and Leta Hollingworth and Abraham Maslow (at the University of Akron). In psychology, the papers of individuals consist mostly of correspondence, but may also contain documents such as lecture notes, unpublished manuscripts, research notebooks, lab protocols, clinical records, diaries, grant proposals, and a multitude of other documents such as reprint request cards, college transcripts, birth certificates, newspaper clippings, Christmas cards, hotel receipts, book royalty statements, love letters, and so forth.

These collections are typically housed under some conditions of environmental control – rooms that are controlled for humidity and temperature, documents stored in acid-free boxes – steps that are taken to preserve the life of the documents. Archival staff prepare **finding aids** for historians to use that will give the reader an idea of what the collections contain and where items can be found in the collection. These finding aids are usually in the form of an inventory that details the contents of the collection. Some collections may be quite small, only a file folder or two. Other collections can be massive. For example, the papers of James McKeen Cattell contain more than 50,000 items and occupy more than 120 linear feet of shelf space.

The papers of important psychologists can be found in many places, including the Library of Congress, the Boston Public Library, the American Philosophical Society, and the US National Archives, as well as at universities such as Harvard, Yale, Cornell, Clark, Duke, Nebraska, Stanford, Radcliffe, Michigan, Columbia, and many others. Yet the discipline of psychology is fortunate because it has a national archives, a central repository that collects the papers of individuals and associations important to the history of American psychology. It is called the **Archives of the History of American Psychology** and it is located on the campus of the University of Akron in Akron, Ohio. For short, most historians just call it the "Psychology Archives."

The Archives of the History of American Psychology

The Psychology Archives were founded in 1965 by psychologists John A. Popplestone and Marion White McPherson to preserve the records and materials crucial to the history of psychology. They recognized that too much of the historical record in psychology was being lost and they wanted to create a place where future scholars would find what they needed to tell psychology's important stories. In more than 40 years, the Archives have grown enormously. Today they are the single largest collection of psychology materials anywhere in the world.

There are more than 750 manuscript collections in the Psychology Archives, including the papers of Henry Herbert Goddard, who pioneered intelligence testing in the United States; Leta Hollingworth, who wrote one of the first books on gifted education and did important research debunking some of the dogmas that asserted the biological inferiority of women; Abraham Maslow, one of the principal founders of the humanistic psychology movement; David Shakow, the architect of the scientist-practitioner model of professional training, also known as the Boulder model; Kurt Koffka, one of the founders of Gestalt psychology; Mary Ainsworth, whose model of human attachment is the impetus for much current research in psychology and related fields; and Robert Guthrie, author of *Even the Rat was White*, whose papers contain much of the history of the early African-American psychologists.

These manuscript collections are crucial for historical work. They allow historians to get inside the individual, to understand the motives for research, theory, and behaviors. These documents allow historians to provide a rich account that simply could never be gathered from the published material alone. To tell the history of humanistic psychology means to have access to the letters and journals of Abraham Maslow. To write a history of intelligence testing in America means having access to the personal papers of Henry Herbert Goddard (see Zenderland, 1998). To understand the early research on the psychology of women, one would need to understand Leta Hollingworth as a woman as well as a psychologist. All of those collections, and much more, can be found in the treasure house that is the Psychology Archives.

Although the manuscript collections are the heart and soul of the Psychology Archives, the collections there are much broader than just the personal papers. The Archives also holds the records of more than 50 organizations including the American Group Psychotherapy Association, the American Psychological Society, Psi Chi, the Association of Women in Psychology, the Association of Humanistic Psychology, the Association of Black Psychologists, and the Society for the Psychological Study of Social Issues. These documents are particularly valuable for understanding the role of psychological organizations in the development of the field, but also as a supplement to the records of individuals.

In addition to the manuscript collections and organizational collections, there are more than 6,000 reels of movie film, including some home movies of Sigmund Freud that exist nowhere else in the world. There are films made by Ivan Pavlov and hundreds of classic reels depicting infant and child development. There are more than 15,000 photographs in the collection, many of them unique. There is a wonderful photo from the 1930s of the two great learning theorists who espoused competing theories – Edward Tolman and Clark Hull – sticking their tongues out at each other. There are photos of Wundt's laboratory in Leipzig, photos that were part of the first public display of psychology in the United States at the Chicago World's Fair in 1893, and portrait photos of most of the individuals important to the history of American psychology. (Many of the photos used in this book come from the Akron collection.) There is also an enormous collection of psychological tests dating from the first such tests to more modern personality and intelligence tests. Further, there is a marvelous collection of more than 1,000 rare pieces of psychological apparatus. Among those instruments is Stanley Milgram's famous "shock" machine, used in his studies on obedience. The teaching machine that B. F. Skinner made for his daughter in the 1950s is there, as well as one of the air-cribs that Skinner invented to ease the burdens of infant care and provide a healthier and safer environment for the baby. There are also many brass and glass instruments from the early psychology laboratories of the 1880s.

The Psychology Archives in Akron are indeed a special place. Psychologist David Baker is the current Director. Scholars visit there each year in hopes they will find what they need to answer their research questions. They often find those answers and a great deal more. If you cannot get to Akron but want to explore some of the collections online, then visit the website of the Archives of the History of American Psychology (http://www3.uakron.edu/AHAP/).

Psychology's Interest in Its History

Psychology has a long-standing interest in its history. History of psychology courses have been taught at least since the 1920s, and today such courses are common offerings in both the undergraduate and graduate curricula in psychology. Often undergraduate students are required to take a course in the history of psychology as part of the requirements for a major in psychology. And many doctoral students in clinical, counseling, and school psychology are required to take such a course because the American Psychological Association, which accredits such programs, requires that students have some education in the history of psychology. So why do psychologists seem to be so interested in the history of their field?

It could be that psychology and history are not all that different in their aims. Consider the following quotations from two eminent British historians. Robin

Collingwood (1946) wrote that the "proper object of historical study . . . is the human mind, or more properly the activities of the human mind" (p. 215). And Edward Carr (1961) argued that "the historian is not really interested in the unique, but what is general in the unique" and that "the study of history is a study of causes . . . the historian . . . continually asks the question: Why?" (pp. 80, 113). Thus, according to Collingwood and Carr, to study history is to study the human mind, to be able to generalize beyond the characteristics of a single individual or single event to other individuals and other events, and to be able to answer the "why" of human behavior, explaining people's behaviors in terms of motive, personality, past experience, social situation, expectations, economic circumstances, biases, and so forth. Like psychologists, historians want to go beyond mere description of behavior and provide a meaningful explanation for events and personal actions.

Historians do not do experimental work, but their work is empirical. They approach their work in the same way that psychologists do, by asking questions, by posing hypotheses. And then they seek to gather evidence that would confirm or disconfirm those hypotheses. Thus the intellectual pursuits of the historian and the psychologist are not really very different. And so as psychologists, or students of psychology, we are not moving very far from our own field of interest when we study the history of psychology.

What is Historiography?

Historiography refers to the philosophy and methods of doing history. In psychology, research is guided by diverse philosophies and methods as well. A behaviorist, for example, has certain assumptions about the influence of previous experience, in terms of a history of punishment and reinforcement, on current behavior. And the methods of study take those assumptions into account in the design and conduct of experiments. A psychoanalytic psychologist, on the other hand, has a very different philosophy and methodology in investigating the questions of interest, for example, believing in the influence of unconscious motives and using such techniques as free association or analysis of latent dream content to understand those motives. Historical research is guided in the same way. Historians bring particular philosophical orientations to their work, and those philosophies guide both their strategies for collecting evidence and their interpretation of that evidence.

Objectivity in Historical Research

Psychologists have to work exceptionally hard to eliminate bias from their research. In truth they never eliminate it entirely, but through a variety of sampling, control, and measurement procedures, they can substantially reduce it. Historians too worry about objectivity in their work. Like psychologists, they bring to their research a bundle of prejudices, preconceptions, penchants, premises, predilections, predispositions, and philosophical orientations. Such personal baggage does not mean that they abandon all hope for objectivity, nor does it mean that their histories are hopelessly flawed. Good historians are aware of their biases. They use their understanding of them to search for evidence in places where they might not otherwise look, or they ask questions that they would not ordinarily ask. And when this searching and questioning causes them to confront facts contrary to their own views, they must deal with those facts as they would with facts that are more consistent with their biases.

Bias in history begins at the beginning: "The historian displays a bias through the mere choice of a subject"(Gilderhus, 1992, p. 80). There are an infinite number of historical subjects to pursue. The historian selects from among those, often choosing one of paramount personal interest. The search within that subject begins with a question or questions that the historian hopes to answer, and the historian likely begins with some definite ideas about the answers to those questions.

Biases exist in many other ways as well, including the historical data. For example, manuscript collections are always selective and incomplete. They contain the documents that someone decided were worth saving, and they are devoid of those documents that were discarded or lost for a host of reasons, perhaps known only to the discarder.

One form of bias that is especially intrusive and problematic is called **presentism** or Whig history (Butterfield, 1931) or present-mindedness (Commager, 1965). Presentists seek to interpret the past in terms of the attitudes and values of the present. Such an error of interpretation is absolutely taboo in good histories. It is certainly among the worst kinds of historical bias. Presentists also seek to interpret the past in a way that emphasizes the progress of the past as a validation for some aspects of the present. Avoiding this error of interpretation calls for a different approach that Stocking (1965) has labeled **historicism**, which is an understanding of the past in its own context and for its own sake. Such an approach requires historians to immerse themselves in the context of the times they are studying.

These are just some of the hurdles that the historian faces in striving for objectivity. They are not described here to suggest that the historian's task is a hopeless one; instead, they are meant to show the forces against which historians must struggle in order to write good history. Daniels (1981) wrote: "The requirements of reasonable objectivity do not rule out individual interpretation and judgment . . . there is no final truth in matters of historical interpretation and explanation" (p. 92). There is only the expectation that the story will be as objective as possible.

Historical Facts and Questions

Psychologists can study the present. In fact they can create the present in their research. Through their experiments, they can produce conditions they hope will allow them to explain cause-and-effect relationships. In contrast, historians study the past. They cannot manipulate the past, but through their research, they can attempt to reconstruct it. They typically begin by collecting facts. What can be found in terms of remnants of the past? Some traces of the past must exist or the historical work cannot be done. Once the facts are accumulated, the historian tries to make sense of them collectively. How do they fit together? Which ones do not seem to fit and why? What facts seem to be missing?

In this initial phase of the historical work, the historian seeks to answer questions like: What happened? When did it happen? Who was involved? We know, for example, that Wilhelm Wundt began doing laboratory work in psychology at the University of Leipzig in the late 1870s. What ideas or theories led to the founding of that lab? How supportive was the university? What was the nature of that lab? What was the physical space like? What kinds of apparatus did he have? Where did the students come from? Did students work with him in his research? What kinds of studies were done in the lab? Who were the subjects (usually called observers) in these experiments? These questions are largely descriptive and are where the historian would begin to tell the story of Wundt's laboratory.

Searching the published literature (articles and books) might turn up some accounts describing the Leipzig laboratory. Wundt's journal – *Philosophsiche Studien* – contained many articles based on experiments done in his laboratory and would be an excellent source for understanding the kinds of research studies undertaken. The issues of that journal would thus give the names of many of his doctoral students. From those names, one could search to see if manuscript collections might exist in any archives for those students. It turns out that the Library of Congress holds the papers of James McKeen Cattell, who was the first American student to graduate in psychology with Wundt, finishing in 1886. In Cattell's papers is a large collection of letters he wrote to his parents from Leipzig describing his work in Wundt's laboratory and his many impressions of Wundt (see Sokal, 1981). In fact much has been written about Wundt's laboratory based on a rich assortment of documents that found their way into archives in Europe, Canada, and the United States. As a result we have diagrams and drawings of the lab rooms, several lengthy descriptions of the Leipzig lab from different periods of Wundt's tenure there, rich descriptions of the work done there, photographs of Wundt and some of the equipment from his lab, and many first-person accounts of students' experiences at Leipzig and their impressions of Wundt. Without archives, it is likely that few of those records would have survived.

External Histories

Historians want to go beyond description and to be able to interpret the Leipzig events in a broader context of German culture and science; in light of the evolution of a new science; in terms of the personalities involved in the laboratory, the university, and the broader scientific community; and in terms of the political, social, and economic issues of the times. To do this requires that the historian go beyond just the history of Wundt and his laboratory and understand the broader context of which the laboratory was a part. Historians refer to such contextualized histories as **external histories** as opposed to **internal histories** that focus narrowly on the events, in this case, within the discipline (see Furumoto, 1989; Hilgard, Leary, & McGuire, 1991). For example, one could research and write a history of American psychology's concerns with the concept of race by relying on the books and articles in psychology that deal with that subject. Such a history would be an internal history and, as such, devoid of the richness that comes from an externalist account. An external history of the same topic would begin with a recognition that psychology's views of race did not exist in a vacuum. Rather they were shaped by a number of socio-politico-cultural forces outside the field of psychology. An external history of American psychology's changing concerns with the concept of race would draw on the information within the discipline and outside the discipline. It would go beyond the published literature and delve into the relevant archival collections of individuals and organizations that were part of that history. It would provide the richest of historical accounts. It would provide a foundation for interpretation.

The great historians, according to Henry Steele Commager (1965), have been the interpreters. And among those, the greatest have been those with exceptional "judgment, originality, imagination, and art" (p. 6). Historian Arthur Schlesinger, Jr. (1963) has argued that it is in the interpretation that history as art is evidenced:

. all the elements of artistic form are as organic in historical as in any other kind of literary composition. There are limits on the historian's capacity for invention, but there need be none on his capacity for insight. Written history, after all, is the application of an aesthetic vision to a welter of facts; and both the weight and vitality of a historical work depend on the quality of vision. (p. 36)

Reading Other People's Mail

This opening chapter was written to provide you with a rudimentary understanding of the nature of historical research, and especially the value of archival collections for doing that kind of work. What follows in the pages of this book is an opportunity for you to "travel" to a number of archives to read the personal correspondence of individuals who had great influence on the field of psychology or whose personal stories are important for understanding psychology's past.

The chapters that follow are often stories of great drama. The letters in each chapter revolve around a central story. They tell of Jewish psychologists forced to flee Germany in the 1930s as the horrors of the Nazi regime became a reality. They tell of Sigmund Freud's only visit to America and the impact his visit had on the development of psychoanalysis in the United States. They tell of William James's work with Mrs Piper, a medium, who James believed could communicate with the dead, and the anger and embarrassment his colleagues in psychology felt over his involvement in such pseudopsychology while they were busily trying to establish psychology as a legitimate science. They tell of John Stuart Mill's passionate love affair with a married woman in Victorian England and the influence of their relationship on his writings.

In the chapters that follow you will read some of the letters that James McKeen Cattell wrote to his mother and father in the 1880s when he was a graduate student in the first psychology laboratory in the world, Wundt's Leipzig lab. Those letters are housed in the Manuscript Division of the Library of Congress in Washington, DC.

You will read from the letters of Mary Whiton Calkins who, in the 1890s, attended classes at Harvard University with William James and others, completing all of the requirements for a doctorate in psychology but being denied the degree because, as a woman, she could not be officially enrolled. Those letters are from the Calkins Papers in the archives at Wellesley College where Calkins spent her career as a faculty member.

You will read letters from the records of the Society for the Psychological Study of Social Issues (SPSSI), an organization formed in 1936 by a small group of American psychologists who felt passionately that psychological science ought to be used to solve some of the social problems that faced the world. This group was instrumental in providing crucial psychological evidence that was a factor in the landmark 1954 Supreme Court decision to end segregated schools. The SPSSI Papers are part of the vast collections of the Archives of the History of American Psychology at the University of Akron.

In the archives of Cambridge University in England is a large collection of letters to and from Charles Darwin. Those letters are currently being published, and when the project is completed they will occupy 30 volumes. The letters that appear in this book all deal with the events immediately prior to the publication of his most famous book, *On the Origin of Species* (1859), and they tell of the personal crisis that almost cost Darwin the credit for his monumentally important theory of species change.

You will also read letters from the Harvard University Archives, from the B. F. Skinner Papers that are housed there, that tell the story of Skinner's invention of a new kind of crib that he called the baby tender. The device, although a success for those parents and infants who used it, proved to be a public relations nightmare, including stories of the suicide of Skinner's daughter who spent part of her infancy in what others called Skinner's "baby box." His daughter grew to be a healthy, happy, and successful person, but that fact has often been lost in the many myths about her "madness" and "death."

Reading these chapters will give you a sense of the fascination that historians feel in their research when they work with personal letters. As noted in an earlier quotation, "it is a rare treat to visit an archive, to hold in one's hand the priceless and irreplaceable documents of our unfolding human drama" (Hill, 1993, p. 6). There is much human emotion in reading other people's mail. There is a vicarious sharing of life experiences with the letter writer. There is the joy of discovery, the thrill of learning, and the obligations of historical scholarship. It is hoped that you will experience some of those emotions as you travel back in time to read first-hand the personal letters of the individuals featured in this book.

2

CHAPTER

John Locke
(National Library of Medicine)

John Locke as Child Psychologist

For more than twenty years, John Locke (1632–1704) studied the question of how the mind works. During that time he wrote and rewrote his most important contribution to psychology, finally published in 1690 as *An Essay Concerning Human Understanding*. This book began a philosophical movement, important to the emergence of scientific psychology, known as British empiricism, which rejected the idea of innate knowledge and argued instead that all ideas were derived from experience. Locke's significance for modern psychology is, according to Edna Heidbreder (1933), that he

> stands at the starting-point of two movements. One, a line of critical inquiry carried on by Berkeley, Hume, and Kant, led to the destruction of the old rational psychology, that system of thought which, claiming a knowledge of the soul that was based on intuition and deduction, held that its knowledge was demonstrable as absolutely valid. The other was a more positive movement, which, expressing itself partly in the common-sense philosophy of the Scottish school, and partly in the teachings of the British associationists, led to a psychology that, though it was empirical as opposed to rational, stopped just short of becoming experimental. (pp. 40–41)

Resurrecting Aristotle's notion of *tabula rasa*, Locke described how experience would write on the blank slate, thus filling the mind with its ideas. Locke argued that although all ideas were derived from experience, they were not necessarily derived from direct sensory experience. Some ideas were the products of reflection, what Locke called the internal operations of the mind. For Locke, there were two kinds of ideas. Simple ideas could be the result of direct sensory experience or reflection. Yet complex ideas could only come from reflection. Earlier philosophers had focused attention largely on the content of the mind – *what* the mind knows. Although he recognized the importance of studying content, he was more interested in *how* the mind knows, that is, how ideas, both simple and complex, were acquired.

As a boy, Locke was educated at home by his father, a country attorney. At the age of 20 he went to Oxford University where he studied medicine, philosophy, and meteorology, earning his baccalaureate (1656) and master's (1658) degrees. Although Locke never practiced as a physician, he had completed his medical studies. He remained at Oxford off and on for the next 25 years until he was expelled in 1684 by an order of King Charles II. Locke was in hiding in Holland at the time of the royal order, because he was suspected of being part of a plot against the King. Although he probably was not part of the movement against Charles II, he may have played a political role in the bloodless revolution of 1688 that placed William of Orange on the throne (Cranston, 1957).

After the revolution, Locke was able to return to England, where he spent the last 15 years of his life in government work and writing. Indeed, these were very productive years for Locke as an author, who had actually published very little before this time. This was partly due to political fears about the fate of his manuscripts should he try to publish them. Certainly the social and political themes surrounding the revolution shaped many of his ideas (see Moore-Russell, 1978). In addition to the *Essay* which appeared in 1690, he also published his most famous political work, *Two Treatises on Government*, in that same year. Parts of that document would later be incorporated into the American Declaration of Independence. His long-time interests in religious tolerance led to two other important works being published during this time: *Letters Concerning Toleration* (1689–92) and *The Reasonableness of Christianity* (1695).

One of Locke's lesser-known works began as a series of letters to Edward and Mary Clarke, written when he was in self-exile in Holland. Edward Clarke (1649–1710) was an attorney who owned an estate near Somerset, England, where Locke's family lived. Clarke had married Locke's cousin, Mary Jepp (?–1705) in 1675. Edward Clarke and Locke became very close friends and Locke took considerable interest in the Clarke children, especially the oldest boy, Edward (referred to as "master" in most letters), and one of the two daughters, Elizabeth, whom he affectionately called his "mistress."

When the Clarkes asked for advice on educating their son, Locke was pleased to oblige, often writing lengthy epistles. He began writing to them in 1684 and continued, with irregular additions, until 1691. He saved drafts of these and used them to write *Some Thoughts Concerning Education*, which was published in July, 1693. This book illustrates Locke's belief in environment as a critical determinant of individual potential, an idea that was consistent with the rest of his empiricist psychology.

The letters reprinted in this chapter are all from Locke to Edward Clarke, with one exception, that being a single letter to his cousin, Mary Clarke. The later letters (not reprinted here) deal with the education of young Edward, for example, how to teach mathematical concepts, and when Latin and Greek should be learned. However, the earlier letters focus more on general advice about child rearing. The opening letter offers advice on the importance of good physical health, whereas the final letter provides Locke's views on poetry, music, dance, and the importance of virtue. In between are some delightful accounts on how to raise boys versus girls, advice drawing both on Locke's medical training and his empiricist views of psychology. He reminds the Clarkes that it is advice from a life-long bachelor with no children of his own. Surely Locke was not the first, nor will he be the last, child expert without children.

In reading these letters you may find the language awkward at first. But after a little reading you should get the rhythm of Locke's prose and more easily discern his meaning. Although the language may be a bit strange to twenty-first-century ears, it is important to remember that these letters were written more than 320 years ago. Languages evolve, and in some sense it is rather remarkable, given such a long time span, that these letters can be so readily understood.

The Letters

John Locke to Edward Clarke, July 19, 1684

... 1 *Mens sana in corpore sano* [a sound mind in a sound body] is a short but full description of the most desirable state we are capable of in this life. He who has these two has little more to wish; and he that wants either of them will be but little the better for anything else. Men's happiness or misery is for the most part of their own making. He whose mind directs not wisely will never take the right way; and he whose body fails his mind will never be able to march in it. I confess there are some men's constitutions of body and mind so vigorous, and well framed by nature, that they shift pretty well without much assistance from others; by the strength of their natural genius, they are, from their cradles, carried towards what is excellent. But those examples are but few, and I think I may say of all the men we meet with, nine parts of ten, or perhaps ninety-nine of one hundred, are what they are, good or evil, useful or not, by their education. 'Tis that which makes the great difference in mankind. The little and almost insensible impressions, on our tender infancies, have very important and lasting influences; and there it is, as in the fountains of some rivers, where a gentle application of the hand turns the

flexible waters into channels that make them take quite contrary courses; and by
this little impression given them at the source they come to arrive at places quite
distant and opposite.

2   I imagine the minds of children are as easily turned this or that way as water
itself; and I fortify against the silly opinions and discourses of others.

3   The first thing then to be had a care of is, that he be not too warmly clad or
covered in winter or summer. The face is no less tender than any other part of the
body when we are born. 'Tis use alone hardens it, and makes it more able to
endure the cold . . .

4   I think it would also be of great advantage to have his feet washed every night
in cold water, and to have his shoes so made that they may leak and let in water
whenever he treads on any marshy place. Here, I imagine, I shall have both Mistress and maids about my ears. One perhaps will think it too filthy, and the other
too much pains to make his stockings clean. But yet truth will have it, that his
health is much more worth than all this little ado, and ten times as much more.
Must my young master never dirty his shoes? and if it cost the wash of a pair of
stockings or two more in a week the trouble may be borne and the thing be worth
it, if we consider how mischievous and mortal a thing taking wet in the feet
proves often to those who have been bred nicely. When a fever or consumption
follows from just an accident, for wet in the feet will sometimes happen, then will
he wish he had, with the poor people's children, gone barefoot, and so 'scaped
the danger and perhaps death which a little unhappy moisture in his feet hath
brought upon him; whilst the hardened poor man's son, reconciled by custom to
wet in his feet by that means, suffers no more by it than if his hands were put in
water. And what is it, I pray, that makes this great difference between the hands
and the feet, but only custom? And I doubt not, but if a man from his cradle had
been always used to go barefoot, but to have his hands close wrapped up constantly in thick mittens and handshoes [as the Dutch call gloves] over them; I
doubt not, I say, but such a custom would make taking wet in the hands as dangerous to him, as now taking wet in their feet is to a great many others. To prevent
this, I would I say have him wear leaking shoes, and his feet washed every night
in cold water, both for health and cleanliness sake. But begin first in the spring
with luke warm water, and so colder and colder every night till in a few days
you come to perfectly cold water, and so continue. For it is to be observed in this
and all other alterations from our ordinary way of living, the change must be
made by gentle and insensible degrees; and so we may bring our bodies to any
thing without pain and without danger.

John Locke to Edward Clarke, January 1, 1685

   . . . I am glad that you approve of my . . . method for keeping your son from
being costive without giving him physic. I believe you will find it effectual, and I

think it a thing of great moment for his health, and therefore I recommend it to you for your son's practice as well as [your own]. Though I [write for] the young sprout, yet I would have the old stock also [equally improved]. [I find] the penny post way has lost several of my letters which came safe to London. For though I care not who sees what I write, yet I would have those also see to whom I write it, specially what cost me some pains in writing, and I think may be of some use to those I send it, as I hope this discourse concerning your son will be, or else I would not give you the trouble to read nor myself to write so much. If your Lady approve of it, when she sees it I will then obey her commands in reference to her daughters, wherein there will be some though no great difference, for making a little allowance for beauty and some few other considerations of the s[ex], the manner of breeding of boys and girls especially in their younger years, I imagine should be the same. But if my way satisfy her concerning my young master, I doubt not but I shall also be thought by her no less careful of my pretty little mistress. But pray let me hear from you concerning this matter, as soon as you can, for if my rules have any advantages in them . . . they . . . are to be put in practice as soon as children begin to speak, and therefore no time is to be lost.

John Locke to Mary Clarke, January 28–February 7, 1685

. . . To make some acknowledgment, 'tis fit I acquit myself of my promise to you in reference to my little mistress . . . [and] you will think that speaking with [the sincere] affection I have for the softer sex I shall not think of any rougher usage than only what [her sex] requires. Since therefore I acknowledge no difference of sex in your mind relating . . . to truth, virtue and obedience, I think well to have no thing altered in it from what is [writ for the son]. And since I should rather desire in my wife a healthy constitution, a stomach able to digest ordinary food, and a body that could endure upon occasion both wind and sun, rather than a puling, weak, sickly wretch, that every breath of wind or least hardship puts in danger, I think the meat, drink and lodging and clothing should be ordered after the same manner for the girls as for the boys. There is only one or two things whereof I think distinct consideration is to be had. You know my opinion is that the boys should be much abroad in the air at all times and in all weathers, and if they play in the sun and in the wind without hats and gloves so much the better. But since in your girls care is to be taken too of their beauty as much as health will permit, this in them must have some restriction, the more they exercise and the more they are in the air the better health they will have, that I am sure; but yet 'tis fit their tender skins should be fenced against the busy sunbeams, especially when they are very hot and piercing: to avoid this and yet to give them exercise in the air, some little shady grove near the house would be convenient for them to play in, and a large airy room in ill weather: and if all the year you make them rise as soon as it is light and walk a mile or two and play abroad before sun-rising, you will by that custom obtain more good effects than one; and it will make them not only fresh and healthy, but good housewives too. But that they may have sleep enough, which whilst they are young must not be scanty, they must be early to bed too.

Another thing is, that of washing their feet every night in cold water and exposing them to the wet in the day. Though my reason is satisfied that it is both the healthiest and safest way, yet since it is not fit that girls should be dabbling in water as your boys will be, and since perhaps it will be thought both an odd and new thing, I cannot tell how to enjoin it. This I am sure I have seen many a little healthy [child do in] winter, and I think that had I a daughter I should order water to be put in her [shoes] when she put them on, and have her feet well washed in cold water. But this must not be begun at any time of the year, but in the hot weather in May, and then begin only with one dabble the first morning, two the next, and so on . . .

Their heads, I think, should never be covered, nor their necks within doors, and when they go abroad the covering of these should be more against the sun then the cold. And herein you may take notice how much it is use that makes us either tender or hardy, for there is scarce a young lady so weak and tender who will not go bare in her neck without suffering any harm at a season when if a hardy strong man not used to it should imitate her it would be intolerable to him, and he would be sure to get a cold if not a fever.

Girls should have a dancing master at home early: it gives them fashion and easy comely motion betimes which is very convenient, and they, usually staying at home with their mothers, do not lose it again, whereas the boys commonly going to school, they lose what they learn of a dancing master at home amongst their ill-fashioned schoolfellows, which makes it often less necessary because less useful for the boys to learn to dance at home when little: though if they were always to play at home in good company I should advise it for them too. If the girls are also by nature very bashful, it would be good that they should go also to dance publicly in the dancing schools when little till their sheepishness were cured; but too much of the public schools may not perhaps do well, for of the two, too much shamefacedness better becomes a girl than too much confidence, but having more admired than considered your sex I may perhaps be out in these matters, which you must pardon me.

This is all I can think of at present, wherein the treatment of your girls should be different from that I have proposed for the boys. Only I think the father [ought] to strike very seldom, if at all to chide his daughters. Their governing and correcting, I think, properly belongs to the mother . . .

John Locke to Edward Clarke, September 1, 1685

Your son's temper by the account you give of it is I find not only such as I guessed it would be, but such as one would wish, and the qualities you already observe in him require nothing but right management whereby to be made very useful.

Curiosity in children is but an appetite after knowledge, and therefore ought to be encouraged in them, not only as a good sign, but as the great instrument nature has provided, to remove that ignorance they brought into the world with them, and which without this busy inquisitiveness would make them dull and useless creatures. The ways to encourage and keep it active and vigorous are, I suppose, these following:

1st. Not to check or discountenance any inquiries he may make, or suffer them to be laughed at; but to answer all his questions and explain matters he desires to know, so as to make them as much intelligible to him, as suits the capacity of his age and knowledge. But confound not his understanding with explications or notions that are above it, or with the variety or number of things that are not to his present purpose. Mark what it is he aims at in the question, and when you have informed and satisfied him in that, you shall see how his thoughts will proceed on to other things, and how by fit answers to his enquiries he may be led on farther than perhaps you could imagine. For knowledge to the understanding is as acceptable as light to the eyes; and children are pleased and delighted with it exceedingly, especially if they see that their enquiries are regarded, and that their desire of knowing is encouraged and commended. And I doubt not but one great reason why many children abandon themselves wholly to silly play, and spend all their time in trifling, is, because they have found their curiosity baulked and their enquiries neglected. But had they been treated with more kindness and respect, and their questions answered as they should to their satisfaction, I doubt not but they would have taken more pleasure in learning several things, and improving their knowledge, wherein there would be still newness and variety, which they delight in than in returning over and over to the same playthings.

2nd. To this serious answering their questions, and informing their understandings in what they desire, as if it were a matter that needed it, should be added some ways of commendation. Let others whom they esteem be told before their faces of the knowledge they have in such and such things; and since we are all even from our cradles vain, and proud creatures, let their vanity be flattered with things that will do them good; and let their pride set them to work on something which may turn to their advantage. Upon this ground you shall find that there can not be a greater spur to anything you would have your son learn or know himself, than to set him upon teaching it his sisters.

3rd. As children's enquiries are not to be slighted, so also great care is to be taken, that they never receive deceitful and eluding answers. They easily perceive when they are slighted or deceived, and quickly learn the trick of neglect, dissimulation, and falsehood which they observe others to make use of. We are not to entrench upon truth in our conversation, but least of all with children. Since if we play false with them, we not only deceive their expectation, and hinder their knowledge, but corrupt their innocence, and teach them the worst of vices. They are travelers

newly arrived in a strange country of which they know very little: we should therefore make conscience not to mislead them. And though their questions seem sometimes not very material, yet they should be seriously answered; for however they
may appear to us to whom they are long since known, enquiries not worth the
making, they are of moment to them who are wholly ignorant. Children are
strangers to all we are acquainted with, and all the things they meet with are at first
unknown to them, as they were to us; and happy are they who meet with kind
people, that will comply with their ignorance, and help them to get out of it . . .

4th. Perhaps it may not, however, be amiss to exercise their curiosity concerning strange and new things in their way, on purpose that they may enquire and
be busy to inform themselves about them; and if by chance their curiosity leads
them to ask what they should not know, it is a great deal better to tell them plainly,
that it is a thing that belongs not to them to know, than to pop them off with a
falsehood, or a frivolous answer . . .

One thing I have observed in children, that when they have got possession of
any poor creature, they are apt to use it ill, and they often torment and treat ill
very young birds, butterflies, and such other poor things, which they got into their
power, and that with a seeming kind of pleasure. This, I think, should be watched
in them, and if they incline to any such cruelty they should be taught the contrary
usage. For the custom of tormenting and killing of beasts will by degrees harden
their minds even towards men, and they who accustom themselves to delight in
the suffering and destruction of inferior creatures, will not be apt to be very com-
passionate or benign to those of their own kind. Our law takes notice of this in
the exclusion of butchers from juries of life and death. Children, then, should be
taught from the beginning not to destroy any living creature unless it be for the
preservation and advantage of some other that is nobler. And, indeed, if the
preservation of all mankind as much as in him lies, were the persuasion of every
one, as it is indeed the true principle of religion, politics and morality, the world
would be much quieter and better natured than it is . . .

John Locke to Edward Clarke, February 8, 1686

. . . Your children have had such good success in that plain way, that if reason
had nothing to say for it, yet our own experience ought to make you exactly follow
it. I had within this very month occasion to observe a child under an year [so often
given] sugar candy to please him, that at last nothing but what was very sweet
[was desired by him] . . . [There was] nothing but perpetual crying and bawling,
and the child from his hunger and craving after sweet things was perpetually
uneasy. I told his mother she giving him those licorish things to quiet him when
he cried was but the way to increase it [un]less she could resolve to feed him
wholly with them, which would certainly destroy his health; and that the only
cure was to endure for a day or two his crying without appeasing [his desires.

After] some time, finding that ill increased by those ways that at present [permitted the] child [to gratify his] appetite, she resolved to take away from him at once all sweet things, and when he cried [to give him] nothing but what she judged wholesomest and best for his health. This made him impatient the first day, but when he saw he got not his desire by crying he left it off, and in two or three days, he, that before could not be quieted, when he saw either sugar, or sugar candy, or apples until they were given to him, so that they were fain carefully to hide them from him, was brought by this means, when apples or the like which he loved came in his way, only to show his desire of them, but not to cry for them, and this in a child wanting one or two of twelve months old. Which example confirms me in the opinion you know I am of, that children find the success of their crying, and accordingly make use of it to have their will sooner than is usually imagined; and that they should be accustomed very early not to have their desires [always granted], and that they should not be indulged in the things they cry for, where they were not absolutely necessary.

You will find one part of this paper filled with the continuation of my opinion in reference to your son. It breaks off abruptly for want of room. But the remainder you shall have whenever you desire it; and when I know how far our rules have been put in practice, and with what success, or what difficulties have hindered. I shall in my next also add what may be convenient, or upon trial you have found deficient, or perhaps impracticable in what I have formerly writ on this occasion. For it often happens that the speculations which please a contemplative man in his study are not so easy to be put in use out of it. If also his particular temper or inclination require any further peculiar application, that also shall be considered. In the meantime I wish you, your Lady, and little ones perfect health and happiness . . .

John Locke to Edward Clarke, February–March 1686

. . . We have also agreed that the books he should at first read should be pleasant, easy and suited to his capacity, and yet not such as should fill his head with perfectly useless trumpery, or lay the principles of vice or folly. And therefore I made choice of *Aesop's Fables*, which being stories apt to delight and entertain a child, may yet afford useful reflections to a grown man; and if his memory retain them all his life after, he will not repent to find them amongst his most manly thoughts and serious business. And if you and others talk with him sometimes about these fables, it will be an encouragement to his reading them.

. . . Poetry and gaming, which usually go together, are alike in this too, that they seldom have any advantage, but to those who have nothing else to live on. Men of estates almost constantly go away losers . . . If, therefore you would not have your son . . . waste his time and estate to divert others, and [view with contempt] the dirty acres left him by his ancestors, I do not think you will much care he should be a poet, or that his schoolmaster should enter him in versifying.

. . . Music I find by some mightily valued, but it wastes so much of one's time to gain but a moderate skill in it, and engages in such odd company, that I think it much better spared. And among all those things that ever come into the list of accomplishments, I give it next to poetry the last place.

. . . Concerning dancing I have (as you know already) a quite other opinion than of music, it being that which gives graceful motion all the life, and above all things, manliness, and a becoming confidence to children. I think it cannot be learnt too early, after they are once of an age and strength capable of it. But you must be sure to have a good master, that knows and can teach, what is graceful and becoming, and what gives a freedom and easiness to all motions of the body. . . . This is all in short that I can think at present concerning matters of learning and accomplishments. The great business of all is virtue . . . Teach him but to get a mastery over his inclination, and make his appetite hearken to reason, and the hardest part of the task is over. To that happy temper of mind I know nothing that contributes so much as the love of praise and commendation, which, therefore, you should, I think, endeavor to instill into him by all the arts imaginable. Make his mind as sensible of credit and shame as may be: and when you have done that, you have put a principle into him which will influence his actions when you are not by; and to which fear of a little smart from a rod is not comparable.

One more thing give me leave to add, and then I think I have done this time, and that is, as he grows up to talk familiarly with him; nay, ask his advice and consult with him about those things wherein he is capable of understanding. By this you will gain two things, both of great moment. The one is, that it will put serious considerations into his thoughts, better than any rules or advices you can give him. [The other is that the] sooner you treat him as a man, the sooner he will begin to be one . . .

Epilogue

As noted above, Locke had kept drafts of his letters to the Clarkes. After his return to England, he showed those letters to other friends, in some cases as advice for the rearing of their children, usually sons. Evidently some of these individuals suggested that he publish the letters, indicating that their content would be useful to parents and educators. Thus the letters appeared in book form in 1693. The book was dedicated to his friend, Edward Clarke, for whom the letters had initially been written. The book's dedication in current editions takes the form of a letter from Locke to Edward Clarke written in 1692 that began:

Sir: These thoughts concerning education, which now come abroad in the world, do of right belong to you, being written several years since for your sake . . . I have so little vary'd any thing, but only the order of what was sent to you at different times . . . I myself have been consulted of late by so many, who profess themselves at a loss how to breed their children, and the early corruption of youth is now become so general a complaint, that he cannot be thought wholly impertinent, who brings the consideration of this matter on the stage, and offers something, if it be but to excite others, or afford matters of correction: for errors in education should be less indulg'd than any. (Locke, 1693, p. i)

Because Locke believed that humans were born as blank slates, education took on great importance. As he noted in one of his letters above, "Children are strangers to all we are acquainted with, and all the things they meet with are at first unknown to them, as they were to us." It was thus critical for adults to groom the minds of children in ways that would produce the kinds of individuals who would be both virtuous and productive citizens.

For Locke, education was supposed to produce a learned person, but of greater importance, it was needed to produce a moral person. His letters to the Clarkes (including many not reprinted in this chapter) reflect, in particular, this latter goal. Locke's letters described this program of education for the upper class, for those individuals of his social station. Even within the children of the elite, he recognized that there were individual differences and that practices would have to be tailored to suit the temperaments and talents of a particular child. The ultimate goal of Locke's educational program was to emphasize reason. The child was to learn to value reason and to be guided by it, thus downplaying the role of emotions and desires in controlling behavior. On several occasions Locke asked Edward Clarke about the temperament of his son and seemed pleased that the boy embodied those qualities that Locke felt needed only nurturance and not teaching.

Locke wrote his book as a means to spread his beliefs about child rearing to others of his social class. Apparently the book was well received, because in only a few short years after its appearance in England, it was translated into French, German, Dutch, Swedish, and Italian. The book is still in print in several languages today. Would it be a useful guide for parenting today? Perhaps. Clearly some of his advice seems to be as valid today as it was when he was writing in the late seventeenth century. Still, most modern parents might not follow his advice about the leaky shoes.

Suggested Readings

Cranston, M. (1957). *John Locke: A biography*. Boston: Longmans Green.
   A very readable and comprehensive biography of Locke's life.
de Beer, E. S. (ed.) (1976–1989). *The correspondence of John Locke, volumes 1–8*. New York: Oxford University Press.
   This is the most complete collection of Locke letters, containing all 3,648 known to exist. Isaac Newton is among the many correspondents in this collection. The correspondence

with Edward Clarke is one of the most extensive in the collection and numbers more than 200 letters.

Locke, J. (1690). *An essay concerning human understanding.* Oxford: Clarendon Press (1975 edition).

Locke's psychological treatise that marked the formal beginnings of British empiricism.

Locke, J. (1693). *Some thoughts concerning education.* Woodbury: Barron's Educational Series (1964 edition).

This book was written from the drafts of letters to Edward and Mary Clarke regarding the rearing and education of their son. The letters cited in this chapter provide part of the basis for Locke's book on education.

Moore-Russell, M. E. (1978). The philosopher and society: John Locke and the English revolution. *Journal of the History of the Behavioral Sciences, 14,* 65–73.

Illustrates the impact of the social and political times on Locke's writings, particularly on the *Essay.*

Morris, C. R. (1931). *Locke, Berkeley, Hume.* Oxford: Clarendon Press.

A brief treatment of the lives of these three empiricist philosophers and a comparison of their theories of knowledge and knowing.

Petryszak, N. G. (1981). Tabula rasa – its origins and implications. *Journal of the History of the Behavioral Sciences, 17,* 15–27.

Discusses Locke's use of the concept of tabula rasa to resolve the conflict between belief in divine determination and belief in individual freedom.

Rand, B. (Ed.). (1927). *The correspondence of John Locke and Edward Clarke.* London: Oxford University Press.

This book includes biographical accounts of Locke and Clarke as well as the complete correspondence between the two men. The letters in this chapter are taken from this source.

3
CHAPTER

Charles Darwin
(Archives of the History of American Psychology/University of Akron)

On the Origin of Species:
Darwin's Crisis of 1858

Many scholars consider Charles Darwin's book, *On the Origin of Species* (1859), to be the most influential book published in the last 400 years. This theory of the evolution of species by means of natural selection has had a profound impact on many fields of study from art to zoology, and psychology is no exception.

The word "evolution" has taken on a very different meaning since Darwin, and is a word that often evokes spirited discourse, if not outright vociferous attacks. It is interesting that Darwin did not use that word anywhere in the 429 pages of his *Origin of Species*. Yet a form of the word appears as the final word in the book. After meticulously building his case for natural selection in species change, Darwin (1859) ended his book with the following sentence:

> There is grandeur in this view of life, with its several powers, having been orig-
> inally breathed into a few forms or into one; and that, whilst this planet has gone
> cycling on according to the fixed law of gravity, from so simple a beginning
> endless forms most beautiful and most wonderful have been, and are being
> evolved. (p. 429)

Part of the mystique of this important book is that Darwin delayed the publication of his ideas about species change for nearly 20 years. Why did he wait so long
to tell the world about such a revolutionary idea?

Charles Darwin (1809–1882) joined a British scientific expedition at the age
of 22. As naturalist aboard the ship HMS *Beagle*, he sailed around the world for
five years, observing and collecting many mineral, plant, and animal forms. From
these extensive studies he published several books, including the five-volume
work entitled *Zoology of the Voyage of H.M.S. Beagle*. The voyage changed Darwin's
life and, subsequently, the world. Yet he literally almost missed the boat.

The young Darwin was contacted in August, 1831 by John Stevens Henslow,
a professor of botany with whom Darwin had worked when he was a student
at Cambridge University. Henslow told him about a scientific voyage being
planned by the British admiralty, with Captain Robert FitzRoy in command of
the *Beagle*. The expedition was to include a naturalist and FitzRoy had wanted
Leonard Jenyns to accept the position. When Jenyns declined, it was offered to
his brother-in-law, Henslow. Henslow also declined and contacted his former
student. Darwin was eager to accept this opportunity; however, his father,
Robert, opposed the trip. He argued that the position must not be much of an
opportunity if so many naturalists were turning it down. He also worried that
the voyage would interfere with Darwin's preparation for a career as a minister,
and he encouraged his son to get on with his life, and to avoid forays that
seemed somewhat frivolous. Darwin, a dutiful son, wrote to Henslow to say that
although his father had not forbade him to accept the position, in good conscience, he could not go against his father's wishes. However, a few days later,
Darwin's uncle persuaded Darwin's father that the voyage was an important
opportunity, and so Robert Darwin withdrew his objections. Darwin hurriedly
wrote to the admiralty to ask if the position was still available. And thus he
embarked on the remarkable five-year sea voyage, which was supposed to last
only two years (see Burkhardt et al., 1985–, pp. 127–136).

Not only did Darwin almost miss the boat, but he almost lost the chance to
be the ship's naturalist by a nose. It seems that the young ship's captain FitzRoy
was a believer in physiognomy, a pseudo-science that proposed that a person's
character and abilities could be determined by the features of a person's face. In
Darwin's interview with FitzRoy, FitzRoy was concerned with the shape of
Darwin's nose, believing that it signified laziness and a lack of determination.
Darwin's performance in the interview, however, was evidently sufficient to
cause FitzRoy to overlook his nose and take a chance on this novice naturalist.

Upon his return from the five-year voyage, Darwin pondered the data that he
had collected, attempting to make sense of the species variations and specializa-
tions that he had observed. He was especially interested in the flora and fauna he
had collected and observed in the Galápagos Islands, a group of volcanic islands
about 600 miles west of Ecuador. There were remarkable species variations found
in nearby islands within that group and Darwin struggled to understand how
those differences came about.

In 1838 Darwin read Thomas Malthus's essay on population (1789), which argued that the world's food supply increased arithmetically while the population increased geometrically, a condition that guaranteed competition and starvation. From Malthus's idea, Darwin recognized the struggle for survival and its relationship to species variations. He began to construct a theory of the transformation of species based on the principle of natural selection. The initial account of the theory was written in 1842 as a manuscript of 35 pages and was expanded to approximately 230 pages in 1844. Portions of that manuscript were shared with several of Darwin's fellow-scientists and friends, particularly Charles Lyell, an eminent geologist, and Joseph Hooker and Asa Gray, both distinguished botanists.

As early as 1844 Darwin knew he was working on a theory of great importance. At that time he made arrangements with his wife for publication of the manuscript should he die before having the chance to reveal his theory to the world. Yet he did not publish his theory, nor did he seem to have any plans to do so. Indeed, 15 more years would pass before Darwin would actually publish this work, and even then he did so with some reluctance.

Why did Darwin delay the publication of his theory? There are many possible answers to that question, some more plausible than others. A number of those answers are summarized and analyzed in an article by historian Robert Richards (1983).

Some Darwin scholars, such as Howard Gruber and Stephen Jay Gould, have argued that Darwin was very much aware of the social consequences of his theory, which linked humans with the rest of the animal kingdom. The theory supported a philosophy of materialism that "assumed the rise of human reason and morality out of animal intelligence and instinct" (Richards, 1983, p. 47). Thus Darwin may have been waiting for a *Zeitgeist* more favorable to his theory.

Another possible reason for the delay is that in 1844, as Darwin was expanding his abstract on species changes, another treatise on the origin of species was published, which was soundly trashed by the scientific community. It would have seemed a bad time to release his theory so close to the publication of such an unscientific account.

Perhaps Darwin was just exceptionally meticulous as a scientist. He formulated his theory in 1838 and then spent the next 20 years collecting information that would support the theory and trying to account for those facts that might seem to reject it. Some facts proved especially problematic, for example, accounting for the development of instincts in sterile worker bees. Richards believes that this concern over the explanatory power of the theory is the most plausible reason for the delay.

Darwin's friends urged him to publish his ideas before someone else published a similar theory and thus gained priority. Yet Darwin seemed in no hurry. Then on June 18, 1858, a package arrived at his home that would turn his world upside down. It was a manuscript from Alfred Russel Wallace (1823–1913), a fellow British naturalist, who outlined a theory very similar to that of Darwin.

Could Darwin honorably publish his theory now that Wallace had sent him this manuscript? As a scientist, Darwin believed that truth was his goal, not fame. But

Darwin was also human and his letters to his friends, Hooker and Lyell, reveal the great conflict he felt upon receiving Wallace's manuscript. He wanted to behave honorably in this matter but in doing so he might lose credit for 20 years of painstaking work. Darwin's terrible dilemma is played out in the letters that follow. In the first letter to Joseph Hooker, Darwin announces that he believes he has discovered "the simple way by which species become exquisitely adapted to various ends." It is an audacious presumption, that he has solved that " 'mystery of mysteries'," and the kind of discovery that comes to only a few scientists in every century.

The Letters

Charles Darwin to Joseph D. Hooker, January 11, 1844

. . . I have been now ever since my return engaged in a very presumptuous work, and I know no one individual who would not say a very foolish one. I was so struck with the distribution of the Galapagos organisms . . . and with the character of the American fossil mammifiers . . . that I determined to collect blindly every sort of fact, which could bear any way on what are species. I have read heaps of agricultural and horticultural books, and have never ceased collecting facts. At last gleams of light have come, and I am almost convinced (quite contrary to the opinion I started with) that species are not (it is like confessing a murder) immutable. Heaven forfend me from Lamarck[1] nonsense of a "tendency to progression," "adaptations from the slow willing of animals," etc.! But the conclusions I am led to are not widely different from his; though the means of change are wholly so. I think I have found out (here's presumption!) the simple way by which species become exquisitely adapted to various ends. You will now groan, and think to yourself, "on what a man have I been wasting my time and writing to."

Darwin to Emma Darwin,[2] July 5, 1844

I have just finished my sketch of my species theory.[3] If, as I believe that my theory is true & if it be accepted even by one competent judge, it will be a considerable step in science.

---

[1] Jean-Baptiste Lamarck (1744–1829), a naturalist, argued that species evolve because of the use or disuse of muscles, senses, and organs. For example, an explanation for the especially long neck of the giraffe would be that as the animals were forced to reach higher and higher into trees for scarce vegetation, their neck muscles would stretch. This change would be passed to the next generation, and so forth, leading over many generations to an elongated neck.
[2] Emma Wedgwood (Darwin) (1808–1896) married Charles Darwin in 1839.
[3] The sketch to which he refers is the 230-page essay on the origin of species.

I therefore write this, in case of my sudden death, as my most solemn & last request, which I am sure you will consider the same as if legally entered in my will, that you will devote 400£ to its publication & further will yourself, or through Hensleigh,[4] take trouble in promoting it. – I wish that my sketch be given to some competent person, with this sum to induce him to take trouble in its improvement & enlargement. – I give to him all my Books on Natural History, which are either scored or have references at end to the pages, begging him carefully to look over & consider such passages, as actually bearing or by possibility bearing on this subject. – I wish you to make a list of all such books, as some temptation to an Editor.

With respect to Editors. – Mr. Lyell would be the best if he would undertake it: I believe he wd find the work pleasant & he wd learn some facts new to him. As the Editor must be a geologist, as well as a Naturalist.

Note: In the next two letters to Leonard Jenyns, an Anglican priest and naturalist, Darwin describes the intellectual evolution of his theory, how his observations and collected data led him to conclude that species change and that related species likely have common ancestors. He also notes that he does not plan to rush his ideas into print.

Darwin to Leonard Jenyns,[5] October 12, 1844

I have continued steadily reading & collecting facts on variation of domestic animals & plants & on the question of what are species; I have a grand body of facts & I think I can draw some sound conclusions. The general conclusion at which I have slowly been driven from a directly opposite conviction is that species are mutable & that allied species are co-descendants of common stocks. I know how much I open myself, to reproach, for such a conclusion, but I have at least honestly & deliberately come to it.

I shall not publish on this subject for several years – At present I am on the geology of S. America. I hope to pick up from your book, some facts on slight variations in structure or instincts in the animals of your acquaintance.

Darwin to Leonard Jenyns, November 25, 1844

With respect to my far-distant work on species, I must have expressed myself with singular inaccuracy, if I led you to suppose that I meant to say that my conclusions were inevitable. They have become so, after years of weighing puzzles,

---

[4] Hensleigh Wedgwood (1803–1891) was Darwin's first cousin and brother-in-law. Darwin's mother was also a Wedgwood (a wealthy family renowned for its manufacture of fine porcelain).
[5] Leonard Jenyns (1800–1893) was the brother-in-law of John Stevens Henslow, Darwin's teacher at Cambridge University.

to myself *alone*; but in my wildest day-dream, I never expect more than to be able to show that there are two sides to the question of the immutability of species, ie whether species are directly created, or by intermediate laws (as with the life & death of individuals). I did not approach the subject on the side of the difficulty in determining what are species & what are varieties, but (though, why I shd give you such a history of my doings, it wd be hard to say) from such facts, as the relationship between the living & extinct mammifers in S. America, & between those living on the continent & on adjoining islands, such as the Galapagos – It occurred to me, that a collection of all such analogous facts would throw light either for or against the view of related species, being co-descendants from a common stock. A long searching amongst agricultural & horticultural books & people, makes me believe (I well know how absurdly presumptuous this must appear) that I see the way in which new varieties become exquisitely adapted to the external conditions of life, & to other surrounding beings. – I am a bold man to lay myself open to being thought a complete fool, & a most deliberate one. – From the nature of the grounds, which make me believe that species are mutable in form, these grounds cannot be restricted to the closest-allied species; but how far they extend, I cannot tell, as my reasons fall away by degrees, when applied to species more & more remote from each other.

Pray do not think, that I am so blind as not to see that there are numerous immense difficulties on my notions, but they appear to me less than on common view. – I have drawn up a sketch & had it copied (in 200 pages) of my conclusions: & if I thought at some future time, that you would think it worth reading, I shd of course be most thankful to have the criticism of so competent a critic.

Note: By the summer of 1858, Darwin's ideas on species change were well developed and written out in a manuscript of approximately 200 pages. But these ideas had yet to be published. The delay, for whatever reasons, proved to be too long. On June 18, 1858, as noted above, Darwin's world crashed in on him.

Darwin to Charles Lyell, June 18, 1858

. Some year or so ago you recommended me to read a paper by Wallace in the *Annals*,[6] which had interested you, and, as I was writing to him, I knew this would please him much, so I told him. He has to-day sent me the enclosed, and asked me to forward it to you. It seems to me well worth reading. Your words have come true with a vengeance – that I should be forestalled. You said this, when I explained to you here very briefly my views of Natural Selection depending on the struggle for existence. I never saw a more striking coincidence; if Wallace had

[6]   Alfred Russel Wallace's article appeared in an 1855 issue of *Annals and Magazine of Natural History.*

my MS. [manuscript] sketch written out in 1842, he could not have made a better short abstract! Even his terms now stand as heads of my chapters. Please return me the MS., which he does not say he wishes me to publish, but I shall of course, at once write and offer to send to any journal. So all of my originality, whatever it may amount to, will be smashed, though my book, if it will ever have any value, will not be deteriorated; as all the labour consists in the application of the theory.

I hope you will approve of Wallace's sketch, that I may tell him what to say.

Darwin to Charles Lyell, June 25, 1858

I am very sorry to trouble you, busy as you are, in so merely personal an affair; but if you will give me your deliberate opinion, you will do me as great a service as ever man did, for I have entire confidence in your judgment and honour . . .

There is nothing in Wallace's sketch which is not written out much fuller in my sketch, copied out in 1844, and read by Hooker some dozen years ago. About a year ago I sent a short sketch, of which I have a copy, of my views (owing to correspondence on several points) to Asa Gray,[7] so that I could most truly say and prove that I take nothing from Wallace. I should be extremely glad now to publish a sketch of my general views in about a dozen pages or so; but I cannot persuade myself that I can do so honourably. Wallace says nothing about publication, and I enclose his letter. But as I had not intended to publish any sketch, can I do so honourably because Wallace has sent me an outline of his doctrine? I would far rather burn my whole book, than that he or any other man should think that I had behaved in a paltry spirit. Do you think his having sent me this sketch ties my hands? . . . If I could honourably publish, I would state that I was induced now to publish a sketch (and I should be very glad to be permitted to say, to follow your advice long ago given) from Wallace having sent me an outline of my general conclusions. We differ only [in] that I was led to my views from what artificial selection has done for domestic animals. I would send Wallace a copy of my letter to Asa Gray, to show him that I had not stolen his doctrine. But I cannot tell whether to publish now would not be base and paltry. This was my first impression and I should have certainly acted on it had it not been for your letter.

This is a trumpery affair to trouble you with, but you cannot tell how much obliged I should be for your advice.

By the way, would you object to send this and your answer to Hooker to be forwarded to me, for then I shall have the opinion of my two best and kindest friends. This letter is miserably written, and I write it now, that I may for a time banish the whole subject; and I am worn out with musing . . .

My good dear friend forgive me. This is a trumpery letter, influenced by trumpery feelings.

[7] Asa Gray (1810–1888) was an American botanist and intimate friend of Darwin.

Darwin to Charles Lyell, June 26, 1858

Forgive me for adding a P.S. to make the case as strong as possible against myself.

Wallace might say, "You did not intend publishing an abstract of your views till you received my communication. Is it fair to take advantage of my having freely, though unasked, communicated to you my ideas, and thus prevent me from forestalling you?" The advantage which I should take being that I am induced to publish from privately knowing that Wallace is in the field. It seems hard on me that I should be thus compelled to lose my priority of many years' standing, but I cannot feel at all sure that this alters the justice of the case. First impressions are generally right, and I at first thought it would be dishonourable in me now to publish.

Darwin to Joseph Hooker, June 29, 1858

I have just read your letter, and see you want the papers at once. I am quite prostrated and can do nothing,[8] but I send Wallace, and the abstract of my letter to Asa Gray, which gives most imperfectly only the means of change, and does not touch on the reasons for believing that species do change. I dare say all is too late. I hardly care about it. But you are too generous to sacrifice so much time and kindness. It is most generous, most kind. I send my sketch of 1844 solely that you may see by your own handwriting that you did read it. I really cannot bear to look at it. Do not waste much time. It is miserable in me to care at all about priority.

The table of contents will show what it is.

I would make a similar, but shorter and more accurate sketch for the *Linnean Journal*.[9]

I will do anything. God bless you, my dear kind friend.

I can write no more.

Note: On July 1, 1858, Charles Lyell and Joseph Hooker read three documents at a meeting of the Linnean Society of London: the manuscript that Wallace had sent to Darwin, excerpts from Darwin's essay of 1844, and a letter from Darwin to Asa Gray dated September 5, 1857. Hooker and Lyell explained the circumstances of the necessity of the joint

---

[8]   Darwin's infant son had died of scarlet fever the previous day.

[9]   The *Linnean Journal* was published by London's Linnean Society, a scientific society founded in 1788 and named in honor of the Swedish naturalist, Carl Linnaeus (1707–1778). Linnaeus is often called the "father of taxonomy" for the classification systems that he developed for plants and animals. Nearly 50 years after his death, the Society acquired his personal library as well as his zoological and botanical specimens.

reading. Both of the theoretical papers were published in an 1858 issue of the Linnean Society's journal.

Darwin to Joseph Hooker, July 13, 1858

Your letter to Wallace seems to me perfect, quite clear and most courteous. I do not think it could possibly be improved, and I have to day forwarded it with a letter of my own. I always thought it very possible that I might be forestalled, but I fancied that I had a grand enough soul not to care; but I found myself mistaken and punished; I had, however, quite resigned myself, and had written half a letter to Wallace to give up all priority to him, and should certainly not have changed had it not been for Lyell's and your quite extraordinary kindness. I assure you I feel it, and shall not forget it. I am more than satisfied at what took place at the Linnean Society. I had thought that your letter and mine to Asa Gray were to be only an appendix to Wallace's paper.

You cannot imagine how pleased I am that the notion of Natural Selection has acted as a purgative on your bowels of immutability. Whenever naturalists can look at species changing as certain, what a magnificent field will be open, – on all the laws of variation, – on the genealogy of all living beings, – on their lines of migration, etc., etc. Pray thank Mrs. Hooker for her very kind little note, and pray, say how truly obliged I am, and in truth ashamed to think that she should have had the trouble of copying my ugly MS. It was extraordinarily kind in her. Farewell, my dear kind friend.

Note: The letters that Hooker and Darwin sent to Wallace have never been found. Wallace referred to them in a letter he wrote from Malaysia to his mother on October 6, 1858: "I have received letters from Mr. Darwin and Dr. Hooker, two of the most eminent naturalists in England, which have highly gratified me. I sent Mr. Darwin an essay on a subject upon which he is now writing a great work. He showed it to Dr. Hooker and Sir Charles Lyell, who thought so highly of it that they had it read before the Linnean Society. This insures me the acquaintance of these eminent men on my return home" (Burkhardt et al., 1991, p. 131).

At the end of September, 1859, Darwin finished reading the proof versions of the final pages of his book and wrote to Lyell reflecting on the intellectual journey that had led to his theory.

Darwin to Charles Lyell, September 30, 1859

I sent off this morning the last sheets, but without index, which is not in type. I look at you as my Lord High Chancellor in Natural Science, and therefore I request you, after you have finished, just to *rerun* over the heads in the Recapitulation part of [the] last chapter. I shall be deeply anxious to hear what you decide (if you are able to decide) on the balance of the pros and contras given in my volume, and of such other pros and contras as may occur to you. I hope that you will think that I have given the difficulties fairly. I feel an entire conviction that if you are now staggered to any moderate extent, that you will come more and more round, the longer you keep the subject at all before your mind. I remember well how many long years it was before I could look into the faces of some of the difficulties and not feel quite abashed. I fairly struck my colors before the case of neuter insects.

I suppose that I am a very slow thinker, for you would be surprised at the number of years it took me to see clearly what some of the problems were which had to be solved, such as the necessity of the principle of divergence of character, the extinction of intermediate varieties, on a continuous area, with graduated condition; the double problem of sterile first crosses and sterile hybrids, etc., etc.

Looking back, I think it was more difficult to see what the problems were than to solve them, so far as I have succeeded in doing, and this seems to me rather curious. Well, good or bad, my work, thank God, is over; and hard work, I can assure you, I have had, and much work which has never borne fruit. You can see by the way I am scribbling, that I have an idle and rainy afternoon. I was not able to start for Ilkley yesterday as I was too unwell; but I hope to get there on Tuesday or Wednesday. Do, I beg you, when you have finished my book and thought a little over it, let me hear from you. Never mind and pitch into me, if you think it requisite; some future day, in London possibly, you may give me a few criticisms in detail, that is, if you have scribbled any remarks on the margin for the chance of a second edition.

Murray has printed 1250 copies, which seems to me rather too large an edition, but I hope he will not lose.[10]

I make as much fuss about my book as if it were my first. Forgive me, and believe me, my dear Lyell.

Epilogue

The conflict raging within Darwin as a result of the arrival of Wallace's manuscript is evident in these letters. Darwin was a scientist, and as such he believed that truth and discovery were what he should work toward, not fame. He tells us that he thought that he would not be bothered if his ideas on natural selection as the mechanism for evolution were usurped by another scientist. Yet clearly he misjudged himself. He was distraught at the realization that his 20 years of work and the originality of his ideas were about to be "forestalled." In his letters he expressed obvious embarrassment about his concern with priority. He wanted to

---

[10]   The publisher, John Murray, did not lose. All 1,250 copies of the first printing sold on the first day of publication, November 22, 1859. Copies of that printing are especially valuable today. One was listed for sale on the Internet by a rare books dealer in 2004 for the sum of $163,000.

do the honorable thing, which he felt was to give over all priority to Wallace. He hoped, however, that his friends would help him discover another course of action that would, at minimum, allow him to share in the credit. He wrote a touching and conflicted letter to Lyell on June 25, 1858, saying at the end of the letter that he just needed to put those issues aside and get his mind on other things. But obviously he could not do that, and he wrote to Lyell the very next day to offer additional thoughts on his horrible quandary. Some scholars, such as Robert Wright (1994), have argued that Darwin manipulated the 1858 crisis to his advantage, by involving his prestigious friends (Lyell and Hooker) in a way that he knew would work to his favor. Perhaps he is right about Darwin's motives and strategy. But the historical record does not really allow us to verify his claim. Nevertheless, the few letters reprinted here tell us a good deal about Darwin as a scientist and as a human being.

When Darwin's *Origin* was published he was given a number of presentation copies from the publisher. He sent copies to Lyell and Hooker, to Jenyns, to his teacher at Cambridge, Henslow, and to several others with whom he had corresponded over the years. There is no evidence that he sent copies to Wallace or to FitzRoy. FitzRoy, a literal interpreter of the Bible, had expressed regret at aiding Darwin in the development of his theory and had urged Darwin to recant. Depressed and in poor physical health, FitzRoy committed suicide in 1865 at the age of 59. He left considerable debts for his widow, which were paid off by his friends, including a generous donation from Charles Darwin. (See the biography of FitzRoy by Peter Nichols (2003) for a fascinating account of this complex and troubled individual.)

As noted at the beginning of this chapter, Darwin's name is widely known today, and his theory has impacted most scientific fields as well as many other disciplinary areas. Psychology has been heavily influenced by Darwin since its beginnings as a science, and today, Darwinian views underlie a growing field known as evolutionary psychology (see Buss, 2003). Despite the fact that most people know Darwin's name, most of them have never read any of his works, nor do they have any real understanding of his ideas or their contemporary importance for science. Wallace, who was pleased that his work was linked with Darwin's (Raby, 2001; Shermer, 2002), has not enjoyed the same name recognition throughout history. Indeed, Wallace's name is as obscure as Darwin's is famous, although he is a familiar name to those who work in the sciences. It is hoped that these letters may spur readers to find a copy of the *Origin* and see what this fuss was all about, as well as seeing first hand the fruits of Darwin's genius as a theorist and scientist.

Suggested Readings

Bowler, P. J. (1989). *Evolution: The history of an idea*. Berkeley: University of California Press. This history of the concept of evolution focuses on the influences on Darwin and the fate of the theory in evolutionary biology.

Browne, E. J. (1995, 2002). *Charles Darwin: Voyaging* and *Charles Darwin: The power of place*. Princeton: Princeton University Press.

These are the first two volumes of Janet Browne's exceptional biography of Darwin. The first describes his early life, the *Beagle* voyage, and the first 20 years at Down House. The second begins with his receipt of the essay from Wallace.

Burkhardt, F., Smith, S., Kohn, D., & Montgomery, W. (Eds.) (1985–). *The correspondence of Charles Darwin*. New York: Cambridge University Press.

This outstanding series of books began publication in 1985 with the first volume containing Darwin's correspondence from 1821 to 1836. Subsequent volumes have been appearing at the rate of one each year, and will continue until all 14,000 letters are in print. Thus, this series constitutes the only comprehensive collection of Darwin letters.

Clark, R. W. (1984). *The survival of Charles Darwin: A biography of a man and an idea*. New York: Random House.

A double biography covering Darwin's life and the life of his theory through the modern synthesis of Julian Huxley in the middle of the twentieth century.

Darwin, C. R. (1859). *On the origin of species*. London: John Murray.

Many subsequent printings and editions exist, including inexpensive paperback versions. It is essential reading for anyone wanting a feel for Darwin as scientist.

Darwin, F. (Ed.) (1950). *Charles Darwin's autobiography, with his notes and letters depicting the growth of the* Origin of species. New York: Henry Schuman.

Edited by Francis Darwin, son of Charles Darwin, this book contains the autobiography Darwin wrote for his children, a collection of reminiscences of his father by Francis Darwin, and a selection of Darwin letters surrounding the writing and reception of the *Origin*.

Keynes, R. D. (1979). *The* Beagle *record*. New York: Cambridge University Press.

This book tells the story of the voyage of the *Beagle*. It is assembled from letters from Darwin and Robert FitzRoy (Captain of the *Beagle*), Darwin's diary, and published works about the voyage by Darwin and FitzRoy.

Nichols, P. (2003). *Evolution's captain: The dark fate of the man who sailed Darwin around the world*. New York: HarperCollins.

An excellent treatment of the life of FitzRoy. Especially fascinating is his troubled life after Darwin's theory is published and FitzRoy's difficulty in dealing with his role in making that theory possible.

Ospovat, D. (1981). *The development of Darwin's theory*. New York: Cambridge University Press.

This book focuses on Darwin's journals, letters, and books during the years 1838–1859, emphasizing the role of natural theology in the early formulations of his theory, and the work of other naturalists in its later development, particularly the changing conception of natural selection.

Raby, P. (2001). *Alfred Russel Wallace: A life*. Princeton: Princeton University Press; Shermer, M. (2002). *In Darwin's shadow: The life and science of Alfred Russel Wallace*. NY: Oxford University Press; and Slotten, R. A. (2004). *The heretic in Darwin's court: The life of Alfred Russel Wallace*. New York: Columbia University Press.

Three biographies on the life and work of Wallace, indicating the recent interest in the work of this important naturalist.

Richards, R. J. (1983). Why Darwin delayed, or interesting problems and models in the history of science. *Journal of the History of the Behavioral Sciences, 19*, 45–53.

In this article, Richards discusses eight explanations for Darwin's delay in publishing the *Origin*. In doing so, he also discusses the determination of what is an interesting question in the history of science and how best to pursue the answers to such questions.

Richards, R. J. (1988). *Darwin and the emergence of evolutionary theories of mind and behavior.* Chicago: University of Chicago Press.

This award-winning book traces the history of evolutionary thought from Lamarck to the modern theories of ethology and sociobiology, with a special emphasis on the treatment of moral behavior.

Harriet Taylor, c.1844
(British Library of Political and Economic
Science)

John Stuart Mill
(National Library of Medicine)

John Stuart Mill and the Subjection of Women

One of the most significant British philosophers in the empiricist tradition begun by John Locke (1632–1704) was John Stuart Mill (1806–1873), whose importance for the history of psychology is considerable, despite the fact that he is typically afforded the briefest of treatments in history of psychology textbooks. John Stuart Mill was the eldest of nine children of James Mill (1773–1836), a Scottish empiricist philosopher whose contribution to the study of the formation and maintenance of associations was the description of a set of factors determining the strength and durability of associations. He was the most mechanistic of the empiricists, describing his mechanical view of the mind in his book, *Analysis of the Phenomena of the Human Mind* (1829). John Stuart Mill was raised according to that mechanistic philosophy; his father wanted him to become a reasoning machine, devoid of emotion.

J. S. Mill's early education was considerable, and he showed remarkable genius for his studies. He began a study of Greek at age 3 and Latin at age 8, and by age

10 had read many of the classic works in their original language. At age 12 he wrote a book-length history of Roman government. His IQ score has been estimated to be 190, the second highest of a study of 300 geniuses (Cox, 1926). J. S. Mill, like his father before him, grew up without playmates other than his siblings. Because one of his duties was to tutor his younger siblings, learning occupied most of his waking hours (Packe, 1954).

James Mill was very possessive of his brilliant son and dominated him in all matters. When John, as a young adult, began to acquire friends, his father would drive them away. Such treatment led John, at the age of 21, to suffer the first of several major clinical depressions in his life. In his autobiography he wrote with great insight about his depression and about his relationship with his father:

> my heart sank within me: the whole foundation on which my life was constructed fell down . . . I seemed to have nothing left to live for. At first I hoped that the cloud would pass away of itself; but it did not . . . Hardly anything had power to cause me even a few minutes oblivion of it . . . I sought no comfort by speaking to others of what I felt. If I had loved any one sufficiently to make confiding my grief a necessity, I should not have been in the condition I was. I felt, too, that mine was not an interesting, or in any way respectable distress. There was nothing in it to attract sympathy . . . My father, to whom it would have been natural for me to have recourse in any practical difficulties, was the last person to whom, in such a case as this, I looked for help. Everything convinced me that he had no knowledge of any such mental state as I was suffering from, and that even if he could be made to understand it, he was not the physician to heal it. (Mill, 1873, pp. 81–82)

His depression lasted for nearly three years, and then in 1830 he met Harriet Taylor. Thus began what Mill called "the most valuable friendship of [his] life" (Mill, 1873, p. 111).

Harriet Taylor (1807–1858) was intelligent, vivacious, rebellious, and a romantic. At age 18 she had married John Taylor, eleven years older, a man who shared none of his wife's love of music, philosophy, literature, and poetry. One of the first extended meetings between John Stuart Mill and Harriet Taylor was at a dinner party, perhaps arranged by Harriet Taylor's Unitarian minister. Mill was immediately taken with Taylor's intellect and beauty, and she, too, was fascinated by this man with such unconventional views on the place of women in society. There were subsequent dinners at the Taylor household and shortly Mill and Taylor began to exchange essays on marriage, divorce, women's roles, and a host of other subjects.

The frequent contact between these two led to gossip in London society. John Taylor grew frustrated with the relationship, but his wife was adamant in her insistence that it was nothing more than friendship. And so it seemed. Then in September of 1833, Mill confessed that he loved her, a sentiment she had expressed earlier to him. Apparently, however, their friendship continued in a platonic fashion. Eventually Harriet Taylor moved into her own house where she and Mill could meet more easily. Such an arrangement was truly scandalous and no doubt most Londoners assumed theirs was a sexual relationship. But their correspondence and other writings indicate that it was not (Hayek, 1951).

When John Taylor became ill with cancer, he asked his wife to come live with him once more and take care of him, which she did for about a year until his death in 1849. After a two-year period of mourning, Harriet Taylor and John Stuart Mill married. After a 20-year friendship, they enjoyed only nine years of a happy marriage before Harriet's death in 1858 from tuberculosis. It was during those years that Mill wrote what is arguably his most important work, *On Liberty*. It began as a brief essay in 1854 and in the ensuing years he and Taylor revised it again and again, "reading, weighing and criticizing every sentence" (Mill, 1873, p. 144), creating the small but powerful book. It was published a few months after Taylor's death and was dedicated to her:

> To the beloved and deplored memory of her who was the inspirer, and in part the author, of all that is best in my writings – the friend and wife whose exalted sense of truth and right was my strongest incitement, and whose approbation was my chief reward – I dedicate this volume. (Mill, 1859)

It had been in the midst of his friendship with Taylor that Mill had written his most important work for psychology, *A System of Logic*, which he published in 1843. In this book, Mill argued for the feasibility of a science of psychology, in his words, a "science of human nature." The possibility of such a science was a hotly debated issue during Mill's time, as many agreed with August Comte that there could be no science of the mind because the mind could not study its own processes (see Heyd, 1989). Although Mill acknowledged that psychology was, in his time, an inexact science, he believed that it was as precise as some sciences, such as astronomy, and worthy of study. Mill did not propose an experimental science of mind in *A System of Logic*, but he did offer a methodological approach to an empirical one relying on ad hoc analysis (see chapter 3 of his book, entitled "That There Is, or May Be, A Science of Human Nature"). There is some evidence that Wilhelm Wundt was strongly influenced by Mill's views on a science of psychology, particularly his ideas of mental chemistry (similar to Wundt's later notion of creative synthesis).

Of Mill's 13 books published during his lifetime, his last one was undoubtedly one of the most meaningful for him. Written in 1861, as he was coming out of the depression caused by the death of his wife, the book was not published until 1869. It was entitled *The Subjection of Women*, a treatise that described the status of women in society, argued for equality of the sexes, and offered a plan of political action to bring about such equality. The book was a culmination of 30 years of discussions between Mill and Taylor, and has become one of the classic texts in the history of feminist thought.

The letters in this chapter focus on Mill's views on women, and also provide a glimpse of his relationship with Harriet Taylor. That relationship had a strong base of shared interest in intellectual pursuits, but of greater importance for Mill, it afforded him the only affection he was to experience in his life.

The Letters

John Stuart Mill to Harriet Taylor, (?) 1832

She to whom my life is devoted has wished for written exposition of my opinions on the subject which, of all connected with human Institutions, is nearest to her happiness . . . [the] question of marriage cannot properly be considered by itself alone. The question is not what marriage ought to be, but a far wider question, what woman ought to be. Settle that first and the other will settle itself. Determine whether marriage is to be a relation between two equal beings, or between a superior & an inferior, between a protector and a dependent; & all other doubts will easily be resolved.

But in this question there is surely no difficulty. There is no natural inequality between the sexes; except perhaps in bodily strength; even that admits of doubt: and if bodily strength is to be the measure of superiority, mankind are no better than savages. Every step in the progress of civilization has tended to diminish the deference paid to bodily strength, until now when that quality confers scarcely any advantages except its natural ones: the strong man has little or no power to employ his strength as a means of acquiring any other advantage over the weaker in body. Every step in the progress of civilization has similarly been marked by a nearer approach to equality in the condition of the sexes; & if they are still far from being equal, the hindrance is not now in the difference of physical strength, but in artificial feelings and prejudices.

If nature has not made men and women unequal, still less ought the law to make them so . . . The first and indispensable step . . . towards the enfranchisement of woman, is that she be so educated, as not to be dependent either on her father or her husband for subsistence: a position which in nine cases out of ten, makes her either the plaything or the slave of the man who feeds her, & in the tenth case, only his humble friend. Let it not be said that she has an equivalent and compensating advantage in the exemption from toil: men think it base & servile in men to accept food as the price of dependence, & why do they not deem it so in women? solely because they do not desire that women should be their equals. Where there is strong affection, dependence is its own reward: but it must be voluntary dependence; & the more perfectly voluntary it is, the more exclusively each owes every thing to the other's affection & to nothing else, – the greater is the happiness.

Harriet Taylor to Mill, (?) 1832

If I could be Providence for the world for a time, for the express purpose of raising the condition of women, I should come to you to know the *means* – the *purpose* would be to remove all interference with affection, or with anything which is, or which even might be supposed to be, demonstrative of affection. In the present state of women's mind, perfectly uneducated, and with whatever of timidity & dependence is natural to them increased a thousand fold by their habit of utter dependence, it would probably be mischievous to remove at once all restraints, they would buy themselves protectors at a dearer cost than even at present – but without raising their natures at all.

Whether nature made a difference between men & women or not, it seems now that all men, with the exception of a few lofty minded, are sensualists more or less – women on the contrary are quite exempt from this trait, however it may appear otherwise in the cases of some. It seems strange that it should be so, unless it was meant to be a source of power in semi-civilized states such as the present – or it may not be so – it may be only that the habits of freedom & low indulgence on which boys grow up and the contrary notion of what is called purity in girls may have produced the appearance of different natures in the two sexes. As certain it is that there is equality in nothing now – all the pleasures such as they are being men's, & all the disagreeables & pains being women's, as that every pleasure would be infinitely heightened both in kind & degree by the perfect equality of the sexes. Women are educated for one single object, to gain their living by marrying . . . To be married is the object of their existence and that object being gained they do really cease to exist as to anything worth calling life or any useful purpose. One observes very few marriages where there is any real sympathy or enjoyment or companionship between the parties. The woman knows what her power is and gains by it what she has been taught to consider "proper" to her state. The woman who would gain power by such means is unfit for power, still they do lose this power for paltry advantages and I am astonished it has never occurred to them to gain some larger purpose; but their minds are degenerated by habits of dependence.

Harriet Taylor to Mill, September 6, 1833

I am glad that you have said it[1] – I am *happy* that you have – no one with any fineness & beauty of character but must feel compelled to say *all*, to the being they really love – while there is reservation, however little of it, the love is just *so much*

[1] This letter is in response to a letter from Mill, which is not extant. Scholars are in agreement that in his letter, Mill had finally been able to tell Taylor that he was in love with her.

imperfect. There has never, *yet*, been entire confidence around us. The difference between you and me in that respect is, that I have always *yearned* to have your confidence with an intensity of wish which has *often*, for a time, swallowed up the naturally stronger feeling – the affection itself – you have not given it, not that you wished to reserve – but that you did not *need* to give – but not having that need of course you had no perception that I had & so you had discouraged confidence from me 'til the habit of *checking first thoughts* has become so strong that when in your presence timidity has become almost a *disease* of the nerves . . . *Yes* – these circumstances *do* require greater strength than any other – the greatest – that which you have, & which if you had not I should never have loved you, I should not love you now.

Note: In 1840, Mill began corresponding on a regular basis with Auguste Comte (1798–1857), a French philosopher we have mentioned earlier. Eventually their letters turned to a discussion of the place of women in society, an issue on which they differed considerably. In 1844, Mill gave the drafts of his letters and the copies of Comte's letters to Taylor for her to read. Her reaction, which was painful to Mill, is printed below.

Harriet Taylor to Mill, (?) 1844

These have greatly surprised and also disappointed me, & also they have pleased me, all this regarding your part in them. Comte's is what I expected – the usual partial and prejudiced view of a subject which he has little considered . . . If the truth is on the side I defend I imagine C. would rather not see it . . .

I am surprised in your letters to find your opinion undetermined where I had thought it made up – I am disappointed at a tone more than half-apologetic with which you state your opinions, & I am charmed with the exceeding nicety elegance & fineness of your last letter. Do not think that I wish you had said *more* on the subject, I only wish that what was said was in the tone of conviction, not of suggestion.

This dry sort of man is not a worthy coadjutor & scarcely a worthy opponent. With your gift of intellect of conscience & of impartiality is it probable, or is there any ground for supposing, that there exists any man more competent to judge that question than you are? You are in advance of your age in culture of the intellectual faculties, you would be the most remarkable man of your age if you had no other claim to be so than your perfect impartiality and your fixed love of justice. These are the two qualities of different orders which I believe to be the rarest & most difficult to human nature . . . I now & then find a generous defect in your mind or your method – such is your liability to take an over large *measure* of people . . . having to draw in afterwards – a proceeding more needful than pleasant.

Mill to Harriet Taylor, c. 1850

Thanks dearest dearest angel for the note – what it contained was a really important addition to the letter & I have put it in nearly your words, which as your impromptu words almost always are, were a hundred times better than any I could find by study. What a perfect orator you would make – & what changes might be made in the world by such a one, with such opportunities as thousands of male dunces have . . .

Mill to Harriet Taylor, October/November 1850

I have been put in spirits by what I think will put you in spirits too – you know some time ago there was a convention of women in Ohio to claim equal rights – (& there is to be another in May) well there has just been a convention for the same purpose in Massachusetts[2] – chiefly of women, but with a great number of men, including the chief slavery abolitionists Garrison, Wendell Phillips, the Negro Douglas,[3] etc . . . most of the speakers are women – & I never remember any public meetings or agitation comparable to it in the proportion with which good sense bears no nonsense – while as to tone it is almost like ourselves speaking – outspoken like America, not frightened & senile like England – not the least iota of compromise – asserting the whole of the principle & claiming the whole of the consequences . . . the thing will evidently not drop, but will go on till it succeeds, & I really do now think that we will have a good chance of living to see something decisive really accomplished on that of all practical subjects – the most important – to see that will be really looking down from Pisgah on the promised land – how little I thought we should ever see it.

Note: The following statement was written by Mill in anticipation of his marriage to Taylor. The wedding took place on April 21, 1851.

John Stuart Mill, March 6, 1851

Being about, if I am so happy as to obtain her consent, to enter into the marriage relation with the only woman I have ever known, with whom I would have entered

---

[2]   The Ohio meetings were in Salem and Akron, and the Massachusetts meeting in Worcester.

[3]   Frederick Douglass (1818–1895), an African-American abolitionist, orator, and essayist, escaped from slavery when he was 20. He worked on suffrage for African Americans, was an advisor to President Abraham Lincoln, and was active in passage of the 15th amendment in 1870 that provided African-American males with the right to vote. No doubt the women involved in those suffrage conventions in the 1840s never imagined that it would take another 70 years before they would be given the right to vote when the 19th amendment to the US Constitution became law in 1920.

into that state; and the whole character of the marriage relation as constituted by law being such as both she and I entirely and conscientiously disapprove, for this among other reasons, that it confers upon one of the parties to the contract, legal power and control over the person, property, and freedom of action of the other party, independent of her own wishes and will; I, having no means of legally divesting myself of these odious powers (as I most assuredly would do if an engagement to that effect could be made legally binding on me), feel it my duty to put on record a formal protest against the existing law of marriage, in so far as conferring such powers; and a solemn promise never in any case or under any circumstances to use them. And in the event of marriage between Mrs. Taylor and me I declare it to be my will and intention, and the condition of the engagement between us, that she retains in all respects whatever the same absolute freedom of action, and freedom of disposal of herself and of all that does or may at any time belong to her, as if no such marriage had taken place; and I absolutely disclaim and repudiate all pretence to have acquired any *rights* whatever by virtue of such marriage.

Note: Both Mill and Taylor had been ill prior to their marriage and much of their correspondence, even from the 1830s, mentions such conditions. Some historians have concluded that Harriet Taylor suffered from syphilis, a disease she may have contracted from her first husband early in their marriage. She also had tuberculosis, as did Mill; indeed, she may have contracted the disease from Mill. By the 1850s both had serious episodes of illness brought on by this tuberculosis, or consumption, as it would have been called. The October/November, 1850 letter printed earlier was written to Taylor when she was particularly ill. No doubt the optimistic message of the women's suffrage movement in America was meant to cheer her.

   Once married, Mill began to encourage Taylor to publish jointly with him on the topics they had discussed together for years. Such joint authorship would not have been appropriate while she was married to John Taylor. They had worked together on Mill's two-volume work on political economy, and were working on other treatises, especially concerning freedom and equality. Taylor's illness no doubt stirred Mill to press the issue of joint authorship: "But I shall never be satisfied unless you allow our best book the book which is to come, to have our two names on the title page. It ought to be so with everything I publish, for the better half of it all is yours, but the book which will contain our best thoughts, if it has only one name to it, that should be yours" (Mill to Taylor, August 29, 1853). There would be no joint authorships and in the autumn of 1858, after years of battling against tuberculosis, Harriet Taylor Mill died.

Mill to W. T. Thornton,[4] from Avignon, France, November, 1858

   The hopes with which I commenced this journey have been finally frustrated. My Wife, the companion of all my feelings, the prompter of all my best thoughts,

---

[4]   One of Mill's colleagues in the East India Company in London.

the guide of all my actions is gone! She was taken ill at this place with a violent attack of bronchitis and pulmonary congestion. The medical men here could do nothing for her, and before the physician at Nice, who had saved her life once before, could arrive, all was over.

It is doubtful that I will ever be fit for anything, public or private, again. The spring of my life is broken. But I shall best fulfil her wishes by not giving up the attempt to do something useful. I am sure of your sympathy, but if you knew what she was, you would feel how little any sympathy can do.

Note: *The first book Mill published after Taylor's death was* On Liberty *(1859), a book that is standard reading in many high-school and college courses in the United States. That book was dedicated to Harriet Taylor and the dedication is reprinted earlier in this chapter. He then turned to writing* The Subjection of Women *which, as noted earlier, was completed in 1861 but not published until 1869. That was their "best book," the one he wanted her name on as co-author. The following excerpts are from letters Mill wrote in response to letters that he received following publication of that book.*

Mill to Alexander Bain,[5] July 14, 1869

The most important thing women have to do is to stir up the zeal of women themselves. We have to stimulate their aspirations – to bid them not despair of anything, nor think anything beyond their reach, but try their faculties against all difficulties. In no other way can the verdict of experience be fairly collected, and in no other way can we excite the enthusiasm in women which is necessary to break down the old barriers. This is more important now than to conciliate opponents. But I do not believe that opponents will be at all exasperated by taking this line. On the contrary, I believe the point has now been reached at which, the higher we pitch our claims, the more disposition there will be to concede part of them. All I have yet heard of the reception of the new book confirms this idea. People tell me that it is lowering the tone of our opponents as well as raising that of our supporters. Everything I hear strengthens me in the belief, which I at first entertained with a slight mixture of misgiving, that the book has come out at the right time, and that no part of it is premature.

One effect which the suffrage agitation is producing is to make all sorts of people declare in favour of improving the education of women. That point is conceded by almost everybody, and we shall find the education movement for women favoured and promoted by many who have no wish at all that things should go any further. The cause of political and civil enfranchisement is also prospering

---

[5]   Alexander Bain (1818–1903) was a noted British philosopher and a frequent correspondent with Mill. Bain wrote several books important to psychology including *The Senses and the Intellect* (1855), *The Emotions and the Will* (1859), and *Mind and Body* (1872). Moreover, he was founding editor of the first psychological journal, *Mind*, in 1876.

almost beyond hope. You have probably observed that the admission of women to the municipal franchise has passed the Commons, and is passing the Lords without opposition. The Bill for giving married women the control of their own property has passed through the Commons, all but the third reading, and is thought to have a good chance of becoming law this session.

Mill to John Nichol,[6] *August 18, 1869*

I have been long without acknowledging your letter of the 20th July, because there were several points in it on which I wished to make some remarks, and I have not had time to do this sooner. Even now I am unable to do it at any length. You have, I doubt not, understood what I have endeavored to impress upon the readers of my book, that the opinions expressed in it respecting the natural capacities of women are to be regarded as provisional; perfect freedom of development being indispensable to afford the decisive evidence of experiment on the subject: and if, as you truly say, conventionalities have smothered nature still more in women than in men, the greater is the necessity for getting rid of the conventionalities before the nature can be manifested. I have, however, thought it indispensable to weigh such evidence as we have and examine what conclusions it points to, and I certainly think that, in all matters in which women do not entirely lean upon men, they have shown a very great command of practical talent . . .

I thought it best not to discuss the questions of marriage and divorce along with that of the equality of women; not only from the obvious inexpediency of establishing a connection in people's minds between the equality, and any particular opinions on the divorce question, but also because I do not think that the conditions of the dissolubility of marriage can be properly determined until women have an equal voice in determining them, nor until there has been experience of the marriage relation as it would exist between equals. Until then I should not like to commit myself to more than the general principle of relief from the contract in extreme cases.

Mill to G. Croom Robertson,[7] *August 18, 1869*

. . . The most important of your points is the suggestion of a possible turning of what is said about the usefulness of the present feminine type as a corrective to the present masculine, into an argument for maintaining the two types distinct by difference of training. You have yourself gone into considerations of great impor-

---

[6]   John Nichol (1833–1894) was professor of literature at the University of Glasgow.
[7]   George Croom Robertson (1842–1892) was a Scottish philosopher and one of the editors of the journal, *Mind*.

tance in answer to this argument, all of which I fully accept. I should add some others to them, as, *first*, it is not certain that the differences spoken of are not partly at least natural ones, which would subsist in spite of identity of training; *secondly*, the correction which the one type supplies to the excesses of the other is very imperfectly obtained now, owing to the very circumstance that women's sphere and men's are kept so much apart. At present, saving fortunate exceptions, women have rather shown the good influence of this sort which they *might* exercise over men, than actually exercised it.

Note: *The three previous letters from scholars were typical of the mail that Mill received in response to his 1869 book. Yet the next letter makes it obvious that the book was also being read outside the academic community. The following letter was written in response to a woman who, after reading* The Subjection of Women, *asked Mill's advice on whether she should divorce her husband on grounds of incompatibility.*

Mill to Unidentified Woman, May 1, 1870

You greatly overrate the qualities required for writing such books as mine, if you deem them to include that of being a competent adviser and director of consciences in the most difficult affairs of private life. And even a person qualified for this office would be incapable of fulfilling it unless he possessed an intimate knowledge of the circumstances of the case, and the character of the persons concerned. It would be a long and a difficult business to define, even in an abstract point of view, the cases which would justify one of two married persons in dissolving the contract without the consent of the other. But as far as I am able to judge from your own statement, yours does not appear to be a strong case, since your husband has still an affection for you, and since you not only do not complain of any ill treatment at his hands, but have so much confidence in his goodness and high feeling, as to feel sure that even in case of your leaving him without his consent, he would not seek to withhold any of your children from you.

If I could venture to give any opinion, it would be that if the only bar between you and such a man is a difference in your "ways of thinking and feeling," unfortunate as such a difference is in married life, the mutual toleration which we all owe to those who sincerely differ from us forms a basis on which the continuance of your union may be made endurable, and the differences themselves, when nothing is done to exasperate them, may, as is usually the case between persons who live intimately together, tend gradually to an approximation.

Epilogue

Shortly after his wife's death, Mill bought a little house in Avignon near the cemetery where Harriet was buried. He would live there for several months each year with his stepdaughter, Helen. The monument at the cemetery was large, with a lengthy inscription, and made of Carrara marble, the marble that Michelangelo used to sculpt his statue of David. It is said to have cost Mill a year's salary.

When *The Subjection of Women* appeared in print, it did not list Harriet Taylor's name on the title page as co-author, but there is no doubt that she influenced the writing. The book's opening paragraph is a single sentence that historian Eugene August (1975) pronounced the best sentence Mill ever wrote. Mill (1869) began:

> The object of this essay is to explain as clearly as I am able, the grounds of an opinion which I have held from the very earliest period when I had formed any opinions at all on social or political matters, and which, instead of being weakened or modified, has been constantly growing stronger by the progress of reflection and the experience of life: That the principle which regulates the existing social relations between the two sexes – the legal subordination of one sex to the other – is wrong in itself, and now one of the chief hindrances to human improvement; and that it ought to be replaced by a principle of perfect equality, admitting no power or privilege on one side, nor disability on the other. (p. 1)

It was a powerful and profound opening to his arguments for "perfect equality." The importance of the book is evidenced by the fact that it is still read today in classes that treat feminist theory and the sociology of the sexes.

There is more to say about the relationship of Mill and Taylor that has not been touched on to this point. Although there are many scholarly sources that treat this subject, and in consistent ways (e.g., August, 1975; Glassman, 1985; Packe, 1954; Pappe, 1960), the focus here will be on one source, an excellent book by a literary scholar, Phyllis Rose, who has described the Mill–Taylor marriage in a book on Victorian marriages. In the Mill–Taylor letters there is insistent praise from Mill stating that his intellect pales in comparison to Taylor's. It is a message that Mill repeated again and again in correspondence, and one that Taylor never disputed. And when she died he continued it in correspondence with other scholars, noting that no man or woman alive was her equal in terms of her intellect. Some of Mill's friends were truly embarrassed by such pronouncements. Rose (1983) offers an interesting hypothesis to explain their relationship.

Rose argues that Mill understood and identified with the subjection of women, largely because he experienced that as a boy and young man in terms of his relationship with his father. Rose (1983) wrote: "His early experiences led him to resent subjection but also to experience it as the most intense connection between two people" (p. 135). Thus he was willing to subject himself wholly to the control of his wife:

> He invented a role for her which she liked both in theory (she liked the idea of equality) and in practice (she liked the feel of mastery). Her subject was willing. Mill's mind approved equality but his soul craved domination. He atoned for the subjection of women by the voluntary, even enthusiastic, subjection of one man and portrayed the result as a model marriage of equals. (Rose, 1983, p. 140)

If such subjugation at long last brought Mill some measure of affection, perhaps it was worth it. The role that Harriet Taylor played in shaping the products of his pen is sharply disputed by scholars (see, for example, Pappe, 1960[8]). There seems no doubt that Mill overstated her contributions, but there is evidence in her letters of the quality of her thought. And there is no denying that, like Mill, she brought with her the first-hand knowledge of subjection. Scholars dispute what her contributions were, but they also ponder what Mill's contributions might have been had he not met her.

Suggested Readings

Elliot, H. S. R. (Ed.) (1910). *The letters of John Stuart Mill*, Vols. I and II. New York: Longmans Green.
The most complete collection of Mill's letters, except that it excludes the correspondence with Harriet Taylor (see Hayek, 1951). The majority of letters printed in this chapter are from this collection.
Hayek, F. A. (1951). *John Stuart Mill and Harriet Taylor: Their friendship and subsequent marriage*. Chicago: University of Chicago Press.
This book reprints all of the known correspondence between Taylor and Mill, as well as many other letters relevant to their relationship.
Heyd, T. (1989). Mill and Comte on psychology. *Journal of the History of the Behavioral Sciences*, 25, 125–138.
Contrasts the psychological views of Mill and Comte in terms of their sociopolitical and pragmatic orientations, noting that their systems are not entirely exclusive of one another.
Mill, J. S. (1843). *A system of logic, ratiocinative and inductive, being a connected view of the principles of evidence and the methods of scientific investigation*. New York: Harper (8th edn., 1900).
Mill's book that, among other things, defined his vision of a science of human nature.
Mill, J. S. (1869). *The subjection of women*. New York: Holt (1885 printing).
Mill's classic feminist treatise.
Mill, J. S. (1873). *Autobiography*. Boston: Houghton Mifflin (1969 edn.).
This book was published posthumously, largely with the help of Helen Taylor, Mill's stepdaughter. Although there is much of interest in this book, Mill's descriptions of his bouts of depression are particularly moving.
Neff, E. (1924). *Carlyle and Mill: Mystic and utilitarian*. New York: Columbia University Press.
One of Mill's most interesting friendships was that with Thomas Carlyle (1795–1881), British essayist and historian. Carlyle's most famous work was a three-volume history of the French Revolution published in 1837. The first draft volume of that work was

[8] Pappe (1960) wrote: "The wide claims made by Mill's new biographers for Harriet's intellectual ascendancy cannot be substantiated. Her early writings evidence her dependence on Mill. For the later period of their partnership we have no valid evidence to show that Harriet turned Mill's mind towards new horizons or gave an unexpected significance to his thought. The specific claims made in this respect crumble under the weight of the counter-evidence" (p. 47).

destroyed by Mill's maid when she assumed the pile of papers was waste meant for burning.

Packe, M. (1954). *The life of John Stuart Mill*. New York: Macmillan.

A very readable and scholarly biography of Mill.

Rose, P. (1983). *Parallel lives: Five Victorian marriages*. New York: Alfred Knopf.

Chapter 3 treats the marriage of Mill and Taylor in a combination of sound history and interesting psychology.

CHAPTER

Wilhelm Wundt
(Archives of the History of American
Psychology/University of Akron)

James McKeen Cattell at age 20
(Library of Congress)

An American in Leipzig

James McKeen Cattell (1860–1944) was among the most important psychologists of his day and a key figure in the development of American psychology as a science. He coined the term "mental test," established the Psychological Corporation (which would become a principal publisher of psychological tests), founded the journals *Psychological Review* and *Psychological Bulletin*, and founded the psychology laboratories at the University of Pennsylvania (1889) and Columbia University (1891), where he trained a number of doctoral students who would make important contributions to psychology, such as Robert S. Woodworth, Edward L. Thorndike, and Harry Hollingworth.

Cattell's honors were many, including his selection as the first psychologist admitted to the prestigious National Academy of Sciences in 1901, and in 1929 his election as President of the Ninth International Congress of Psychology – the first international psychology congress to be held in the United States. Arguably Cattell's most important contribution to psychology was his editorship of the journal *Science* from 1894 until his death in 1944. When he bought that journal from Alexander Graham Bell, it was of marginal importance, but under his editorship, he turned it into the most important voice for scientific discovery in the world. Moreover, he used his position as editor to promote the image of psychology among the natural sciences; there is no denying that it significantly enhanced psychology's visibility and status among the older sciences.

Cattell was born in Easton, Pennsylvania, home of Lafayette College, where his father was president from 1863 until 1883. The Cattell family was well educated, ambitious, well connected politically and socially, and financially successful. It seems likely that in his crib, James McKeen Cattell realized that he would make important contributions to the world.

After his graduation from Lafayette College in 1880, Cattell pursued additional study for a time in Germany, but returned in 1882 when he received a fellowship to study with G. Stanley Hall (1844–1924) at Johns Hopkins University. There he began his work on the measurement of mental processes in America's first psychology laboratory. However, he and Hall soon clashed and the incident resulted in Hall's withdrawal of his fellowship (see Ross, 1972). Feeling anger and resentment toward Hall, Cattell returned to Germany for a second time to pursue a doctorate in psychology in Wilhelm Wundt's (1832–1920) laboratory at the University of Leipzig, arriving there in November, 1883. Cattell graduated from Leipzig in 1886, the first American to earn a doctorate from Wundt with a dissertation in the new science of psychology.

At the time of Cattell's arrival at Leipzig, Wundt's fame as a psychologist was already well established. Students from a number of countries came to Leipzig to study with Wundt, including 16 Americans for whom Wundt served as the major professor (Benjamin et al., 1992). Many of these Americans described Wundt as an excellent mentor and a gifted lecturer. Consider the following passage from one of those students:

> Clad in a conventional black frock-coat and black trousers, he [Wundt] would steal into his great lecture hall, attended by his *famulus* [assistant], as if he wished to avoid observation. As soon as his familiar figure appeared, applause in the form of shuffling feet on the part of his hundreds of students would greet him . . . Utterly unmoved, as if he had not heard us, Wundt would glide to his place on the dais, assume his accustomed position, fix his eyes on vacancy and begin his discourse. There could not be a better scientific lecturer. Without a scrap of writing, he would speak for three-quarters of an hour so clearly, concisely, and to the point, that, in listening to him, one would imagine one were reading a well-written book in which the paragraphs, the important text of the page, the small print, and the footnotes were plainly indicated. Wundt told no stories, gave few illustrations, scorned any attempt at popularity. His only thought was to deal with the topic of the day as thoroughly and as exhaustively as the time permitted . . . With all this, he was followed almost breathlessly, sometimes by eight hundred students, and, if the lecture had been unusually amazing, they would burst into spontaneous applause. As unconscious as at the beginning, Wundt

would glide from the hall, and another great and unforgettable experience of life had ended. (Worcester, 1932, p. 90)

Throughout his career at Leipzig, Wundt remained one of the university's most popular lecturers. Finding a room large enough to hold his classes was a perennial problem.

Apparently Cattell did not hold Wundt in the same esteem as did many of his other students. His letters express doubts about Wundt's abilities as a scientist and the value of his work. The letters that follow are excerpts from the Cattell letters and journal entries published by historian Michael Sokal (1981). The originals are part of the Cattell Papers in the Manuscript Division of the Library of Congress in Washington, DC. All letters, except two, are from Cattell to his parents, whom he typically addressed as "Dear Mama and Papa." One letter is to Cattell from his father, William Cattell, and the other, not really a letter, is an outline of a dissertation proposal that Cattell submitted to Wundt.

These letters were all written during Cattell's years as a student at Leipzig with Wundt, from 1883 to 1886. They give considerable insight into Cattell's personality and his working relationship with Wundt. They portray Cattell as self-centered, arrogant, disrespectful of others, and supremely confident, some would say narcissistic. In contrast, they show Wundt as a flexible mentor, and not as the autocrat that some historians of psychology have portrayed him to be. These letters also give an idea of what it was like to be a graduate student in the beginning days of the new science of psychology.

The Letters

Journal entry, November 23, 1883

To think of it; here I am in Leipzig! We sailed from N. Y. on the Servia Wed. Oct. 31st arriving in Liverpool early Friday morning (the 9th). The ship was tossed about somewhat but it was a pleasant passage for this time of year. I was only sick two days . . .

I know as yet nothing about the university . . . I will hear Wundt . . . I must work harder than I have since my freshman year in college. My program is to study mostly empirical psychology, reading a little on the history of philosophy. I want to work on Lotze,[1] translating his Psychologie & writing some review, and to work and write on stimulants & my Baltimore experiments.[2]

---

[1]   Rudolf Hermann Lotze (1817–1881) was trained in medicine at the University of Leipzig and spent most of his career on the faculty at the University of Göttingen. He was a physiologist, philosopher, and psychologist who influenced the beginnings of experimental psychology.

[2]   Refers to the work Cattell did at Johns Hopkins University on the speed of mental processes while a student with G. Stanley Hall.

Cattell to parents, December 30, 1883

Tomorrow afternoon Prof. Wundt is going to explain to Berger and me an "Arbeit"[3] with which Berger[4] expects to pass his examination. If we get valuable results they will be published under our two names. I am getting a piece of apparatus made, which I have invented in order to carry on the work I began in Baltimore. I have written to Dr. Hall, hinting that I would like to have my notes and papers. I am not anxious that he should publish a paper, which would give him credit, which he does not deserve. If magazine editors do not see fit to print my work under my name it need not be published at all. It looks as though I had found several serious mistakes in results published by Wundt, but of this I cannot be sure until I make further experiments. I will have to work hard during the rest of the semester as I am moving on a number of different lines having little in common. Experimental psychology lies about as far apart from philosophy as chemistry from Greek.

Cattell to parents, January 6, 1884

I am working hard and I think successfully. There were four of us, working at a subject in experimental psychology, I being the last to join, and one, who was to publish the results under his name, having been working on the subject for about a year. I told you Wundt was going to give Berger and me a subject; we were pleasantly surprised when he told us that we could keep on with the same work, that the others had not been very successful, and would have to take up a new and less important subject. This was of course quite a compliment to us. We hope to have results worth publishing in two or three months. It would be quite nice for me to be the joint author of a German paper. We work every day and very hard. Day before yesterday we worked, with only twenty minutes intermission, from eight in the morning until after seven in the evening. We have a room to ourselves, and can come when we please and do what we please. Besides the work given us by Wundt, we are making some experiments I suggested, and which we hope will give interesting results. Of course I have lots of other work before me. I can now continue my Baltimore experiments, and must do a good deal of preparatory study before I will be ready to translate Lotze's psychology.

Cattell to parents, January 20, 1884

I spend four mornings and two afternoons working in Wundt's laboratory. I like Berger very much, he works hard, has good ideas and – what is equally important

---

[3] Literally meaning "work," it refers here to a research problem.
[4] Gustav Oscar Berger was a German student and friend of Cattell.

– is ready to follow my good ideas. He does most of the averaging & table-making, which is no small or easy work. On the whole I like Wundt, though he is inclined first to disparage our ideas and then adopt them, which is rather aggravating. It is of course possible that we may not get along well together, as differences of fact and opinion will occur, and I don't know how to give up when I think I'm right. German Professors are not used to "indocile" students, as it is usual here in the Professor's presence to "hold awe-striken breaths at a work divine."

But as I said I respect and like Wundt, and as he mostly lets us alone every thing may move along smoothly. Our work is interesting. If I should explain it to you you might not find it of vast importance, but we discover new facts and must ourselves invent the methods we use. We work in a new field, where others will follow us, who must use or correct our results. We are trying to measure the time it takes to perform the simplest mental acts – as for example to distinguish whether a color is blue or red. As this time seems to be not more than one hundredth of a second, you can imagine this is no easy task. In my room I am continuing my Baltimore experiments, and here too I measure times smaller than 1/1000 of a second. With all this and my lectures I have as you may suppose but little time for reading or writing.

Note: In a January 5, 1884 letter to his parents, Cattell wrote: "Professor Wundt thought that when a magnet was made by passing a current around a piece of iron, it was made instantaneously. I find with the current he used it takes over one tenth of a second. All the times he measured were much too long" (Sokal, Davis, & Merzbach, 1976, p. 60). In a later letter to a research physician, Cattell explained the error in more detail, noting that the problem was that the times in which the magnet in the chronoscope (the instrument that measured time) attracted the armature and released the armature were different, and that Wundt had not recognized that systematic difference in calculating reaction times (ibid.). Thus Cattell was correct about some errors in Wundt's work. (For additional information on apparatus issues in the early mental chronometry work, especially the work of Cattell and Wundt, see Benschop & Draaisma, 2000.)

William Cattell to his son, James McKeen Cattell, January 27, 1884[5]

I address you this separate letter, because your mother & I have had our anxiety as to your relations with Prof. Wundt much increased by yr references to him in yr last letter. If in this matter I trusted alone to my own judgment, so often clouded of late with groundless apprehensions, it might seem as if I was giving myself

[5] The previous few letters from Cattell to his parents had contained passages about Wundt that had begun to worry them. Cattell's losing his fellowship at Johns Hopkins University in his conflict with Hall was an embarrassing moment for William Cattell. He wrote this letter to his son to try to help him see the attitude that caused troubles in his relation to authority figures.

needless anxiety. But dear Mama, from yr very first reference to Prof. W. & without a word from me, has felt intensely anxious & has often expressed her great apprehension lest, instead of securing him as a friend you wd say or do something that wd first alienate him and then (alas! Such is human nature in the best of men) lead him to place something in yr way – Of course on other grounds than any personal reason, such as want of "docility" etc. –

I fear you cannot understand how deeply we feel this danger. Both of us are distressed at the very thought of your having – even if you are in the right – a repetition of the ill feeling wh. it is evident was brought about between some of the authorities & yrself at Balt. – We both fear you are not as cautious in this matter as you should be. You speak in yr letter of not being able to accept the views of the German Professors as to their students being "docile" – but in the very kind letter you recd fr. Dr. Hall he used this very word with ref. to you: – he was favorably impressed with yr abilities & had the highest expectations of what you cd have accomplished had you only been more "docile" – Parental partiality is proverbially blind, especially where a son is so loving & thoughtful & dutiful as you are: yet dear Mama & I cannot but fear that there is some real ground for apprehension here; that what you may regard as "independence," or even "self-respect" in yr relations to yr professors, we shd call by another word; – and I should be wanting in parental love & faithfulness if I did not earnestly warn you against it – *for your own sake*.

So my dear son let me beg you to act with great circumspection in all your relations to the Professors for our sakes as well as your own. You write of having found errors in some of Prof. W's published investigations. If he is really wrong & you have discovered it, to publish this with becoming modesty when you are no longer under his instructions will of course do you honor. *Now* it is dangerous ground. No matter if Prof. W. is convinced that he is wrong; it will require great tact for you to let him & others know it without wounding his amour propre: and engendering unkind feelings towards you. And no honor that you could get from any such correction of his errors could possibly compensate for the loss of his kindly personal interest in you. It wd be far better for you, while a student, to be as "docile" as the most exacting Professor could demand.

I have written you a long letter – & yesterday & today have been poor days with me: – but dear Mama was anxious that I shd write. She has read what I have already written and says it expresses just what she feels. I know you will appreciate our devoted love for you that leads me to call yr attention to this matter, & to urge you to act with great caution – for yr own sake as well as ours.

May God ever bless you my dear son.

Cattell to parents, February 6, 1884

I thank you, Papa, for your letter anent my relations with Wundt and other people. No one, not even myself, has my welfare so much at heart as you and

Mama, and by following your advice I would probably always be more successful and happy than in following my own impulses. The only question is whether a life of uniform success and happiness would not be as undesirable as it is impossible. I admire men who struggle, and suffer, and fail, rather than those who are always comfortable and in good humor. It is perhaps better to fight one's way through life, than to slip through. As to this special case my relations with Wundt could not be pleasanter, nor do I see any reason why they should change. Both Berger and I intend to take our Dr.'s degree here, and would not want to get in trouble with Wundt.

Cattell to parents, October 16, 1884

I got my largest piece of apparatus from the machinist's today.[6] I feel like an author with his first book. The machine is really a great advance on methods heretofore used. I imagine Prof. Wundt would give $500 if he had it four years ago – or indeed so much if he had himself thought of it now. I shall set up my elements tomorrow, and have things in working order. It is very much better having my apparatus in my room.[7] In the first place every-thing is in good order, I shall never be disturbed, and it is far more convenient. But there are two greater advantages even than these. There will arise no differences of opinion between Prof. Wundt and myself, and Prof. Wundt will not be given credit for half the work.

Draft of a statement Cattell gave to Wilhelm Wundt, October 25, 1884

I should like to present as a thesis in application for the degree of doctor of philosophy an essay on Psychometry, or the time taken up by simple mental process. I am well aware that this subject is too large and difficult for me to thoroughly investigate as a university student, but I trust I shall be able to prepare an acceptable thesis by giving (1) a brief summary of the work which has been done in this field (2) a fuller account of experiments I myself have made and the results reached (3) the subjects which seem to me to need investigation.

I give below an imperfect analysis, of the factors on which the reaction time depends, underlining with blue ink the subjects on which I have worked, and with red ink those which I should like to investigate this winter.[8]

---

[6] The apparatus was a gravity chronometer, a device that measured time in 1/1000ths of a second.

[7] Wundt allowed Cattell to move the experiments from the Psychology Laboratory to Cattell's apartment.

[8] No different ink colors appeared in the draft.

Reaction Time
Analysis.
The *sense stimulus*. Sound, Light, Touch (touch
proper, electric shock, temperature) Taste, Smell

Sound – loudness, pitch, timbre ⎫
Light – intensity, color (saturation) ⎪
Touch proper – force, kind ⎪
Electric shock – intensity ⎬ momentary
Temperature – degree (heat & cold) ⎪ continuous
Taste – intensity, variety ⎪
Smell – intensity, variety ⎭

Sense organ, nerve, and muscle { normal / abnormal }

Sense organs & efferent nerve used – touch on lip and back, light image on yellow
or field of indirect vision, taste on tip of tongue or palate.
Muscle & efferent nerve used, finger wrist, foot

The Subject   (physiological / psychological)

Sex, Age, Temperament, Character, Mental Acumen, Physical power, Avocation
The Same Individual

Normal
Abnormal

                                         Normal
                                         Fresh, wearied, interested, indifferent,
Mental State ⎫   dull, excited
Physical State ⎬   Eating, Sleep, exercise, temperature,
                                         weather (saturation & electric condition)
                                         Attention – Practice – Fatigue

                  { Voluntary
Attention   { caused (signal, distraction, etc.)
                  ⎧ series
Practice ⎫   ⎨ day
Fatigue   ⎬   ⎩ continuous

                                  Abnormal
                  (pain or disease)
Physical   (distress, elation, or disease) { natural
Mental   (insanity)   { artificial
artificial by use of drugs, alcohol, ether, caffein, morphine, etc.

Cattell to parents, October 28, 1884

The lectures began yesterday. I have already heard the most important of them
and the light is too bad to admit of taking notes. I am very busy, and as I want to

work in the morning and evening, ought to take exercise in the afternoon. The air is so bad, as to be really injurious. In Prof. Wundt's lecture room there are packed some three hundred men – the ceiling is low and not a crack is left open. For all of which reasons I shall attend but few lectures. German students in their last year scarcely ever hear any.

Cattell to parents, October 29, 1884

At four I heard Prof. Wundt lecture on Ethics. After the lecture he talked to me for three quarters of an hour and was extremely pleasant. In the paper I gave him on Saturday, I classified the work I have done, and propose doing this winter under four heads. Prof. said he would accept any one of these as a doctor's thesis, but recommended one as especially original.[9] He said he would accept this for his "Philosophische Studien."[10] This offer is all the more of an honor from the fact that scarcely any of the work has been done – he must therefore have considerable confidence in me. He said he would let me use the set up type for printing my doctor's thesis, which would make it comparatively inexpensive. He also said he hoped when I printed work in English I would send him a translation for his "Studien." He is going to come to see me.

Cattell to parents, November 6, 1884

Prof. Wundt came to see me this morning. He stayed three quarters of an hour and was very cordial, as he has always been recently. He has treated me very nicely, considering that I have called his attention to mistakes in his work, and have left his laboratory, where he would much rather have had me stay. That he has acted this way is not only pleasanter for me, but also better for him. If, as many would have done, he had insisted that my corrections were wrong and my work of no account, and had put obstacles in the way of my setting up my own laboratory, the facts would not have been changed; but I would have published sometime or other my work in a way not pleasant to him. As it is he offers to print my work in his own magazine and is in every way pleasant and obliging. I shall therefore probably correct his work in a way that will be almost a compliment, and I shall be considered a pupil of his, and he will be given credit for what work I print now or later.

He praised today my arrangement of apparatus highly, and will copy it in some respects for his institute. He also offered to accept my doctor's thesis and print in his "Studien" the work I began in Baltimore. This I have been working

[9]   The topic was association (learning).
[10]   This was Wundt's journal, which he had founded in 1881, and which published many of the psychological studies from his laboratory.

on and can easily finish by Christmas. So I could probably get my degree the first of August. In six months I could study up enough Philosophy, physics, and biology or mathematics, I imagine. Still unless there is some special reason for this I would rather finish up all my experimental work by August, then come home to see you, and return and pass the examination in the Winter. Besides the division of my work above mentioned – which is on the Time of Simple Mental Processes – there are three others. The Association time, which Prof. Wundt recommended for a doctor thesis and offered to accept for his Journal. This is scarcely begun. Then there is a good deal of work already done on the Reaction Time – this is what Berger and I worked on last winter. Fourthly there is work on the Legibility of letters, words, and phrases, practically the most interesting and valuable of all. I have quite a good deal of work on this, but there is any amount more to be done.

Cattell to parents, January 16, 1885

Prof. Wundt lectured yesterday and today on my subject – I suppose you won't consider it egotistical when I say that I know a great deal more about it than he does, but you will be surprised when I say that half of the statements he made were wrong. I cannot understand how he is willing to give as positive scientific facts the results of experiments which he knows were not properly made. I could write a paper on these two lectures most damaging to Prof. Wundt. It is to be hoped for his sake as well as mine that he passes me in the examination on philosophy.

Cattell to parents, January 22, 1885

I worked in Wundt's laboratory this afternoon probably for the last time. Berger has enough material for his thesis – he is to hand it in next month. I have no doubt that it will be accepted, and if so mine will be as a matter of course. Wundt's laboratory has a reputation greater than it deserves – the work done in it is decidedly amateurish. Work has only been done in two departments – the relation of the internal stimulus to the sensation, and the time of mental processes. The latter is my subject – I started working on it at Baltimore before I read a word written by Wundt – what I did there was decidedly original. I'm quite sure my work is worth more than all done by Wundt & his pupils in this department, and as I have said it is one of the two departments on which they have worked. Mind I do not consider my work of any special importance – I only consider Wundt's of still less. The subject was first taken up by Exner, and Wundt's continuation of it has no originality at all; and being mostly wrong has done more harm than good.

Cattell to parents, February 13, 1885

As I told you I was invited by Prof. Wundt to supper with other members of the laboratory. I can't say that I enjoy such things, I have no special reverence for any one I know personally, and it gives me no special delight to hear Wundt talk about the opera and such like. Mrs. Wundt is however nice and Prof. Wundt seems to like me and to appreciate my phenomenal genius.

Cattell to parents, June 13, 1885

I called on Mrs. Wundt this morning – she is very nice, as I have told you. The professor also came to see me – I am going to row them up to Connewitz some day next week. There are two bright children – a girl of eight, and a boy of six. Prof. Wundt is coming to see me tomorrow. I am invited to dinner at Prof. Heinze's[11] the day after – so you can see I am on excellent terms with my professors. Indeed I imagine – though I have often been told the contrary – that I am quite clever in getting along with all sorts and conditions of people. The only question is how far it is manly – or worth the while – to spend one's life playing a part or rather a dozen different parts.

Cattell to parents, November 14, 1885

I received today both "Brain" and the "Studien" with my paper.[12] My work is of considerable importance, and some parts of it are very easy to understand and of general interest. I think it would be well if you could get it noticed in the papers, quoting possibly some paragraphs. Indeed it might not be impossible and might be worth the while to get it re-printed in one of our papers – the Sunday Tribune for example. I shall myself send copies to some journals (mostly European) and to some people – I shall not however send any to Philadelphia, Princeton or Bethlehem.

A paper like this gives me a very secure place in the scientific world, makes me equal with any American living. One likes however to be given credit for what one has done even by people who know nothing about the work. I scarcely know why we like to be praised by fools, but we do. Still there is some reason in my case. I may want a position or a wife, and certainly do want to be able to pick out the people I associate with.

---

[11]   Max Heinze (1835–1909) was a leading authority on the history of philosophy.
[12]   Cattell's paper, "The inertia of the eye and brain," appeared in Wundt's journal in German and in the English-language journal, *Brain*.

Epilogue

Readers of the Cattell letters are often dismayed at Cattell's egotistical manner; there are certainly no signs of humility here. He constantly worries about Wundt or Hall getting credit they do not deserve and that he alone get credit for his work. He tells his parents that his work (which at that time had not resulted in a single publication) is worth more than all of that in Wundt's lab. He threatens actions against Wundt if Wundt doesn't pass him in an exam. He sees himself as clever in manipulating and deceiving people, even though he thinks that such charades might be "unmanly." He sees himself as a "phenomenal genius," and after publication of a single paper, he declares himself "equal with any American living." Maybe "egotistical" is not an adequate description, given such extreme statements; perhaps there is pathology in this personality. One wonders what his parents thought of the claims in his letters. We know that they were worried about him destroying his relationship with Wundt. Were they embarrassed by his boasts?

Perhaps this arrogance was helpful in Cattell's career. Perhaps he could not have played his important entrepreneurial role in psychology without such an inflated ego. It is possible that he transferred his belief in himself to his belief in psychology, predicting it would ultimately be the most important of the sciences. And he spent most of his life promoting that vision. As noted earlier, his position as editor of *Science* afforded him a unique opportunity to portray the new science of psychology to the better established physical sciences. And that visibility was critical for psychology's growth as a science in the early part of the twentieth century.

Cattell never completely abandoned his indocile ways. He had a number of disputes with Columbia University's president Nicholas Murray Butler. When Cattell wrote a letter in 1917 protesting the sending of conscientious objectors into battle in World War I, Butler accused him of treason and fired him. Cattell later sued, won a large financial settlement from the university, but never returned to academic life. Instead he continued to edit his several journals and launched the Psychological Corporation. Although he had angered some (perhaps many) in his career, he seems to have matured as a scientist and human being. His contributions in the early history of psychology have ensured him a place on American psychology's Mount Rushmore.

Suggested Readings

Baldwin, B. T. (1921). In memory of Wilhelm Wundt by his American students. *Psychological Review, 28*, 153–188.

Upon Wundt's death in 1920, a number of his American students contributed to a collection of memories about him. Cattell's recollections of Wundt are part of this tribute.

Blumenthal, A. L. (1975). A reappraisal of Wilhelm Wundt. *American Psychologist, 30*, 1081–1088.

This article marks the emergence of a renewed interest in the work of Wilhelm Wundt and a critical examination that corrected earlier views of Wundt's psychology. Particularly significant is a section of the article that relates Wundt's ideas to contemporary psychology, notably cognitive psychology.

Bringmann, W. G., & Tweney, R. D. (Eds.) (1980). *Wundt studies: A centennial collection.* Toronto: Hogrefe.

This book is a collection of articles commemorating the centennial of Wundt's founding of his laboratory in Leipzig in 1879. It provides extensive biographical material about Wundt, discusses the founding of the Leipzig laboratory, describes the research topics investigated in that laboratory, and provides case studies of several of Wundt's doctoral students.

Cattell, J. McK. (1885). The time it takes to see and name objects. *Mind, 11,* 63–65.

This article is a brief account of some of Cattell's research at Baltimore and Leipzig on the speed and nature of mental processing.

Sokal, M. M. (1971). The unpublished autobiography of James McKeen Cattell. *American Psychologist, 26,* 626–635.

This article is an unfinished Cattell autobiography which Sokal found in a box of unmarked papers at the Library of Congress. It is the only extant autobiographical material of Cattell other than that contained in his letters.

Sokal, M. M. (1980). *Science* and James McKeen Cattell, 1894–1945. *Science, 209,* 43–52.

This article describes the 50 years of Cattell's editorship of *Science* and the importance of that activity for a science of psychology.

Sokal, M. M. (Ed.) (1981). *An education in psychology: James McKeen Cattell's journal and letters from Germany and England, 1880–1888.* Cambridge, MA: MIT Press.

This book is an edited collection of Cattell's letters from his graduate study in Baltimore, Germany, and England. It includes excerpts from more than 450 documents – letters and journal entries – selected from the Cattell Papers in the Library of Congress. Themes of the book include Cattell's personal development, the early development of experimental psychology, and the nature of American study in European universities in the late nineteenth century.

Wundt, W. (1874/1904). *Principles of physiological psychology,* trans. E. B. Titchener. New York: Macmillan.

This is the first edition of Wundt's most influential work in psychology. It was a thorough compendium of the research underlying the new science of psychology. The book eventually went through five editions.

6
CHAPTER

Harry Kirke Wolfe
(Archives of the History of American Psychology/University of Akron)

The Struggle for Psychology Laboratories

In nineteenth-century America, psychology was a subfield of philosophy, embodied in what was called moral philosophy, a brand of Scottish faculty psychology. According to moral philosophers, like James McCosh of Princeton University and Noah Porter of Yale University, psychology was the science that would reveal the nature of the soul. But it was not an experimental science, nor was it much grounded in empiricism. In fact, some historians have argued that moral philosophy was taught in colleges to counter the so-called atheistic tendencies of the British empiricists (Leahey, 2000).

These early psychologists were interested in such topics as sensory functioning, the role of experience, how associations were formed, emotions, and the nature of will, all of which would be important areas of study in the new psychology of the twentieth century (see Fuchs, 2000). However, they were principally interested in questions of the soul – knowing right from wrong, avoiding temptation, sustaining religious faith. The 1850 edition of Webster's dictionary affirmed this view in defining psychology as "a discourse or treatise on the human soul; or the doctrine of man's spiritual nature" (p. 886). That definition persisted into the 1880s until supplanted by one that changed "philosophical discourse" to "laboratory science." It was a remarkable metamorphosis both in terms of the nature of the change and the time it took to occur.

Historians generally credit German psychologist Wilhelm Wundt (1832–1920) with founding the first laboratory of psychology in 1879 at the University of Leipzig (see Chapter 5). In this laboratory, Wundt began experimental investigations of the questions that had long been part of philosophical psychology, particularly questions of sensory functioning (an influence of the British empiricists who argued that all knowledge was acquired through the senses). Students from all over the world came to study with Wundt, including American, G. Stanley Hall (1844–1924).

When Hall arrived in Leipzig he already had received his doctorate (under William James at Harvard University). Hall spent minimal time with Wundt, working instead with the physiologist Carl Ludwig, but he was much committed to the new scientific psychology. A few years after his return to the United States, Hall opened the first American psychology laboratory at Johns Hopkins University in 1883. From that point the laboratory movement spread quickly in America, partly stimulated by the publication of James's *Principles of Psychology* in 1890. By 1900, only 17 years after Hall had established his laboratory, there were more than 40 psychology laboratories in the United States (Benjamin, 2000).

A number of these early laboratories were founded by American students who got their doctorates with Wundt: James McKeen Cattell (University of Pennsylvania, 1889 and Columbia University, 1891), Harry Kirke Wolfe (University of Nebraska, 1889), Edward A. Pace (Catholic University, 1891), Frank Angell (Cornell University, 1891 and Stanford University, 1893), Edward Wheeler Scripture (Yale University, 1892), and George M. Stratton (University of California, 1896). And thus began the science of psychology, referred to as the "new psychology" to distinguish it from the old psychology of the moral philosophers. (See Morawski, 1988, and Danziger, 1990 for treatments of the rise of scientific psychology in America.)

Some universities embraced the new psychology and eagerly supported the development of their psychological laboratories. However, for the majority of universities the enthusiasm was less and the pace of development much slower. There were still many university scholars who believed, like August Comte, that there could never be a science of mind, that the mind was capable of studying everything except itself. Or they might have agreed with John Stuart Mill that psychology could be a science but only an empirical one, never an experimental one. Many of these late nineteenth-century psychology laboratories struggled against these beliefs, trying to establish their legitimacy alongside the established natural sciences.

One of the earliest of the American psychology laboratories was founded at the University of Nebraska in September of 1889. It was the sixth such laboratory to be founded and possibly the first that was devoted exclusively to laboratory instruction and research by undergraduate students. Its founder was Harry Kirke Wolfe (1858–1918), who graduated from Nebraska with his baccalaureate degree in 1880. Wolfe taught school for a few years and then went to Berlin in 1883, where he studied with Hermann Ebbinghaus (1850–1909), and then to Leipzig the following year. He received his doctorate with Wundt in 1886, conducting a study on the memory for tones for his dissertation research. Wolfe was in Leipzig with James McKeen Cattell (see Chapter 5) and the two of them became the first Americans to earn psychology degrees with Wundt, Cattell finishing in April and Wolfe in August.

Wolfe returned to the United States and once again taught in the public schools for a few years before accepting a job at the University of Nebraska in 1889 as assistant professor in philosophy. He was also chair of the Philosophy Department, a dubious honor at best because he was the only member of the department. In his first year Wolfe taught a course in scientific psychology and a year-long course entitled "experimental psychology," emphasizing the methods of the new psychology that he had learned in Germany. Several senior students in this class were allowed to pursue original research for college credit.

Wolfe's laboratory attracted a number of students who went on to distinguished careers in psychology. Two surveys during the 1920s (Fernberger, 1921, 1928) ranked Nebraska third among the universities in the training of psychologists, an achievement due principally to Wolfe's dedication and inspiration as a teacher. Three of Wolfe's undergraduates – Walter Pillsbury, Madison Bentley, and Edwin Guthrie – would become presidents of the American Psychological Association, an honor that no other undergraduate mentor in the history of psychology can claim. The success of his students belies the success Wolfe had in building and equipping his laboratory. His tenure as a faculty member at the University of Nebraska was a continuing struggle to convince an agriculturally minded administration of the value of the new psychology and the need for a laboratory. The letters and other documents that follow tell the story of this struggle. It is not just Wolfe's story but more broadly is the story of psychology's early struggle for recognition as a laboratory science. These letters also give an idea of the nature of research and equipment common to the early psychology laboratories (see Capshew, 1992).

The documents in this chapter are taken from the Archives of the University of Nebraska and the personal papers of the Wolfe family. The letters begin with a report that Wolfe sent to the acting chancellor of the university at the close of his first year at Nebraska, describing his year as chair of the Philosophy Department and his plans for the near future.

The Letters

Harry Kirke Wolfe to Charles E. Bessey (Acting Chancellor, University of Nebraska),
May 15, 1890

I respectfully offer the following report of the Dept. of Philosophy for the current collegiate year.

I. (a)   A beginning has been made in collecting the more important works on Modern Psychology. A few recent works of Ethics and Logic have also been added to the library. The number of periodicals has increased from three to fourteen, including several foreign magazines of my own.[1]

(b)   The following illustrative apparatus is now ready for use.

1 *Set Marshall's Physiological Charts* (13)
1 *Synthetic preparation of the Brain*
1 *Greatly enlarged model of the eye*
1 *Greatly enlarged model of the ear*
1 Stop-clock (1/4 sec)
1 Metronome
1 *Chronoscopograph with electrical accessories*[2]
1 Large Seconds Pendulum (regulator of above)
1 Oliver's Color-sense Test
1 Helmholtz Standard color sheets
1 Drop apparatus (Intensity of sound)[3]
1 Revolving apparatus (memory for color)

Several hundred hand-painted cards for testing color sense and color-memory, and for illustrating the phenomena of contrast, mixture of sensations, after images etc.

1 Large case for preserving the instruments and materials of the Dept.
A few drawings illustrating the development of the nervous system and sense organs

Attention may be called to the fact that this dept. has received *no* "Equipment fund." $217.50 "Library fund" and $100.00 "Dept. fund" have been granted.

II.   The work of this Dept. ought to be chiefly scientific, but lack of equipment has compelled me to make it largely literary. A mixed system of recitation and informal lectures has been followed. The stimulation of curiosity rather than its satisfaction has been my aim. . . .
IV.   The isolation of the department and the reputed difficulty of its subjects make it impossible to insist on organic development. I have in mind the following lines for extension.

---

[1]   One of those added was Wundt's journal, *Philosophische Studien*, which began publication in 1881.
[2]   This device was for measuring time, perhaps in 1/1000ths of a second, and was a standard piece of apparatus for the early psychological laboratories.
[3]   The drop apparatus was likely an acoumeter, a device that produced sounds of differing intensity by dropping a metal ball from different heights onto a glass plate.

(a)   Two years of Psychology as *science* (Clark University, the Universities of Penn, Wis & Ind place this subject alongside the *other nat. sciences*) . . .

I hope the scientific nature of this dept. may be recognized in the next apportionment of funds. We *need* a tone instrument, a time-sense instrument, a number of cheaper instruments. . . and *an additional room*.

Wolfe to the Regents of the University [of Nebraska], May 29, 1891

I offer the following report of the department of Philosophy for the academic year 1890–'91.

I. *Improvements* during the year

In the fall term an effort was made to begin the work in Experimental Psychology; though the lack of equipment prevented the rise of sanguine expectations. First of all a laboratory room was necessary. After consulting with one of the Regents I decided to use a part of the Library Fund of my department for fitting up an unoccupied room in the basement, and if necessary to replace the loan from the department fund of the following year. In my opinion the success of the dept. depended on the introduction of experimental work this year. About $80.00 was used in fitting up a laboratory. Most of the apparatus added during the year was made by the University mechanic, by students, or by the professor.

II. *Nature of the Work of the Department* during the year . . .

(b)   Laboratory work may be roughly grouped as follows; (1) Measurement of simplest mental phenomena, as the Least Observable Difference in sensations. (2) Determination of the relation between stimulus and sensation. (3) Testing Weber's Law. (4) Determination of the area of extent of consciousness for simple ideas. (5) Sense of Time. (6) Time occupied by simple mental processes.[4]

Even with our crude apparatus some of the results are very interesting and with supplementary experiments for verification have sufficient value to warrant publication. With some addition to our equipment these laboratory experiments ought to offer enough new material each year for at least one monograph worthy of publication. This, however, would be merely incidental to the repetition of the better known experiments in Psychophysics as scientific discipline and as an introduction to the study of mind . . .

---

[4]   This work on measuring the speed of mental processes came from the Leipzig laboratory and, more specifically, from Cattell's dissertation research (see Chapter 5). In fact, Wolfe was a subject in Cattell's doctoral research.

IV. Plans for the future, including estimate of necessary expenses.

I cannot emphasize too strongly the necessity of providing some facilities for experimental work . . . It is possible to build up an experimental dept. in Psychology with little outlay. No field of scientific research offers such excellent opportunities for original work; chiefly because the *soil is new*.[5] If it is not deemed advisable to encourage original research in this line, $500.00 will provide sufficient equipment for illustrating the most common phenomena of our elementary course. I think this sum would enable me to furnish work for two hours per week during the entire year.

Wolfe to the Regents of the University of Nebraska, May?, 1891

The Department of Philosophy now possesses sufficient equipment for such work as has been heretofore required. It is believed, however, that opportunity is now afforded for greatly increasing its usefulness at comparatively small expense . . .

The scientific nature of Psychology is not so generally recognized; hence I feel justified in calling attention to two points. 1st The advantages offered by experimental Psychology, as a discipline in scientific methods, are not inferior to those offered by other experimental sciences. The measurement of the Quality, Quantity and Time Relations of mental states is as inspiring and as good discipline as the determination of, say the per cent of sugar in a beet or the variation of an electric current. The *exact* determination of *mental processes* ought to be as good *mental* discipline as the exact determination of processes taking place in matter.

2nd The study of mind is the most universally *applied* of all sciences. Because we learn so much about it from everyday experience is the reason, perhaps, that it only recently has become an "exact" science. Whatever is known of mind is especially valuable in professional life, and particularly so in that profession whose object is the *training* of mind. The science of teaching depends immediately upon the results of psychological investigation. The progressive teacher must know, not only these results and the "methods" based thereon, but also how to investigate for himself.

On the recommendation of the Faculty you have adopted an Elective Course in Pedagogics based on the study of Mind. The importance of that Course itself would justify the equipment asked for. I do not think, however, that only those expecting to teach would elect work in experimental Psychology. On the contrary there is a natural demand for such work by students of philosophical tendencies.

---

[5] Wolfe was trying to add a two-hour per week laboratory component to the beginning course in psychology. Notice his use of the agricultural metaphor, a tactic he used in other letters as well. As a Land Grant college in a farming state, agriculture played a significant role in the affairs of the University of Nebraska.

On the whole I think it is probable that a course in experimental Psychology would be elected by as many non-professionals as elect work in some of the other departments of science.

With the following apparatus and with such books as the Library Fund will enable me to procure, I shall be able to offer a two years course in Psychology and to inaugurate the elective course in Pedagogics based thereon. [*Note: The remainder of the letter is a two-page listing of needed equipment with prices totaling $1,818.*][6]

Note: Wolfe's class enrollments were growing at this time at a rate more than double the University's growth. In the summer of 1891 he was promoted to the rank of Professor. However, he received no equipment fund. He kept the laboratory functioning by building most of the necessary equipment himself. He also borrowed some equipment from the departments of Biology (microscopes, thermometers, and embryological specimens) and Physics (tuning forks, resonators, electric motors, magnets, and batteries). He bought some items using his own money, diverted some of his meager library funds to purchase equipment, and regularly overspent his departmental budget. Even without the laboratory funds, he added the two-hour laboratory to the beginning course and continued the lab for the experimental course, both of which were two-semester courses. He received no teaching credit for the extra hours he spent each week with students, nor did the students receive any extra credit for all those laboratory hours added to their regular classwork. Still, the students filled his classes.

Wolfe to the Chancellor and Board of Regents of the University of Nebraska, March 31, 1895

The relative growth of the department of Philosophy during the past three years has been even greater than that of the University. It is now impossible to carry the work in a manner at all creditable to the professor in charge. The demand has been created and we are not able to satisfy it as becomes a University . . .

The work here has become inexplicably popular and our courses now contain more elective students than all the courses given by the eight men at Cornell. This is of course pleasant to us all in a sense. The work however is not up to the standard even of last year, and another year it cannot be done as well as this year without more encouragement than the Regents have already given.

---

[6] It is likely that this letter was encouraged by Chancellor Bessey, who wanted Wolfe to give the Regents extra justification for his equipment requests. The reference to sugar in a beet was not just another agricultural metaphor. The University was one of three funded by the US government in their efforts to develop an American sugar beet that would reduce American sugar imports. Consequently, the Chemistry Department at the University was greatly supported with a well-equipped laboratory that would have been the envy of most university chemistry departments.

Instead of ten hours per week I am carrying this semester twenty seven hours (last semester more than thirty hours) *exclusively* and *continuously* with students. After looking over papers, themes, etc there is very little time left for preparing lectures. I can feel the difference between the quality of last year's work and that of this year in spite of the facts that all day Saturday and six hours Sunday are regularly given to University work and that I know more than I knew last year.

The equipment of psychological departments has not thus far depended upon the total revenue of the Universities. Harvard had no laboratory until ours was commenced. Indiana University with half our income has as good a laboratory as we have, while Michigan with twice our income has not half as good a beginning, though Wisconsin has made a better start than we have. The growth of the laboratory has depended upon the success of its application to the work in hand. Ours was the fifth to begin (in this country) and is not far from fifth in material equipment, while only one laboratory is helping more students . . .

The Chancellor has announced that for the next year, at least, we must be content to be a *teaching* university. I agree with him in this and with the sentiment back of it – that we must always be chiefly a teaching school. In so far as that principle *is recognized* facilities will be afforded departments in proportion to their teaching needs and teaching results . . .

I know it will be impossible to furnish equipment for a second year in psychology or for special work by advanced students, though there is already demand for both . . . But I do confidently expect that means will be furnished to make my own work as effective as possible in the lines already opened.

The following items are believed to be necessary to maintain the work of philosophy at its present standard.

1. Student assistance $700.00
2. Mechanical assistance (wood & metal work)   200.00
3. Additional Equipment   500.00
4. Incidental (or current) Expenses   250.00
5. Repairs on basement rooms   65.00
6. Books, periodicals, etc.   350.00

In regard to the third item I wish to say that the lack of equipment this year has been largely made up by additional time and energy on the part of the professor, and that cannot possibly be continued another year even by working all day Sundays.

Note: Undoubtedly this is the most negative report filed by Wolfe and, like almost all of his other pleas for funding of the laboratory, it resulted in no laboratory funds being granted by the University. In part Wolfe's dismay reflects a broken promise by the university administration in the spring of 1894, which had indicated that he would receive a sum of $1,200 for equipment for the laboratory. Wolfe had spent part of the spring writing to colleagues at other psychology laboratories, such as E. B. Titchener at Cornell Univer-

sity, indicating that he would be receiving money for his laboratory and asking for information about new psychological equipment. When the budget situation worsened in the summer, the promised funds were withdrawn.

Unable to convince the University of Nebraska administration, Wolfe made his arguments public in a journal article entitled "The New Psychology in Undergraduate Work" (Wolfe, 1895). One of the arguments against funding his laboratory was that it was for undergraduate students, and there were many in psychology who believed that psychology laboratory instruction should be reserved exclusively for graduate students (see French, 1898).

Wolfe in the Psychological Review *(1895)*

It ought to be unnecessary to describe the effects on the student of a laboratory course in psychology, and yet, like chemistry and physics and biology and zoology, this new science will have to fight for every inch of ground . . .

A valid objection [to the psychology laboratory] is . . . the time required for this work. Better supervision is required than for laboratory work in either chemistry or physics. This demands personal attention from the instructor in psychology. I think this objection is unanswerable. If instructors in psychology are unwilling to do this kind of work, we must wait until another species of instructor can be evolved . . .

Logic and metaphysics and the dictionary may be well taught without a laboratory; physiological and experimental psychology require some *things* to see and feel . . .

The junior . . . comes to psychology with more or less information concerning isolated facts of several sciences. [In a] general course of physiological and experimental psychology with laboratory practice . . . the needed facts of the associated sciences will be brought together; their relations will become clear, and gradually there will grow up a rational appreciation of the interdependence of the forces of nature.

Note: To understand Wolfe's exasperation at the lack of support for his laboratory, it is important to understand how he felt about research, specifically, how research was important in learning. For Wolfe, doing research meant ensuring mental growth. He believed that getting students involved in research was a means to stimulate their continued learning once they left the university, what would today be called an impetus to lifelong learning. The excerpt that follows is from an undated lecture of Wolfe's found in the Archives of the University of Nebraska.

Wolfe lecture notes entitled "The Psychology of Research" *(no date)*

If we go back to childhood it is plain that research is the sole method of growth. Watch the child in his cradle investigating his fingers, his toes, his toys, the wall paper, anything that attracts his interest. Try the lecture method with him and observe his disgust! No worse, his indifference. The beginning of interest and of development is in self-initiated movements . . .

Vaccination is said to last seven years. Research is not so effective. The growing mind should be reinoculated with the virus of independent search for facts and new relations every week, and even old age is not immune from the attacks of staleness. In fact the best elixir for doping father time is again this same faithful old tincture of *work with first hand data*, doubly distil it, and take it three times a day . . .

Mental power comes solely from wrestling with complex problems in a primitive way – the way of intimate, individual, self-initiated *interest. This is original research.*

Note: In 1897 the University of Nebraska had a new chancellor, George MacLean, who objected to Wolfe's habit of overspending his budget. He asked Wolfe to provide a written explanation of a reported budget deficit of $75.86.

Wolfe to George MacLean and Board of Regents, March 24, 1897

At the request of the Chancellor I herewith submit a list of expenses incurred by me for the Department of Philosophy after my departmental fund was exhausted . . . I do not consider these expenses as a "deficit" even in the technical use of the term. I am personally responsible for them and if the University doesn't wish to buy the articles from me when it is able to do so I shall preserve the remains as "heirlooms" in my family treasure house . . . As long as I work thirty five hours (35) per week[7] with my students I shall provide any needed inexpensive article for my work without reference to the condition of my departmental fund. When my relations to the University become purely business relations I shall have much more time for personal affairs.

Epilogue

No doubt Wolfe's attitude about overspending his budget, as expressed in the letter above, irritated MacLean. Wolfe's response, in essence, indicated that he was dismayed that the University could not provide him with the funds that *he* considered necessary to do his job. Moreover he indicated he would basically ignore his budget and, if he overspent, make up the difference from his own pocket. MacLean was not amused, and in the spring semester of 1897 he called Wolfe to his office to tell him that he should resign immediately or be fired. Wolfe, who was arguably the most popular professor on campus among the students, did not

---

[7]   The 35 hours to which Wolfe referred were his actual class and lab contact hours each week, and would not have counted his many hours of preparation, grading, and so forth.

believe that the Board of Regents would support MacLean, and he refused to resign. MacLean announced his firing the next day and indicated it had been supported by the Board.

More than 1,000 of the University's 1,600 students signed a petition in a single day calling for Wolfe's reinstatement, but the Regents upheld the firing. At the next meeting of the mandatory chapel services, students hissed Chancellor MacLean when he appeared on stage. In the end, Wolfe was gone. He was unemployed for a year and then found work in the public schools, first in Omaha and then in Lincoln.

Wolfe was replaced by Thaddeus L. Bolton, who had earned his doctorate with G. Stanley Hall. Bolton, too, was a strong advocate of the laboratory and for awhile it seemed that he might be more successful than Wolfe. He managed to get a commitment from the administration for seven laboratory rooms in the new physics building scheduled for completion in 1905. He proudly described his laboratory-to-be in a 1904 article in *Science* (see Miner, 1904). However, a few months before the building opened, the rooms were assigned to the Physics Department, and Bolton was left in his old space in the basement of the library. Eventually he too would be fired for his continued complaints about the lack of support of his laboratory.

After eight years in the public schools, Wolfe was rehired at the University of Nebraska in 1906. He continued his requests for laboratory support. Mostly these were ignored, although he did get some minimal equipment funds and funds for several student assistants for the laboratory. Finally, in 1916, the University announced it would build a new social sciences building that would include Philosophy/Psychology. Wolfe was told to design the psychology laboratories for that building, which he did. It was his last contribution because he died in the summer of 1918 at the age of 59. His dream laboratory opened approximately 18 months later.

Suggested Readings

Benjamin, L. T., Jr. (1991). *Harry Kirke Wolfe: Pioneer in psychology*. Lincoln: University of Nebraska Press.
   This biography describes the life of one of the earliest American psychologists and arguably the most inspirational psychology teacher of his generation.
Benjamin, L. T., Jr. (2000). The psychology laboratory at the turn of the 20th century. *American Psychologist, 55*, 318–321.
   Coverage of the origins of psychology laboratories in America from 1883 to 1900.
Billia, L. M. (1909). Has the psychological laboratory proved helpful? *Monist*, July, 351–366.
   Offers a mixed view of the accomplishments of more than 25 years of the new psychology.
Bruce, R. V. (1987). *The launching of modern American science, 1846–1876*. New York: Cornell University Press.
   Traces the development of science laboratories in America in the natural sciences and their impact on the course of higher education.

Capshew, J. (1992). Psychologists on site: A reconnaissance of the historiography of the laboratory. *American Psychologist, 47,* 132–142.

Discusses the development of historical accounts of American psychology laboratories and includes an extensive bibliography of such published accounts.

Capshew, J. H., & Hearst, E. (1980). Psychology at Indiana University from Bryan to Skinner. *Psychological Record, 30,* 319–342.

A history of the Indiana psychology laboratory, founded in 1887 by William L. Bryan, a student of G. Stanley Hall.

Danziger, K. (1990). *Constructing the subject: Historical origins of psychological research.* New York: Cambridge University Press and Morawski, J. G. (Ed.) (1988). *The rise of experimentation in American psychology.* New Haven: Yale University Press.

These two books provide excellent coverage of the birth and development of laboratory psychology in America.

Murray, F. S., & Rowe, F. B. (1979). Psychology laboratories in the United States prior to 1900. *Teaching of Psychology, 6,* 19–21.

Brief descriptions of the founding of 44 psychology laboratories.

Raphelson, A. C. (1980). Psychology at Michigan: The Pillsbury years. *Journal of the History of the Behavioral Sciences, 16,* 301–312.

Although Pillsbury did not establish the psychology laboratory at the University of Michigan, his arrival there in 1897 marked a new era in excellence for that department. Pillsbury was one of Wolfe's undergraduate students. This article describes the growth of the Michigan department during Pillsbury's tenure as department head.

Wolfe, H. K. (1895). The new psychology in undergraduate work. *Psychological Review, 2,* 382–387.

Wolfe's rationale for providing psychology laboratory instruction for undergraduate students. See the opposing view as offered by Ferdinand C. French in the same journal (1898, 5, 510–512).

7
CHAPTER

William James
(Archives of the History of American Psychology/University of Akron)

William James and Psychical Research

In the 1850s in a darkened room, people gathered around a table, hands joined, eyes closed, sitting in silence. One of the persons in the circle had special powers – the medium (usually a woman) – the person who would serve as the conduit to make contact with spirits in the other world, the spirits of loved ones now departed. After a period of silence there would be noises, perhaps voices, the windows to the room might blow open, the table might begin to move, the medium would jerk, moan, shake, or display some other unusual behavior that signaled she had gone into a trance. Then the spirits would make contact with the group through the medium and the entertainment would begin. These events were called séances and they were the modus operandi for spiritualists in the latter half of the nineteenth century (Leahey & Leahey, 1983).

When scientific psychology emerged in the United States in the 1880s, psychologists made great efforts to distance themselves from such pseudosciences as phrenology, psychic research, mesmerism, physiognomy, mental healing, and spiritualism. The public, however, had a difficult time making that separation. For the average citizen, if psychology was the science of the mind, then it obviously was about mind reading, telling the future, and communicating with the dead.

Psychologists were not amused at this confusion and sought to erect clear boundaries between their science and these fields that masqueraded as science, often through methods of deception. Thus when one of their own – one of the most visible of the new psychologists – became heavily involved in psychic research and attended multiple séances, it was a source of great embarrassment, consternation, and even anger.

William James (1842–1910) is arguably the most important individual in the early history of American psychology. That reputation results, in part, from his classic book, *The Principles of Psychology* (1890), a two-volume work that set the stage for an American functional psychology. Through James's incomparable prose, the *Principles* recruited a generation of researchers to share in James's enormous promise for the new science of psychology.

James's contributions to the science of psychology were acknowledged by his peers in many ways, including his election to the National Academy of Sciences and to the presidency (twice) of the American Psychological Association. Yet a few years after the publication of the *Principles*, some of America's most prominent psychologists – James McKeen Cattell, Edward Bradford Titchener, and Hugo Münsterberg, for example – were openly concerned that James had become a liability for scientific psychology. That concern grew from James's identification with psychical research, particularly investigations of mediums and their professed abilities to communicate with spirits of the dead.

James had expressed an interest in psychic phenomena as early as 1869, when he was 27 years old. However, he did not become seriously interested in the field until a trip to London in 1882–1883 exposed him to the newly established Society for Psychical Research (SPR). On that trip he met Henry Sidgwick (then president of the SPR), Frederic Myers, and Edmund Gurney, all of whom would figure prominently in James's growing interest in the topic.

In 1884, James joined the British SPR and also became a supporter of the American SPR, which was founded in Boston that same year. The following year, James met Mrs Leonore Piper (1859–1950), a Boston medium who had already impressed some members of James's family with her abilities in contacting the spirit world. It was at this point that James got seriously involved in the field, conducting a prolonged investigation of Mrs Piper through participation in a number of séances. He reported on that work in 1886 to the American SPR and had his novelist brother, Henry James, read a further report on Mrs Piper to the British SPR in 1890.

James became an active promoter of the progress of both the British and American SPRs. For the former, he was a vice-president for 18 years and served two terms as president (1894–1896). He also was a frequent contributor to the *Proceedings* of both groups, writing on such topics as clairvoyance, automatic writing, and mediumistic phenomena, such as trance, materialization, and sensory occurrences. Some of his articles were also published in popular magazines, such as *Scribner's*, and in these accounts he often attacked scientific psychology for its unwillingness to pursue research on psychic phenomena, or at least to keep an open mind about such occurrences.

James's colleagues counterattacked him in a series of letters in Cattell's journal, *Science*, with James joining in the debate. The new psychology, which had only recently declared its independence from philosophy and which sought to improve its standing among the sciences (see Coon, 1992; Moore, 1977), was naturally concerned about James's work, which was seen as taking psychology back to the mysticism and metaphysics of its past. Some of the attacks were quite pointed and voices on both sides of the controversy expressed bitterness in their exchanges. James countered the arguments of his colleagues, lamenting the fact that as scientists they had closed their minds to psychic events without ever evaluating the evidence or demonstrating a willingness to test the claims of psychics. He believed that such an attitude was, in itself, unscientific. In the end, none of the criticism deterred James, who persisted in psychical research until his death.

The Letters

William James to Thomas Davidson, February 1, 1885[1]

As for any "anti-spiritual bias" of our Society, no theoretic basis, or *bias* of any sort whatever, so far as I can make out, exists in it. The one thing that has struck me all along in the men who have had to do with it is their complete colorlessness philosophically. They seem to have no preferences for any general *ism* whatever. I doubt if this could be matched in Europe. Anyhow, it would make no difference in the important work to be done, what theoretic bias the members had. For I take it the urgent thing, to rescue us from the present disgraceful condition, is to ascertain in a manner so thorough as to constitute *evidence* that will be accepted by outsiders, just what the *phenomenal conditions of certain* concrete phenomenal occurrences are. Not till that is done can spiritualistic or anti-spiritualistic theories be even mooted. I'm sure that the more we can steer clear of theories at first, the better.

James to Shadworth Hodgson,[2] *August 16, 1885*

We have been stirred up by the English Society for Psychical Research's example, to start a similar society here, in which I am somewhat interested, though

---

[1] This letter was prompted by a complaint from Davidson that the American Society for Psychical Research had an "anti-spiritual bias."

[2] Shadworth Hodgson (1832–1912) was an English philosopher who was greatly admired by James.

less practically than I could wish. Returns come slowly – I mean stuff to inquire into comes slowly; and altogether my small experience has filled me with a prodigious admiration of the devotion and energy of Gurney, Myers, and others with you. Something solid will come of it all, I am sure.

James to Carl Stumpf,[3] January 1, 1886

I don't know whether you have heard of the London "Society for Psychical Research," which is seriously and laboriously investigating all sorts of "supernatural" matters, clairvoyance, apparitions, etc. I don't know what you think of such work; but I think that the present condition of opinion regarding it is scandalous, there being a mass of testimony, or apparent testimony, about such things, at which the only men capable of a critical judgment – men of scientific education – will not even look. We have founded a similar society here within the year – some of us thought that the publications of the London society deserved at least to be treated as if worthy of experimental disproof – and although work advances very slowly owing to the small amount of disposable time on the part of the members, who are all very busy men, we have already stumbled on some rather inexplicable facts out of which something may come. It is a field in which the sources of deception are extremely numerous. But I believe there is no source of deception in the investigation of nature which can compare with a fixed belief that certain kinds of phenomenon are *impossible*.

James to George Croom Robertson,[4] October 4, 1886

I mailed you t'other day Part II of the *Proceedings* of the American Society for Psychical Research, a rather sorry "exhibit" from the "President's" address down. There is no one in the Society who can give any time to it, and I suspect it will die by the new year.

James to Christine Ladd-Franklin,[5] April 12, 1888

Your letter interests me very much, because the account you give is similar to accounts which I have heard from others of the influence upon them of the hand

[3] Carl Stumpf (1848–1936) headed the psychology laboratory at the University of Berlin and is best known for his work on the psychology of tone. James had met Stumpf on an earlier trip to Europe.
[4] George Croom Robertson (1842–1892) was a Scottish philosopher and professor of mental philosophy at University College, London. He was the initial editor of the journal, *Mind*, and one of James's closest friends.
[5] See Chapter 10 for a discussion of Ladd-Franklin.

of a certain Mrs. Wetherbee who is a "magnetic healer" here, and who, on members of my wife's family, has certainly "charmed away pain" in a most surprising manner. I know Dr. Crockett also, and like him. I have had hitherto only his own accounts of his performances, not knowing any of his patients but one, on whom he failed.

But I am very dubious of the poor little Soc. for Psych. Re. accomplishing much by seeking to "investigate" these things. Of all earthly things, therapeutic effects are the hardest to run to ground, and convince a skeptic of. There will always be a dozen loopholes of escape from any conclusion about therapeutics, and the mind will take which ever one it prefers.

Note: In the following letter, James provides a lengthy and revealing account of his experiences with Mrs Piper and his impressions of her as someone with supernatural powers.

James to Frederic William Henry Myers,[6] December 1890

You asked for a record of my own experiences with Mrs. Piper, to be incorporated in the account of her to be published in your *Proceedings*.

I made Mrs. Piper's acquaintance in the autumn of 1885. My wife's mother Mrs. Gibbens, had been told of her by a friend, during the previous summer, and never having seen a medium before, had paid her a visit out of curiosity. She returned with the statement that Mrs. P. had given her a long string of names of members of the family, mostly Christian names, together with facts about the persons mentioned and their relations to each other, the knowledge of which on her part was incomprehensible without supernormal powers. My sister-in-law went the next day, with still better results, as she related them. Amongst other things, the medium had accurately described the circumstances of the writer of a letter which she held against her forehead, after Miss G. had given it to her. The letter was in Italian, and its writer was known to but two persons in this country . . .

I remember playing the *esprit fort* [religious free thinker] on that occasion before my feminine relatives, and seeking to explain by simple considerations the marvelous character of the facts which they brought back. This did not, however, prevent me from going myself a few days later, in company with my wife, to get a direct personal impression. The names of none of us up to this meeting had been announced to Mrs. P., and Mrs. J. and I were, of course, careful to make no reference to our relatives who had preceded. The medium, however, when entranced, repeated most of the names of "spirits" who she had announced on the two former occasions and added others. The names came with difficulty, and were only gradually made perfect. My wife's father's name of Gibbens was announced first as

---

[6] Myers (1843–1901) was a philosopher, founding member of the British SPR, and a friend of James.

Niblin, then as Giblin. A child Herman (whom we had lost the previous year) had his name spelled out as Herrin. I think that in no case were both Christian and surnames given on this visit. But the *facts predicated* of the persons named made it in many instances impossible not to recognize the particular individuals who were talked about. We took particular pains on this occasion to give the Phinuit[7] control no help over his difficulties and to ask no leading questions. In the light of subsequent experience I believe this not to be the best policy. For it often happens, if you give this trance personage a name or some small fact for the lack of which he is brought to a standstill, that he will then start off with a copious flow of additional talk, containing in itself an abundance of "tests."

My impression after this first visit was that Mrs. P. was either possessed of super-normal powers, or knew the members of my wife's family by sight and had by some lucky coincidence become acquainted with such a multitude of their domestic circumstances as to produce the startling impression which she did. My later knowledge of her sittings and personal acquaintance with her has led me absolutely to reject the latter explanation, and to believe that she has supernormal powers.

I visited her a dozen times that winter, sometimes alone, sometimes with my wife, once in company with the Rev. M. J. Savage. I sent a large number of persons to her, wishing to get the results of as many *first* sittings as possible. I made appointments myself for most of these people, whose names were in no instance announced to the medium. In the spring of 1886 I published a brief "Report of the Committee on Mediumistic Phenomena" in the *Proceedings* of the American Society for Psychical Research.

I dropped my inquiries into Mrs. Piper's mediumship for a period of about two years, having satisfied myself that there was a genuine mystery there, but being over-freighted with time-consuming duties, and feeling that any adequate circumnavigation of the phenomena would be too protracted a task for me to aspire just then to undertake. I saw her once, half accidentally, however, during that interval, and in the spring of 1889 saw her four times again. In the fall of 1889 she paid us a visit of a week at our country house in New Hampshire, and I then learned to know her personally better than ever before, and had confirmed in me the belief that she is an absolutely simple and genuine person. No one, when challenged, can give "evidence" to others for such beliefs as this. Yet we all live by them from day to day, and practically I should be willing now to stake as much money on Mrs. Piper's honesty as on that of anyone I know, and am quite satisfied to leave my reputation for wisdom or folly, so far as human nature is concerned, to stand or fall by this declaration.

As for the explanation of her trance phenomena, I have none to offer. The *prima facie* [ostensible] theory, which is that of spirit-control, is hard to reconcile with the extreme triviality of most of the communications. What real spirit, at last able to

---

[7] Phinuit was Mrs. Piper's control, that is, the spirit who communicated through her to the others in a séance.

revisit his wife on this earth, but would find something better to say than that she had changed the place of his photograph? And yet that is the sort of remark to which the spirits introduced by the mysterious Phinuit are apt to confine themselves. I must admit, however, that Phinuit has other moods. He has several times, when my wife and myself were sitting together with him, suddenly started off on long lectures to us about our inward defects and outward shortcomings, which were very earnest, as well as subtle morally and psychologically, and impressive in a high degree. These discourses, though given in Phinuit's own person, were very different in style from his more usual talk, and probably superior to anything that the medium could produce in the same line in her natural state. Phinuit himself, however, bears every appearance of being a fictitious being. His French, so far as he has been able to display it to me has been limited to a few phrases of salutation, which may easily have had their rise in the medium's "unconscious" memory; he has never been able to understand *my* French; and the crumbs of information which he gives about his earthly career are, as you know, so few, vague, and unlikely sounding as to suggest the romancing of one whose stock of materials for invention is excessively reduced. He is, however, as he actually shows himself, a definite human individual, with immense tact and patience, and great desire to please and be regarded as infallible . . .

The most convincing things said about my own immediate household were either very intimate or very trivial. Unfortunately the former things cannot well be published. Of the trivial things, I have forgotten the greater number, but the following . . . may serve as samples of their class: She said that we had lost recently a rug, and I a waistcoat. (She wrongly accused a person of stealing the rug, which was afterwards found in the house.) She told of my killing a gray-and-white cat, with ether, and described how it had "spun round and round" before dying. She told how my New York aunt had written a letter to my wife, warning her against all mediums, and then went off on a most amusing criticism, full of *traits vifs* [vivid features], of the excellent woman's character. (Of course no one but my wife and I knew the existence of the letter in question.) She was strong on the events in our nursery, and gave striking advice during our first visit to her about the way to deal with certain "tantrums" of our second child, "little Billy-boy," as she called him, reproducing his nursery name. She told how the crib creaked at night, how a certain rocking chair creaked mysteriously, how my wife had heard footsteps on the stairs, etc. Insignificant as these things sound when read, the accumulation of a large number of them has an irresistible effect. And I repeat again what I said before, that, taking everything that I know of Mrs. P. into account, the result is to make me feel as absolutely certain as I am of any personal fact in the world that she knows things in her trances which she cannot possibly have heard in her waking state, and that the definitive philosophy of her trances is yet to be found. The limitations of her trance information, its discontinuity and fitfulness, and its apparent inability to develop beyond a certain point, although they end by rousing one's moral and human impatience with the

phenomenon, yet are, from a scientific point of view, amongst its most interesting peculiarities, since where there are limits there are conditions, and the discovery of these is always the beginning of explanation.

This is all that I can tell you of Mrs. Piper. I wish it were more "scientific." But
valeat quantum! it is the best I can do.

· James to F. W. H. Myers, January 30, 1891

... To speak seriously, however I agree in what you say, that the position I am
now in (professorship, book published and all) does give me a very good pedestal
for carrying on psychical research effectively, or rather for disseminating its results
effectively ... I ... expect in the summer recess to work up the results already
gained in an article for *Scribner's* magazine ... Of course I wholly agree with you
in regard to the *ultimate* future of the business, and fame will be the portion of
him who may succeed in naturalizing it as a branch of legitimate science. I think
it quite in the cards that you, with your singular tenacity of purpose, and wide
look at all the intellectual relations of the thing, may live to be the ultra-Darwin
yourself. Only the facts are *so* discontinuous so far that possibly all our generation can do may be to get 'em called facts. I'm a bad fellow to investigate on
account of my bad memory for anecdotes and other disjointed details. Teaching
of students will have to fill most of my time, I foresee; but of course my weather
eye will remain open upon the occult world.

Note: What follows is an exchange of letters between James McKeen Cattell (see Chapter
5), editor of Science, and William James, that were published in Science. They demonstrate the conflict within psychology, a new science trying to establish its legitimacy as a
genuine science, with James on the one side arguing for psychic investigations, and most
of the rest of psychologists on the other side trying to distance the field from what they
considered utter nonsense. Cattell's first letter includes responses from five scientists[8] who
visited one or more of Mrs Piper's séances.

James McKeen Cattell, Letter in Science, April 15, 1898 (v. 7, pp. 534–535)

MRS. PIPER, THE MEDIUM.

The last number of the *Proceedings of the Society for Psychical Research* contains
a statement to the effect that the present writer does not pay "the slightest atten-

---

[8]   The five scientists, as identified by Cattell, included: Baldwin (1861–1934), a professor of philosophy and psychology at Princeton, University of Toronto, and Johns Hopkins University;
Trowbridge (1843–1923), a Harvard physicist; Nathaniel Southgate Shaler (1841–1906), a Harvard
geologist; James Mills Peirce (1834–1906) a Harvard mathematician; and Silas Weir Mitchell
(1829–1914), a physician and author.

tion to psychical research *á la* English Society;" he "taboos it throughout, but has never even read the reports and their experiments in telepathy." If this information were obtained by telepathy it does not increase my confidence in that method of communication. It is exactly the thirteen volumes issued by the Society for Psychical Research that seem to me to prove the trivial character of the evidence for the heterogeneous mass of material taken under the wing of the Society.

The present number of the *Proceedings* seems to me, however, of some interest in that it concludes or continues an account of the séances of Mrs. Piper, under the title, "A Further Record of Observations of Certain Phenomena of Trance," on which subject Dr. Richard Hodgson has now contributed over 600 pages. The case of Mrs. Piper is of interest, because Professor James has said:

"If you wish to upset the law that all crows are black, you mustn't seek to show that no crows are; it is enough if you prove one single crow to be white. My own white crow is Mrs. Piper. In the trances of this medium, I cannot resist the conviction that knowledge appears which she has never gained by the ordinary waking use of her eyes and ears and wits." (*SCIENCE*, N.S., III., 884.)

It is Professor James who gives dignity and authority to psychical research in America, and if he has selected a crucial case it deserves consideration. The difficulty has been that proving innumerable mediums to be frauds does not disprove the possibility (though it greatly reduces the likelihood) of one medium being genuine. But here we have the "white crow" selected by Professor James from all the piebald crows exhibited by the Society.

I find, among the great number of names and initials whose séances with Mrs. Piper are reported, five and only five well-known men of science. The following are the concluding sentences of their reports:

From James Mark Baldwin – These elements of truth were, however, so buried in masses of incoherent matter and positive errors as to matters in which she tried to give information that the sense of her failure on the whole is far stronger with me. Even as to the fact of her being in a trance at all my impression is not strong, despite the fact that I came fully expecting to be convinced on that point.

My state of mind, therefore, is almost the same that it was before the sitting, *i.e.*, a condition of willing approach to any evidence on either side of the question at issue; I am only disappointed that she did not give me more data for forming a positive opinion. I am fully aware, however, that one such sitting has very little negative weight, considering the variations which this sort of phenomena are subject to.

From John Trowbridge – I was struck by a sort of insane cunning in the groping of the woman after something intangible. It did not seem to me that she simulated a trance state. She was apparently, as far as I could judge, in some abnormal condition. I could not discover that she hit upon anything that was connected with the handkerchief.

From N. S. Shaler – Let me say that I have no firm mind about the matter. I am curiously and yet absolutely uninterested in it for the reason that I don't see how

I can exclude the hypothesis of fraud, and, until that can be excluded, no advance can be made. When I took the medium's hand, I had my usual experience with them, a few preposterous compliments concerning the clearness of my understanding, and nothing more.

From J. M. Peirce – Since writing the foregoing, I have gone over the notes in detail, making a memorandum of successes and failures. I am surprised to see how little is true. Nearly every approach to truth is at once vitiated by erroneous additions or developments.

From S. Weir Mitchell – On re-reading your notes I find absolutely nothing of value. None of the incidents are correct, and none of the very vague things hinted at are true, nor have they any kind or sort of relation to my life, nor is there one name correctly given.

[And Cattell concluded] Truly, "we have piped unto you, but ye have not danced."

James to the "Editor of Science*" (Cattell), Letter in* Science, *May 6, 1898*
(v. 7, pp. 640–641)

Your reference to my name in the editorial note in *Science* for April 15th, entitled "Mrs. Piper, the Medium," justifies me in making some remarks of my own in comment on your remarks upon Mr. Hodgson's report of her case. Any hearing for such phenomena is so hard to get from scientific readers that one who believes them worthy of careful study is in duty bound to resent such contemptuous public notice of them in high quarters as would still further encourage the fashion of their neglect.

I say any hearing; I don't say any fair hearing. Still less do I speak of fair treatment in the broad meaning of the term. The scientific mind is by the pressure of professional opinion painfully drilled to fairness and logic in discussing orthodox phenomena. But in such mere matters of superstition as a medium's trances it feels so confident of impunity and indulgence whatever it may say, provided it be only contemptuous enough, that it fairly revels in the untrained barbarians' arsenal of logical weapons, including all the various sophisms enumerated in the books . . .

I am sure that you have committed these fallacies with the best of scientific consciences. They are fallacies into which of course, you would have been in no possible danger of falling in any other sort of matter than this. In our dealings with the insane the usual moral rules don't apply. Mediums are scientific outlaws, and their defendants are quasi-insane. Any stick is good enough to beat dogs of that stripe with. So in perfect innocence you permitted yourself the liberties I point out.

Please observe that I am saying nothing of the merits of the *case*, but only of the merits of your forms of controversy which, alas, are typical. The case surely deserves opposition more powerful from the logical point of view than your remarks; and I beg such readers of SCIENCE as care to form a reasonable opinion to seek the materials for it in the Proceedings of the Society for Psychical Research, Part XXXIII. (where they will find a candid report based on 500 sittings since the last report was made), rather than in the five little negative instances which you so triumphantly cull out and quote.

James McKeen Cattell to James, May 6, 1898 (Letter in Science, *v. 7, pp. 641–642)*

My note in SCIENCE was not "editorial," but was placed in that department of the JOURNAL for which editors take the least responsibility. I gave my individual opinion, Professor James gives his, and I fear that our disagreement is hopeless . . . I wrote the note with reluctance and only because I believe that the Society for Psychical Research is doing much to injure psychology. The authority of Professor James is such that he involves other students of psychology in his opinions unless they protest. We all acknowledge his leadership, but we cannot follow him into the quagmires.

James to Theodore Flournoy,[9] February 9, 1906

Yes! Hodgson's[10] death was ultra-sudden. He fell dead while playing a violent game of "hand-ball." He was tremendously athletic and had said to a friend only a week before that he thought he could reasonably count on twenty-five years more of life. None of his work was finished, vast materials amassed, which no one can ever get acquainted with as he had gradually got acquainted; so now good-bye forever to at least two unusually solid and instructive books which he would have soon begun to write on "psychic" subjects. As a *man* Hodgson was splendid, a real man; as an investigator, it is my private impression that he lately got into a sort of obsession about Mrs. Piper, cared too little for other clues, and continued working with her when all the sides of her mediumship were amply exhibited. I suspect that our American Branch of the S. P. R. will have to dissolve this year, for lack of a competent secretary. Hodgson was our only worker, except Hyslop, and *he* is engaged in

[9] Flournoy (1854–1921), professor of psychology at the University of Geneva, shared James's interests in psychic phenomena, and the two were frequent correspondents between 1880 and James's death in 1910 (see the suggested readings section of this chapter for a book collection of their letters).

[10] This is not the English philosopher. Richard Hodgson (1855–1905), a psychologist and psychic researcher, was one of the leaders of the American SPR and was involved with James in the investigation of Mrs. Piper for many years. After his death, James worked with Mrs. Piper to contact Hodgson in a series of séances James called the Piper–Hodgson control.

founding an "Institute" of his own, which will employ more popular methods. To tell the truth, I'm rather glad of the prospect of the Branch ending, for the Piper-investigation – and nothing else – had begun to bore me to extinction . . .

Note: *James sought to make contact with the departed Hodgson. The "contact" was made through Mrs Piper through her control. It is not evident if this control was Phinuit or another spirit.*

James to Ferdinand C. S. Schiller,[11] *August 24, 1906*

The ghost of dear old Hodgson is reappearing through Mrs. Piper and I am to co-ordinate his utterances and make report. *Not* convincing, to me: but baffling exceedingly . . .

James to Charles Lewis Slattery,[12] *April 21, 1907*

My state of mind is this: Mrs. Piper has supernormal knowledge in her trances; but whether it comes from "tapping the minds" of living people, or from some common cosmic reservoir of memories, or from surviving "spirits" of the departed, is a question impossible for *me* to answer for now to my own satisfaction. The spirit theory is undoubtedly not only the most natural, but the simplest, and I have great respect for Hodgson's and Hyslop's arguments when they adopt it. At the same time the electric current called *belief* has not yet closed in my mind.

Whatever the explanation be, trance mediumship is an excessively complex phenomenon, in which many concurrent factors are engaged. That is why interpretation is so hard.

James to Thomas S. Perry, January 29, 1909

I have just got off my report on the Hodgson control, which has stuck to my fingers all this time. It is a hedging sort of an affair, and I don't know what the Perry family will think of it. The truth is that the "case" is a particularly poor one for testing Mrs. Piper's claim to bring back spirits. It is *leakier* than any other case, and intrinsically, I think, no stronger than many of her other good cases, certainly weaker than the G. P. case. I am also now engaged in writing a popular article, "the avowals of a psychical researcher," for the *American Magazine*, in which I simply state without argument my own convictions, and put myself on record. I think that public opinion is just now taking a step forward in these

---

[11]   Schiller (1864–1937) was a philosopher and president of the British SPR.
[12]   Slattery (1867–1930) was an Episcopal minister.

matters . . . and possibly both these *Schriften* [articles] of mine will add their influence.

Epilogue

Interests in psychic phenomena were not a sideline of James's intellectual work. Indeed, as Perry (1935) has noted, such ideas were central to his philosophy, and "from his youth James contemplated such 'phenomena' without repulsion and with an open mind" (p. 204). His final published statement on psychical research came in October, 1909, only ten months before his death. In this *American Magazine* article he concluded his 25 years of work arguing that psychic phenomena were elusive but real, and investigable with the methods of science. He predicted that psychical research would provide "the greatest scientific conquests of the coming generation" (James, 1909, p. 589). On that account, James was monumentally wrong.

James is often portrayed today as a figure who embraced psychology early in his life only to abandon it after 1890 for a preference for philosophy and mysticism. Certainly James said some disparaging things about science, including the new scientific psychology. Yet, although he lost faith in the promise of experimental psychology as his colleagues were practicing it, he never abandoned his belief in the scientific method and continued his version of science in his psychic investigations, despite its rejection by experimental psychology. The letters in this chapter reveal something of this important area of James's life and career, a story that is often omitted from the contemporary histories of scientific psychology. Moreover, this story from James's life illustrates the conflict between scientific psychology and the popular psychology of the public, a conflict that continues today, much to the consternation of most psychologists.

Suggested Readings

Bjork, D. W. (1983). *The compromised scientist: William James in the development of American psychology.* New York: Columbia University Press.
  A look at James as artist, philosopher, and psychologist, including excellent coverage of his debates on the scientific validity of psychical research with Cattell, Münsterberg, and Titchener. The phrase "compromised scientist" has several meanings in this book, one of which refers to the perception of James's abandonment of scientific standards.
Coon, D. J. (1992). Testing the limits of sense and science: American experimental psychologists combat spiritualism, 1880–1920. *American Psychologist, 47,* 143–151.
  Details the efforts of psychologists to distance themselves from pseudopsychology, particularly the claims of spiritists.
James, H. (Ed.) (1920). *The letters of William James* (2 vols.). Boston: Atlantic Monthly Press.
  This collection of James's letters was edited by his son, Henry, and selectively covers the years 1861 to 1910. It is the earliest of the many published collections of James letters and contains some of the most significant pieces in James's vast correspondence which is now housed in the archives at Harvard University.

James, W. (1890). *The principles of psychology* (2 vols.). New York: Henry Holt.

James's classic treatment of psychology in 1,400 pages, a book that required him 12 years to write. Many contemporary scholars in psychology regard it as the greatest book written in the history of psychology. It is must reading for any card-carrying psychologist. And it will interest students who read only a chapter or two.

James, W. (1909). The confidences of a "psychical researcher." *American Magazine, 68,* 580–589. Reprinted in Murphy and Ballou (1960) and in James (1911), *Memories and studies* (New York: Longmans Green), under the title "The final impressions of a psychical researcher."

James's final contribution to the literature on psychical research. He laments that after 25 years he is no closer to understanding psychic phenomena than he was at the beginning of his research. Yet he forecasts a future of significant scientific advance for the field.

Le Clair, R. C. (Ed.) (1966). *The letters of William James and Theodore Flournoy.* Madison: University of Wisconsin Press.

A collection of more than 120 letters between James and Swiss psychologist Theodore Flournoy (1854–1920) covering the years 1890–1910. These two men shared a number of interests, especially psychical research.

Murphy, G., & Ballou, R. O. (Eds.) (1960). *William James on psychical research.* New York: Viking Press.

This book is a compilation of most of James's published and unpublished writings on psychical research, and includes more than 100 pages on James's investigations of Mrs Piper. It also includes a number of letters with various correspondents on the topic.

Perry, R. B. (1935). *The thought and character of William James* (2 vols.). Boston: Little, Brown.

An early biography of James written by one of his students who later became a colleague in James's philosophy department at Harvard. It emphasizes James's role as a philosopher. Also contains many excerpts from James's letters.

Scott, F. J. D. (Ed.) (1986). *William James: Selected unpublished correspondence, 1885–1910.* Columbus: Ohio State University Press.

The best of the James letters appear in earlier collections. Still, these are of interest to anyone who enjoys the charm and vitality of James's writing.

8
CHAPTER

Hugo Münsterberg
(Archives of the History of American Psychology/University of Akron)

Hugo Münsterberg and the Psychology of Law

By 1892 there were more than a dozen American universities that had psychology laboratories, one of those the Nebraska laboratory founded by Harry Kirke Wolfe in 1889 (see Chapter 6). Yet although there were psychology laboratories at lesser universities, there was not one at what was the preeminent university in America – Harvard. William James, the leading figure in psychology and philosophy at Harvard, was determined to remedy that situation. He decided to hire a German psychologist from the University of Freiburg, a young man of 28 who had earned his doctorate in psychology and philosophy with Wilhelm Wundt at Leipzig and also a medical degree from the University of Heidelberg. James wrote that he wanted a man of genius. He got that, and more, in Hugo Münsterberg. When Münsterberg died, "He was arguably the best known psychologist in America" (Hale, 1980, p. 3). He also was one of the most hated individuals in America, as will be explained later.

Münsterberg was born June 1, 1863 in Danzig, Germany (now Gdansk, Poland), into a moderately prominent Jewish family. He completed his PhD degree in 1885 and his MD in 1887. In that same year he began teaching at the University of Freiburg in the Black Forest region of Germany, founding a psychology laboratory, which he funded mostly from his own money. There he established a reputation as a solid and creative researcher, rising to the position of Associate Professor at age 28, an unusual honor for someone so young.

Münsterberg arrived at Harvard in August 1892 to assume the position of Director of the Psychology Laboratory, and within a year, bolstered by the financial resources of Harvard, he had built a first-class laboratory that was described in detail in an article for *McClure's Magazine* (Nichols, 1893). Herbert Nichols, Münsterberg's laboratory assistant, wrote:

> Both for original research and for demonstration, this laboratory is the most unique, the richest, and the most complete in any country; and in witness of the fame and genius of its present director, and of the rapidly spreading interest in experimental psychology, particularly in America, there are already gathered here, under Professor Münsterberg's administration, a larger number of students specially devoted to mental science than ever previously studied together in any one place. (p. 406)

In comparing the ease and time course of the establishment of the psychology labs at Nebraska (as described in Chapter 6) and Harvard, there could, perhaps, be no greater contrast. In his article, Nichols acknowledged that Harvard was off to a late start, but promised that it would soon lead all American psychology laboratories and that Münsterberg was the reason: "in his genius, the hopes and destiny of experimental psychology at Harvard are now centered" (p. 409). It would appear that, when it came to his boss, Nichols was not above practicing a little excessive ingratiation.

Münsterberg stayed three years at Harvard but in 1895 returned to Freiburg University. From there he hoped to secure a position at one of the more prestigious German universities. Harvard had sought to retain him with the offer of a permanent position, but he was eager to go home. So Harvard gave him a two-year leave of absence in which to change his mind. When nothing better materialized in Germany by 1897, he returned to Harvard, where he would remain for the rest of his life. He resumed his duties as director of the laboratory. The respect of his American colleagues was demonstrated the following year when he was elected president of the American Psychological Association.

In his early years at Harvard, Münsterberg worked largely on experimental questions in the laboratory, but gradually he began to find himself cast in a broader role as scientific expert on a host of popular issues. Like many of the experimental psychologists of his generation, he wrote articles for the popular press, that is, for the popular magazines of his time. He also gave frequent interviews to newspaper reporters. Because he was often a source of sensationalistic comments, he became something of a media darling, one who could be counted on for a good quotation. He was invited by editors to contribute to their magazines, and did so frequently. In a span of 20 years he wrote on such topics as the personality of Americans, school reform, hypnotism, democracy, Native Americans, African Americans, political parties, motion pictures, journalistic inaccuracy, gambling, prohibition, beauty, vocational choice, communicating with the dead, patriotism, coeducation, insanity, and many other subjects.

Münsterberg remained active in the Harvard laboratory until around 1906. At that time, however, his interests shifted virtually full-time to work in applied psychology. Between 1906 and 1916 he published 20 books, mostly on topics of applied interest. Several of those books were compilations of articles that he had published in popular magazines, especially *McClure's Magazine* and *Atlantic Monthly*. In 1909 he published a book entitled *Psychotherapy* (1909a), one of the first books to treat that subject, and another book on educational psychology, *Psychology and the Teacher* (1909b). In 1913 and 1915 he published two books on the psychology of business. The first of those was entitled *Psychology and Industrial Efficiency* (1913) and was a watershed book in promoting the development of the field that would become known as industrial-organizational psychology. In 1916 he published the first book on the psychology of movies entitled *The Photoplay: A Psychological Study*. That book was reprinted recently and is considered a classic work in the history of film. These books that demonstrated the application of psychology to medicine, business, education, and the arts added to the fame of Münsterberg as public scientific expert. The 1913 book on industrial psychology was an especially influential work and was even on the bestseller lists for a time.

In addition to the industrial book, there was another applied book that proved to have lasting importance. It was the first applied psychology book that Münsterberg wrote and was on the application of psychology to the field of law. It was published in 1908, entitled *On the Witness Stand* (1908a). Then as now, crime got a lot of media coverage. Münsterberg began his work in forensic psychology by studying the accuracy of memory, especially the validity of the testimony of eyewitnesses. He was also interested in the problem of false confessions, crime prevention, lie detection, and the decision processes of jurors, and he published articles on all of these topics. His formal involvement in the psychology of law began in 1906, the result of a controversial murder trial in Chicago. That trial and other forensic adventures of Münsterberg are described in the story and letters that follow. This chapter is based largely on the Münsterberg Papers, which are housed in the Department of Rare Books and Manuscripts of the Boston Public Library. The collection contains approximately 6,000 letters; however, fewer than 450 were written by Münsterberg. That is, the bulk of the collection is letters he received.

But before we get to the letters on psychology and law, we begin with William James's invitation to Münsterberg to come to America.

The Letters

William James to Hugo Münsterberg, February 21, 1892

Is it conceivable that if you should be invited, you might agree to come and take charge of the Psychological Laboratory and the higher instruction in that subject in Harvard University for three years at a salary of say 3,000 dollars?

This is a private question of my own, and not an inquiry on the part of our University authorities . . .

The situation is this: We are the best university in America, and we must lead in psychology. I, at the age of 50, disliking laboratory work naturally . . . am certainly not the kind of stuff to make a first-rate director thereof. We could get younger men here who would be safe enough, but we need something more than a safe man, we need a man of genius if possible . . .

Once more, this is a private question from me to you, and you will oblige me by not making it public. The scheme will require much labor to carry it into effect, and I cannot begin the work at all unless I have something definite to go upon on your side . . .

William James to Henry James,[1] April 11, 1892

I have almost succeeded, however, in clinching a bargain whereby Münsterberg, the ablest experimental psychologist in Germany, allowance made of his being only 28 years old – he is in fact the Rudyard Kipling of psychology – is to come here. When he does he will scoop out all the other universities as far as that line of work goes.

Note: And so Münsterberg came to Harvard, where he would remain for the rest of his life except for a two-year spell in Germany. He may not have proved to be the Rudyard Kipling of psychology, but he made a name for himself in psychology and with the American public.

The letters that follow immediately are related to two murder trials: those of Richard G. Ivens in 1906 and Bill Haywood in 1907.

In the first case, John Sanderson Christison, a Chicago physician and famous criminologist, author of Crime and Criminals *(1897), sent a pamphlet he had written on the Ivens murder case to Münsterberg, William James, and others, asking for their opin-*

---

[1] Henry James (1843–1916) was the younger brother of William James, and by 1892, a well-known novelist, living abroad in England. He is one of only a few Americans to be immortalized in Poet's Corner in London's famed Westminster Abbey.

ions on the guilt or innocence of the convicted man, thought to be mentally challenged, who was soon to be executed. Ivens was being tried for the brutal murder of a young woman, a crime to which he had confessed, although he later retracted his confession. James replied by telegram, stating: "Ivens probably innocent. Reprieve necessary for thoroughly investigating mental condition" (Christison, 1906, p. 50). Münsterberg was more certain in his response, believing that Ivens's confession was obtained under duress and deception, and that it represented a false confession (see Münsterberg, 1908a, pp. 139–145).

Münsterberg to John Sanderson Christison, June 8, 1906

After reading your pamphlet, I feel obliged to say that I agree with you in all essential points.

I have studied mental abnormalities and especially the borderland cases for twenty years, and have hypnotized a very large number of patients. On this basis I feel sure that the so-called confessions of Ivens are untrue and that he had nothing to do with the crime.

It is an interesting and yet rather clear case of dissociation and auto-suggestion. It would probably need careful treatment to build up his dissociated mind and thus awaken in him a clear memory of his real experiences.

The witches of the seventeenth century were burned on account of similar confessions, and the popular understanding of mental aberrations has not made much progress since that time. (From Christison, 1906, p. 51.)

John Sanderson Christison to Münsterberg, June 25, 1906

The young man, Ivens, was hanged as you have probably learned by this time. His lawyers failed to make use of the letters I had received, thinking they could succeed without any such help. They were conceited incompetents. I wired the state Board of Pardons that I held letters from nine eminent authorities on mental subjects who supported my opinion after carefully reading the data in my pamphlet which was complete in all the essentials of the case. Your letter and [that of] Prof. James did much to break the intense feeling against Ivens. [And] now the whole public who believed him guilty without doubt – have been thrown into uncertainty – by the manner of his death and immediately previous events. I am to enlarge the pamphlet & insert the opinions I have received together with others yet to be heard from in Europe . . . I feel that the public as well as jurists, doctors, and clergymen ought to be made to think upon this case. For it may be a long time before we can get another with such clear and unquestionable evidence to the point. Thanking you for your prompt and outspoken opinion on behalf of justice of humanity.

Ira W. Foltz [Chicago attorney] to Münsterberg, July 9, 1906

Do you find the Ivens case of sufficient importance to science to justify you in thoroughly examining the entire evidence produced on the trial? Ivens was an innocent man and the evidence shows this fact almost to a mathematical conclusion. I believe his confessions were grafted on his mind by and through the threatening demeanor of the police. It was proven that his confessions were untrue in the main, yet public sentiment lashed into a frenzy by the press on false information, demanded his conviction and execution. I think that even mathematical proof would not have saved him under the circumstances. Surely some day the guilty party or parties will be apprehended and then the awful mistake will be revealed . . . If you desire to see the records of the case please let me know and I will gladly send them to you.

John Sanderson Christison to Münsterberg, July 16, 1906

I was glad to hear from you today and beg to thank you for your kind letter. I am preparing an enlarged pamphlet on the Ivens case and will, I think, make the case as clear as the space I will use will permit. It will be about 120 pages in all and will contain a chapter on hypnotism with several experimental cases as illustrations for the general reader.

The court record is 2000 pages but I have taken out of it all I think necessary for the case . . . Young Ivens could have been spared had my offer and advice been followed by his father and the lawyer. They did not even take a copy of the pamphlet with them to the Supreme Court or the Board of Pardons.

I shall spare no one connected with the case in my discussions of it. I shall print the facts required to complete the explanations and they will have more lessons than one . . . If I can get Mrs. Ivens (mother of Richard) to let me use some of the letters he wrote to a young woman friend (which I read) the unthinking world would be converted to the truth of Ivens' innocence.

Note: After the views of Münsterberg, James, and others were made public in a Chicago newspaper story, there were angry responses from those who were dismayed that psychologists who had no direct familiarity with the trial would pronounce a judgment of certainty from the hallowed halls of Harvard University. One writer (unidentified) wrote that James and Münsterberg were ignorant of the facts: "The long-distance impudence of Profs James and Munsterburg (sic) can have no effect [except] to make themselves and their science ridiculous" (newspaper clipping, no date, no source, found in the Münsterberg Papers). Hale (1980) has written that Münsterberg was especially upset by the execution: "The failure of his and James's intercession involved more than a personal rebuff; it amounted to an attack on psychology itself" (p. 112).

The second of the murder trials took place in Boise, Idaho in May and June, 1907. William Haywood was on trial for ordering the killing of former Idaho governor, Frank Steuenberg. The murder was carried out by Harry Orchard, who surprised the courtroom by confessing to a total of 18 murders, all of them ordered by Haywood and other union leaders in the Western Federation of Miners. Steuenberg had angered Haywood and the miners when he had called in federal troops to put down violent demonstrations by the miners. The editor of McClure's *Magazine asked Münsterberg to go to Boise toward the end of the trial, a trip that interested him because of his interest in criminal behavior, and a trip that interested the staff of* McClure's *because of the possibility of a great story from one of the most infamous murder trials in recent memory (see Münsterberg, 1907).[2] Münsterberg sat in the courtroom, watching Orchard testify and watching Haywood's reactions. It was Münsterberg's goal to determine whether Orchard, a self-confessed multiple murderer, was telling the truth about Haywood's involvement.*

Münsterberg's notes, "Experiments with Harry Orchard" (1907, unpublished)

As my seat was at the small table of the attorneys for the prosecution, I had him [Orchard] only a few feet from me for careful observation. I cannot deny that the impression of that first morning was very bad. I saw him from the side and his profile, especially the jaw, appeared to me most brutal and most vulgar; I saw also at once the deformation of the ear, the irregularity in the movement of the eyes and the abnormal lower lip. That this was the profile of a murderer seemed to me not improbable . . . I looked instinctively to the other side where Haywood sat, with the head of a thinker and leader. No sharper contrast was possible: all my sympathies went to this brilliant face of the defendant and all my disgust to the witness.

Note: It is interesting that Münsterberg, who often wrote disparagingly about the pseudosciences of phrenology and physiognomy (judging character by facial features), would have offered a physiognomic analysis of the two key figures in this trial. Münsterberg would view Orchard differently after testing him at the penitentiary for seven hours, relying principally on a word-association test and timing Orchard's responses with a chronoscope he had brought with him from Harvard. Those tests led him to conclude, with boastful certainty, that Orchard was telling the truth about Haywood's involvement in the murder of Steunenberg.[3]

[2] One source states that it was the new governor of Idaho who invited Münsterberg to attend the Haywood trial (Hothersall, 2004). That is possible, but the Münsterberg Papers indicate that the trip was initiated by *McClure's* editor.

[3] The origin of the word-association test is in dispute. There is evidence of independent development from Francis Galton, Wilhelm Wundt, Max Wertheimer, and Carl Jung. Jung published an article on the technique in the inaugural volume of the *Journal of Abnormal Psychology* (1906). It was also the subject of his lectures at Clark University in 1909 (see Chapter 11). He certainly did much to familiarize Americans with the technique.

Münsterberg's notes, "Experiments with Harry Orchard" (1907, unpublished)

... no outside evidence could have such convincing character as the results of the tests, and no witnesses for the defense and, of course, no opinion of twelve jurymen could have shaken this scientific finding ... As far as the objective facts are concerned my few hours of experimenting were more convincing than anything which in all those weeks of the trial demonstrated.

Note: After arriving back in Cambridge, Münsterberg announced his conclusions to a reporter who published his remarks in one of the Boston newspapers. There were arguments that his statements had prejudiced the outcome of the Boise trial,[4] and Münsterberg had fears of facing a lawsuit, especially after the jury acquitted Haywood. He had good reason to worry, because one of Haywood's attorneys was Clarence Darrow (1857–1938), the most famous American trial lawyer of his day.[5] Darrow wrote to Münsterberg after the conclusion of the trial.

Clarence S. Darrow to Münsterberg, August 16, 1907

... As a scientific man I think that you cannot afford to put yourself in such position as you have already placed yourself in your statements to the press. You came to Boise at the request of Mr. McClure. Mr. McClure had already published or had in his possession the autobiography of Harry Orchard.[6] It is entirely possible that you did not intend to boom [promote] that article or be used by McClure, but the inference that it was done wittingly or unwittingly will always remain if you proceed further in this matter.

So far as your statements of observing Orchard in Court, they are not true. Orchard was on the stand about eight days. He was recalled one day when you were there to ask a few impeaching questions; at that time he was not on the stand for over thirty minutes and the questions were unimportant and could in no way test him, and the record will show that my statement is true.

You consorted and associated with the enemies of the defense and the friends of Orchard and the prosecution. You got no information whatever from us and made no investigation of our witnesses or our clients, and in my humble opinion you are in no more position to give any intelligent judgment upon the truthfulness of Orchard's story than the man in the moon, and whatever you say upon this question does not interest me especially, excepting to give my view that you

---

[4] See "Professor Münsterberg and the Idaho Trial," *The Nation*, 85, July 18, 1907, p. 55.
[5] See C. Darrow, *The Story of my Life*, New York: Charles Scribner's Sons, 1932 (reprinted in 1996 by Da Capo Press).
[6] The autobiography of multiple murderer Harry Orchard was serialized in *McClure's Magazine* in five parts: 1907, 29, pp. 294–316, 367–379, 507–523, 658–672; 1907, 30, pp. 113–129.

are saying it at your own risk of your reputation and whatever there may be in the science you profess to serve.

If you could tell by the measurements of Orchard's head whether he was an honest man or not it might have been well to take some measurements of our witnesses and see whether they were liars too.

I did not seek any controversy with you upon this question and am not anxious to have any now, but if any article is published in reference to it I shall feel as if I ought to publish my views upon it the same as I did before . . .

Note: After the not-guilty verdict for Haywood, the letter from Darrow, and the negative reaction he received after the press carried the story of his claim for Orchard's truthfulness, Münsterberg (1908a) was cautious about what he said about Orchard and Haywood.[7] But he did not backtrack on his belief in his lie-detection technique, what one newspaper called the "truth compelling machine" (Gilliams, 1907). He argued that as a way to get at the truth in criminal cases, it was more accurate and more humane:

> The time will come when the methods of experimental psychology cannot longer be excluded from the court of law. . . . The vulgar ordeals of the "third degree" in every form belong to the Middle Ages, and much of the wrangling of attorneys about technicalities in admitting the "evidence" appears to not a few somewhat out of date, too: the methods of experimental psychology are working in the spirit of the twentieth century. The "third degree" may brutalise the mind and force either correct or falsified secrets to light; the time measurements of associations is swifter and cleaner, more scientific, more humane, and more reliable in bringing out the truth which justice demands.[8] (Münsterberg, 1908a, pp. 108–109; see also Münsterberg, 1907)

Others disagreed about the wisdom of psychologists as expert witnesses in the courts.[9]

---

[7] Although Haywood was acquitted of murder charges in the 1907 trial, in 1918 he was found guilty of sabotaging America's war efforts and sentenced to 30 years in prison. While awaiting an appeal he escaped to Russia in 1921, where he lived until his death in 1928. Orchard remained in the penitentiary in Idaho, where he died in 1954 at the age of 88.

[8] Münsterberg worked on other measures of lying, including various physiological measures such as blood pressure, similar to the measures used in today's modern polygraph. One of his graduate students who worked in those studies and who later claimed credit for inventing the lie detector (which he did not) was William Moulton Marston (1893–1947). Marston would gain fame as the creator of the comic-book superhero Wonder Woman, who used her lasso with magical powers to force people to tell the truth (see Bunn, 1997).

[9] An anonymous letter in *The Nation*, 85, July 11, 1907, p. 24 summarized Münsterberg's findings from the Boise trial and concluded: "unless more interesting results than those reported are forthcoming, it would seem that the eight days spent in traveling between Boise and Boston were, scientifically considered, so much time wasted. Professor Münsterberg thinks that in the future the psychological expert may have an important place in courts of justice . . . But to admit psychological expert evidence in most trials would open the door to every sort of charlatanry. The cry to-day is not more, but fewer, experts."

Münsterberg's book, On the Witness Stand, *stimulated interest in the field of forensic psychology and caused him to be sought out by lawyers and individuals caught up in the justice system. The following letter is typical of some of the correspondence he received as a perceived expert on criminal behavior.*

Charles Durfee [attorney in Golconda, Illinois] to Münsterberg, December 15, 1913

I have a client who upon a charge of murder, is now serving a forty-two year sentence in the Southern Illinois Penitentiary. He shot and killed a man, as he insists, while he was asleep – or rather in a half awakened condition.

The convict advises me, and I think he is absolutely square in that regard, that he has ever been subject to doing rather rash things when suddenly or violently awakened; that he was lying on a cot asleep, the party whom he shot, came to his cot, caught him by the legs playfully but violently drew him from the cot, and that he quickly snatched a revolver and shot the man to death. His story is corrobarated (sic) by certain physical surroundings, needless here to relate.

I am writing to you, to beg that you name to me some publication of your writings, in which I may find what you have to say along the line of circumstances here related. I am familiar with some of your works – rather but one, "On the witness stand" and am in harmony with your theory. I await an answer.

Note: Münsterberg *published other articles on psychology and the law, including an article on the deliberations of juries (1913b). Included in that article was discussion of an experiment conducted by Münsterberg in which juror decision-making was studied before and after jury discussion. He found that the discussion caused more than 50 percent of the men to change their minds, whereas not one woman in his study changed her vote after the discussion, leading him to conclude that women made poor jurors. At least one attorney wrote to concur, although the "data" he presented on decision-changing hardly agreed with Münsterberg's findings.*

William A. Johnson [attorney in Everett, Washington] to Münsterberg, November 15, 1913

I am enclosing a clipping that may be of interest to you in that it tends so forcibly to corroborate and illustrate the point that you made not long ago in your article in reference to women acting on juries.

. . . The jury was out quite a long time, and on the first ballot, the vote was 9 to 3 in favor of acquittal; all three who thought him guilty were women, and practically all those who thought him innocent were men; subsequently two of the women went over to the side of the majority, in view of the fact that the vote was so large and in favor of acquittal. The other woman stayed with her original convictions however, and as you see, her naïve explanation was that she "Didn't try to change any one else's opinions, she just kept her own." It appears that she is a dressmaker, who "reads the classified ads, and glances at the headlines, and hasn't much time for anything else." As a result, a hung jury, and a new trial.

It has seemed to me, during my experience at the bar, that the woman juror is hardly a success, although we rarely have such a striking illustration of the "Why," as this case has furnished, and I must confess that when I first read your analysis of the reason why a woman would be in some respects difficult on a jury, I hardly agreed with you . . .

Note: One of the most interesting forensic cases to involve Münsterberg occurred in 1908 in response to an article that he had published in McClure's Magazine (1908b).

Mrs Esther R. to Münsterberg, January 8, 1908

Your article in Jan. McClure's magazine on "Hypnotism and Crime" was read with interest by me, but failed to satisfy me along one line of your argument, wherein you state that "hypnotic power" cannot be exerted in a manner which seems wrongful, by a distant hypnotizer. Recent occurrences at this and other places cause me to differ from you on that point.

Enclosed find [a] clipping containing an account of two similar wrecks on the G. T. R. [Grand Trunk Railroad] at this station, both of which followed a severe paroxysm of grief on my part, over outrages and humiliation heaped upon myself and family by the Co. which refused to right the wrong. Vivid dreams also foretold of the calamities. The power to do these thing[s] has been tested frequently by me during the past few years, mostly during the past year until I am afraid to let my mind dwell upon my wrongs, for just so surely does "something happen," and I want your assistance in placing the responsibility. While the destruction of the R. R. property would trouble me not at all, the thought that my anger sends men unprepared into eternity is decidedly unpleasant.

That when the R. R. company ignored all my requests for justice on their part, I earnestly besieged God to take up the matter for me, accounts in part, but if he intends on punishing me in some other way it will be worse for me in the end . . . The wreck did not get on my nerves, for although I was on the spot within a half hour and remained most of the night, I experienced none of the horror one would suppose, but a sort of exultation at seeing such vast destruction, although I did not forget to ask God to be merciful to the men hurried out of existence. Neither did I lose the opportunity presented to tell the R. R. Detective Foley and claim agent and attorney's Williams and Butler, that the [rail]road was getting its just deserts . . .

Note: *Münsterberg was understandably interested in the letter. He replied to the woman but also wrote to officials of the Grand Trunk Railway to share the information with them. Evidently the railroad officials were already familiar with Mrs Esther R.*

Münsterberg to Mrs Esther R., January 17, 1908

I was very much interested indeed in receiving your letter of January eighth . . . Your statements are very suggestive and my psychological interest in your case leads me to beg you for further details. Of course, there are many mysterious connections in the world and science is only at the beginning of the discovery of them. The more it is necessary that we gather all possible details in every important case.

Now, I understand that you believe yourself that the last railroad wreck, which occurred through the opening of a switch by an unknown hand, was really the result of your justified excitement and anger, as the Company had ignored your requests for justice. Now I should like to know more in detail how you would be able to prove to science this connection. Had you, for instance, a clear visual image of the coming wreck a short time before the collision occurred? Or did you dream in your imagination of yourself as opening the switches? Or did you see any one else opening them? Do you remember where you were when the collision occurred? And how long before you had been in the neighborhood of that switch? It, of course, would not have been impossible that the influence of your justified excitement made not only your mind but also your hand, without your knowledge, and of course without your responsibility, a passive instrument of the punishment of the Company. I wish very much that you would tell me every little thing about it, as such mysterious connections and evil influences are often best understood when all the little particulars are brought to light. I shall be very much interested to hear all the details from you which refer to your mysterious relation to those last two wrecks. I shall then write you my opinion.

Note: *It is difficult to know exactly how to interpret Münsterberg's letter. Clearly, in contacting the railroad authorities, he was concerned that Mrs R. might be responsible for the train wrecks. Was he trying to coax her into a confession in telling her that her grievances were justified and that her actions could be seen as not her responsibility? As a psychologist and physician, who was then working on his book* Psychotherapy *(1909), he must have found the case a clinically interesting one. Following is the reply to Münsterberg's letter.*

Mrs Esther R. to Münsterberg, January 28, 1908

I was both pleased and flattered to receive an answer to my letter of the 8th . . . and was deterred from answering, partly because I wanted to ask you if there is any connection between prayer and psychology . . . for I would not like to deny God's part in the transactions . . . The first R.R. wreck (5 yrs ago) I am not so clear about, only remembering dimly, it seemed incredible to me that I was in any way responsible, and it did not take so firm a hold of me for that reason.[10] About one year before it my husband . . . was dragged to a near by city to jail on Sat. night too late to get bail, 8:30 o'clock the arrest was made at almost train time and we were left nearly frantic over Easter Sunday, not even knowing the reason . . .

About 1 years afterwards in cleaning house I came across a [railroad] switch key, and it recalled all the rail road trouble . . . and I snatched it to my breast with both hands and fell upon my knees agonizingly beseeching God to punish the Company, as we had obtained no redress for disgrace and loss of a good deal of money. I cannot remember what became of the key. I must have flung it in the fire or cistern or somewhere as I do not remember seeing it since. Immediately after, the next day or so, the accident happened. Two engines were smashed and two men killed . . .

In R. R. Atty L. G. Stanley's office in Detroit is a letter written by me to him in which I told him I had caused the first accident and would cause another just like it. I have often tested my powers by lying awake at night and "thinking an accident", looking in the papers for it the next night, until I have become almost frightened over the success of it and almost doubted if it were God's work. Only trainmen and engines destroyed, 7 during the past month within 25 miles of here on the G. T. R. Am I guilty, does their blood rest upon my head, I do not want loss of life, only satisfaction?

The night of 27 of Dec. 08[11] I was lying on a lounge in my sitting room . . . I lay there thinking of it all [the grievances with the railroad] and clasped my hands over my face and groaned in agony, not praying, but groaning out my awful sense of wrong, when my husband, who knows nothing about my feelings and would not understand, came home [and] said "there has been a wreck, do you want to go and see it." A sense of exhilaration took hold of me and we went to where the demolished engines and crushed men lay. I was not affected in the least (although I could not kill a chicken) and went where the men turned away from sick. I exultantly told the head officials who soon arrived that I was getting even for my wrongs . . . Last night, while wakeful, I again was in deep thought over my wrongs, and again was two engines wrecked and a fireman killed . . .[12]

---

[10] Her recall would place the wreck in 1903. There were two wrecks in Michigan that year involving the Grand Trunk Railroad. One occurred in Detroit on May 4, 1903 when seven people died from a rear-end collision from an unscheduled train. The second occurred near Durand, Michigan on August 7, 1903 when two circus trains collided, the second one running into the first one which had stopped. Twenty-six people and numerous circus animals died. Neither seemed to involve any switching problems or suggest foul play.

[11] I have not been able to identify a Michigan train wreck associated with this date.

[12] Again, I have not been able to find a fatal Michigan train wreck that occurred close to the date of this letter.

You asked if I might have turned the switch, that is out of the question, as a train passed over it 10 minutes before the accident and it is nearly a half mile from my home, and I was not out after supper . . . Prof. Munsterberg, I am so glad that I can say all of this to you, and you won't laugh at me . . .

Note: According to Münsterberg's daughter Margaret, who published the first biography of her father in 1922, Münsterberg believed that "all doubt was removed that the woman in a morbid condition had turned the switch, although, when the deed was done, she had no recollection of herself as agent" (p. 175).

Mrs R. wrote to Münsterberg about a year after their initial correspondence. It is not clear where Mrs R. was at the time but it is not evident that she was incarcerated, either in a mental asylum or a prison. Clearly the local police and railroad authorities knew of her and her claims of "mental" responsibility for the wrecks.

Mrs Esther R. to Münsterberg, December 27, 1908

When your favor of the 19th reached me, my first thought was, did I make him write me, or, did he make me review the happenings of a year ago, which also included your correspondence concerning it all as I recalled the whole scene a few evenings before as I stood looking out into a foggy close of a dreary day, at a passing train, but, though the sense of injury, at the hands of the station agent, and railroad officials, is as strong as ever, the absence of the bitter, revengeful feeling before felt, surprised me. Have you helped me to overcome it?

Note: That Mrs R. was still a free citizen is suggested by the following letter from Münsterberg. It also suggests that he believed in the possibility that she might have been responsible for the train wrecks, in some way more than "wishing" them to occur.

Münsterberg to Grand Trunk Railway Legal Department (no date)

I am afraid that if Mrs. [R] is approached directly, either by the court or by a lunacy commission, the mental traces of the true facts will be lost and you would probably be unable to deliver her to a place of safety. Detectives might, of course, put an end to further crime by watching her, but they would be unable to clear up the past.

Epilogue

Archival records are often incomplete, a fact that is considerably frustrating for historians. Such is the nature of the case of Mrs Esther R. We do not know what happened to her, nor if she was ever found to be involved in causing the train wrecks. Münsterberg continued to work in the field of forensic psychology for several years after the publication of his 1908 book, and often promoted his belief that psychologists should be involved in the legal system if the best outcomes were to be achieved. He wrote:

> The lawyer and the judge and the juryman are sure that they do not need the experimental psychologist. . .They go on thinking that their legal instinct and their common sense supplies them with all that is needed and somewhat more; and if the time is ever to come when even the jurist is to show some concession to the spirit of modern psychology, public opinion will have to exert some pressure. Just in the line of law it therefore seems necessary not to rely simply on the technical statements of scholarly treatises, but to carry the discussion in the most popular form possible before the wider tribunal of the general reader. (Münsterberg, 1908a, pp. 10–11)

Whereas Münsterberg was adamant about psychology's place in the courts, there were many who remained unconvinced. In reviewing Münsterberg's book, a writer in *The Nation* asserted: "On the whole, it seems clear that we are not yet prepared to apply psychology in judicial procedure, and that we are warranted in begging the experimental psychologists to forego any suggestion that such application be made until they are more settled in their convictions than they are to-day" ("On the Witness Stand," 1908, p. 472).

Convinced that he had demonstrated the critical relevance of psychology for the field of law, Münsterberg moved on to other fields, as noted above, applying psychology to medical practice, business, education, and the arts. His appeal to the public has been explained by Matthew Hale (1980): "Psychology promised power – over self and others – in years when men and women felt increasingly powerless to control their own lives, and it offered an explanation for the irrational behavior that seemed more and more to dominate public life. . . . millions of Americans sensed a crisis of the will as industrial and urban society emerged" (pp. ix–x). And chief among those who offered answers to the problems of an increasingly complex and bewildering world was Hugo Münsterberg, "the most aggressive publicist in the discipline [of psychology]" (p. x).

Whereas Münsterberg enjoyed a long run as America's best known psychologist – psychological expert to the masses – his popularity did not last. The agent of change was Münsterberg's German nationalism and growing war clouds in Europe (see Keller, 1979). He was a German and maintained his German citizenship throughout his life in America. During his time in America he viewed himself as something of an ambassador for both Germans and Americans, interpreting German culture for Americans and vice versa. When tensions became more intense among European countries in the early twentieth century, Münsterberg became more outspoken on behalf of Germany. By 1907 his speeches, letters to newspapers, and magazine articles created an embarrassment for Harvard. The situation grew worse each year, especially after war erupted in 1914. There were calls from the public that Harvard fire him and that he be deported. He received a great deal of hate mail and even some death threats from Americans angered by his pro-German writings. One wrote:

> it would appear opportune for you to leave America . . . you are neither needed or wanted here. So don't you had better get out? Take a month to do so if you wish but by all means get out! Hurry to the side of your friends the Bastard Kiser (sic) and his #@&#@ looking son the Crown Prince. Of course if you do not you might be accommodated with a little taste of war right here some fine day in the college yard. That might do you and at the same time result in your getting out via the undertaker. But by all means get to hell out. ("Alumnus," no date, Münsterberg Papers)

As the war in Europe raged on, Münsterberg continued to defend Germany even after a German submarine sank the British liner, the *Lusitania*, in May 1915, resulting in the loss of more than 1,200 lives, many of them Americans. This proved to be the last straw for the few Harvard colleagues who still supported Münsterberg. Ostracized at Harvard, he withdrew to his home and went to campus only to meet his classes. On Saturday, December 16, 1916, he was lecturing to one of those classes when he leaned suddenly against the desk and then fell to the floor. He died within minutes, apparently from a cerebral hemorrhage. He was 53 years old (Hale, 1980; Münsterberg Papers).

Today Münsterberg is remembered primarily for his work in applied psychology, especially his promotion of industrial psychology and forensic psychology, two fields that enjoy considerable success today. For forensic psychologists, there is an American Psychology-Law Society that numbers more than 2,000 members and is a division of the American Psychological Association. There are several journals that cover research and practice in this field; probably the best known of these is *Law and Human Behavior*, which began publication in 1977.

Forensic psychologists practice their trade in attorneys' offices, in jails or prisons, in the courtroom, and many other settings. A common function is the assessment of the behavioral and mental capacities of individuals in the judicial system, and addressing "questions of law such as the insanity defense, competency to stand trial, civil competency, risk to self or others, and child custody" (Roesch, 2000, p. 383). Forensic psychologists often work with courts and parole boards to evaluate the readiness of individuals for probation or parole. They work with corporations that are being sued to help them decide their chances of winning their cases. They work with attorneys to help them select (or exclude) potential jurors. They work with the FBI, the Secret Service, and police departments as behavioral profilers. They are sometimes involved in hostage negotiations.

In summary, psychological practitioners can be found working in all aspects of the justice system today. And psychologists who do research on the interface of psychology and law work today on many of the same topics pioneered in Münsterberg's work, for example, false confessions, eyewitness testimony, and jury behavior. These researchers and practitioners thus follow in the footsteps of Hugo Münsterberg, America's first forensic psychologist.

Suggested Readings

Benjamin, L. T., Jr. (2000). Hugo Münsterberg: Portrait of an applied psychologist. In G. A. Kimble and M. Wertheimer (Eds.) *Portraits of pioneers in psychology* (Vol. 4, pp. 112–129). Washington, DC and Mahwah, NJ: American Psychological Association and Lawrence Erlbaum.
A brief account of Münsterberg's career, focusing on his work in applied psychology.

Hale, M., Jr. (1980). *Human science and social order: Hugo Münsterberg and the origins of applied psychology.* Philadelphia, PA: Temple University Press.
A very fine biography of Münsterberg that places his life and work in the historical and geographical contexts of his time.

Keller, P. (1979). *States of belonging: German-American intellectuals and the First World War.* Cambridge, MA: Harvard University Press.
Part one of this book (pp. 5–118) is entitled "Hugo Münsterberg – On Being German in America," and is the best account of Münsterberg's German nationalism and the politics that produced the stress that likely resulted in his premature death.

Landy, F. (1992). Hugo Münsterberg: Victim or visionary? *Journal of Applied Psychology, 77,* 787–802.
A very interesting account of Münsterberg's life and work, focusing on his contributions to industrial psychology and the difficulties engendered by his personal style.

Münsterberg, H. (1908). *On the witness stand.* New York: Doubleday, Page & Co.
This classic book in the history of forensic psychology in America includes chapters on eyewitness testimony, crime detection, false confessions, crime prevention, and hypnosis, among other topics.

Münsterberg, H. (1913). *Psychology and industrial efficiency.* Boston: Houghton Mifflin.
A seminal book in establishing the field of industrial-organizational psychology.

Münsterberg, M. (1922). *Hugo Münsterberg: His life and work.* New York: D. Appleton.
A biography of her father by Margaret Münsterberg. Although hardly objective and balanced, this book is, nevertheless, an interesting look at a fascinating figure in the history of psychology. The book includes many quotations from letters in the Münsterberg Papers.

Otto, R. K., & Heilbrun, K. (2002). The practice of forensic psychology: A look toward the future in light of the past. *American Psychologist, 57,* 5–18.
This excellent article argues that forensic psychology is at a crossroads. The progress of the field is said to be grounded in the need to establish stronger ties between forensic knowledge and practice, leading to guidelines for practice; more attention to treatment; and better education of legal consumers.

Wrightsman, L. S., & Fulero, S. M. (2005). *Forensic psychology* (2nd edn.). Belmont, CA: Wadsworth.
The leading textbook in the field, authored by two very prominent authorities on forensic psychology.

9
CHAPTER

Mary Whiton Calkins, c.1889
(Wellesley College Archives)

A Woman's Struggles for Graduate Education

Mary Whiton Calkins (1863–1930) was a distinguished psychologist and philosopher of her day. She wrote a number of important books in both fields and was perhaps best known for her system of self-psychology, a belief that "psychology should be conceived as the science of the self, or person, as related to its environment, physical and social" (Calkins, 1930, p. 42).

Calkins's many accomplishments included inventing the paired-associate technique for studying learning and memory, founding the first psychology laboratory at a women's college (Wellesley College, 1891), being the first woman elected to the presidencies of the American Psychological Association (1905) and the American Philosophical Association (1918), and being elected the first honorary woman member of the British Psychological Association (1928).

Note: This chapter was written with considerable assistance from Laurel Furumoto, Professor Emerita of Psychology at Wellesley College and an outstanding scholar in the history of psychology. See the suggested readings section in this chapter for a listing of some of her works.

Calkins was born in Connecticut but grew up in Buffalo, New York where her father was a Congregationalist minister. At age 19 she enrolled at Smith College, where she studied the classics, especially Greek and philosophy. After graduation in 1885 she spent a year in Europe studying languages. Shortly after her return to the United States, she accepted a position at Wellesley College as a tutor in Greek.

Because of her interest in philosophy and her skills as a teacher, a colleague in the Department of Mental Philosophy suggested to Calkins that she consider a new faculty position for someone to teach psychology. At first Calkins showed little interest; however, her colleague convinced her to change her mind and the idea was presented to the president of the college, who agreed and offered Calkins the position contingent upon her studying the new subject for a year (Furumoto, 1990).

In late 1888 and early 1889, Calkins sought advice from several of her former professors at Smith College: Mary Augusta Jordan, a professor of English; Harry Norman Gardiner, a professor of philosophy; and especially Charles Edward Garman, a visiting professor of philosophy (from Amherst College), who had exerted a powerful influence on her in the one course she had taken from him. Calkins asked them if they thought she needed additional study in psychology or if they thought she could teach the course satisfactorily without such work. Jordan felt she could teach without any additional formal study; Garman was less certain in his answer. By June of 1889, Calkins had decided to remain in her current teaching field, but did not close the door on the psychology opportunity.

In February of 1890, Calkins accepted the position of Instructor in Psychology at Wellesley and began planning for a year of graduate study in the field. She hoped she might study psychology with Garman, but he was forced to decline owing to poor health. For a while she considered going to Germany to study, but she learned that many universities there would not admit women students to their degree programs. She was aware of the recent emergence of a new scientific psychology (often called "physiological psychology"), which contrasted with the old psychology of mental and moral philosophy, and she was interested in obtaining some of her training in this new field. Therefore she sought a graduate program that could offer her laboratory training in the new psychology.

In May of 1890, Calkins wrote to two professors at nearby Harvard University: William James (1842–1910) and Josiah Royce (1855–1916). Both expressed interest in having her as a student but were unable to invite her because of rules against coeducation at Harvard. That decision was later reversed and she was allowed to attend classes but could not be officially recognized as a student. One of the first courses Calkins took was James's seminar on psychology, a class with four men. Shortly all the men dropped out of the course, perhaps because of the presence of a woman. In recalling this experience Calkins (1930) wrote:

Most unhappily for them and most fortunately for me the other members of his [James's] seminary in psychology dropped away in the early weeks of the fall of

1890; and James and I were left . . . at either side of a library fire. The *Principles of Psychology*[2] was warm from the press; and my absorbed study of those brilliant, erudite, and provocative volumes, as interpreted by their writer, was my introduction to psychology. What I gained from the written page, and even more from the tete-a-tete discussion was, it seems to me as I look back on it, beyond all else, a vivid sense of the concreteness of psychology and of the immediate reality of "finite individual minds" with their "thoughts and feelings." (p. 31)

Could any student in the history of psychology have been afforded a greater opportunity for learning!

After a year of study with James and Royce at Harvard and with Edmund C. Sanford (1859–1924) at Clark University in Worcester, Massachusetts, Calkins returned to Wellesley, where she began her laboratory (with considerable help from Sanford) and her instruction in psychology. But after only a semester at Wellesley she began to think about further study and wrote to her psychology professors for advice. Sanford recommended study in Europe, and mentioned that Hugo Münsterberg (who had received his doctorate from Wundt at Leipzig) had admitted a woman to his psychology program at the University of Freiberg in Germany. Calkins also considered going to Cornell University where Frank Angell, another of Wundt's doctoral graduates, had established a new psychology laboratory. James encouraged her to delay her decision as long as possible and soon his reason became apparent: Münsterberg accepted a position at Harvard in the fall of 1892 to direct the psychology laboratory.

Calkins applied to Harvard to study with Münsterberg (1863–1916), and he strongly supported her application. Again, she was allowed to take courses but only as a "guest"; she was not to be officially registered. And so for the next three years she studied with Münsterberg, mostly on a part-time basis while she continued her duties at Wellesley, but for a year, when she was on leave from her college, she worked full time in his laboratory.

In 1895 Calkins asked the Philosophy Department at Harvard to give her a doctoral examination, albeit an unofficial one. Her examining committee consisted of James, Royce, Münsterberg, and George Santayana, and others. On behalf of the committee, Royce reported to the Harvard Corporation that the committee voted unanimously to pass Calkins and that her performance demonstrated a scholarship that was "exceptionally high."[3] Thus she had completed all of the requirements for a doctoral degree at Harvard and had the enthusiastic support of her professors. But of course she would not be granted a doctoral degree, because she was never an official student.

[2] William James's masterwork, his two-volume *Principles of Psychology*, was published in September 1890, just before Calkins began her one-on-one course with him.

[3] William James later wrote (in 1895) to one of Calkins's classmates describing her examination: "it was much the most brilliant examination for the Ph.D. that we have had at Harvard" (Scarborough & Furumoto, 1987, p. 46).

The letters in this chapter tell part of the story of Calkins's struggle. The majority are part of the Calkins Papers which are part of the Wellesley College Archives. The letters begin with Calkins seeking advice about her anticipated preparation in psychology.

The Letters

Mary Augusta Jordan to Mary Whiton Calkins, December 18, 1888

My opinion is most gladly at your disposal in the matter of your possibly teaching psychology. It seems to me that you are remarkably adapted to such work and that in the department of Philosophy in general you are sure to do your best work ever . . . Special preparation may well afford to wait. Personally I may say that I have come in contact with few minds among women that I would as gladly see devoted to hard work as yours . . . No class would suffer at your hands and I believe that in a few years classes would get from you what they comparatively seldom do get from teachers here – original work and a spur to original work . . .

Calkins to Charles Garman, January 1, 1889

Do you think it right, under any circumstances for a person to undertake to teach psychology without a thorough and long preparation especially for the work? . . . Since my senior year (1885) in Smith College, when I studied psychology under your guidance, I have not done any psychological or philosophical *study*; I have read a little in these subjects and constantly increased my interest in them. This year and last I have been teaching Greek at Wellesley and the further study of Plato has led, as it needs must, to serious thought on philosophic questions . . . Do you think it possible – admitting an antecedent enthusiasm for the subject that anyone with such insufficient preparation can properly teach a class?

Charles Garman to Calkins, April 27, 1889

I remember with much pleasure the interest with which you took up the study of Psychology in the fall of 1884 and I also have distinctly in mind the success with which you dealt with the most difficult problems. It does not seem to me that you have any reason for hesitation on this question so far as your natural qualifications for teaching this study are concerned. I feel that you would be eminently successful. Now as to the particular question that you desire me to answer viz. as to the wisdom of taking the place in your college without a more extended preparation than you have already had. This is a question I do not feel able to answer. There must be considered the temper and habits of the classes . . .

My judgment on the whole is that you had better take the risks and accept the position should it be offered to you in June. You will have all summer to study psychology and if you will not be too ambitious the first year or two and be content to take the classes over no more ground than you are familiar with, you will by that time be in a position to branch out.

Calkins to Charles Garman, June 1, 1889

... but I have not wholly surrendered the hope that I may sometime be able to study and to teach psychology. Your helpful and discriminating counsel has been of utmost value to me and I shall keep your letter, with the words which I gathered up from lectures and discussions, as my guides, if ever I do enter this path.

Calkins to Charles Garman, February 22, 1890

I am venturing now to trouble you with some questions about my study. I myself have positively decided on two points only: first, that, of all things, I wish and need to study with you; second, that some part of my work must be in the line of physiological psychology. I feel myself very presumptuous in asking whether it will be possible for you, in any measure, to direct my work. I owe to you so much of my interest in psychology, my understanding of the subject, any apprehension of its relation to the great life problems, that your personal help seems to me almost necessary, if I am to enter on work of such importance.[4]

Harry Norman Gardiner to Calkins, May 1890

I do not know at all how to advise you or help you about your suggestion of study in Germany. Of two things only I am clear, first that you will be able to prosecute your studies to greater advantage if you have the direct inspiration of a teacher even though he may be able to teach you little or nothing, and secondly that Germany is a good place to study, if only you can find the teacher you want there. Whether you could have the privilege of attending lectures or obtaining private instruction in Psychology and Philosophy at any of the German universities ... I do not know.

Note: In the next several letters, Calkins investigates educational possibilities at Harvard University.

---

[4] As noted earlier, Garman was too ill to take on Calkins as a student.

William James to Calkins, May 24, 1890

The President [of Harvard University, Charles Eliot] writes that he "sees no way to do anything for you not even in Philosophy 20a."[5] It seems very hard. But he has to keep guard all along the line, and I suppose that laxity would soon produce an involuntary and unintended occupation of a great many of these higher courses by women . . . I can only say now that if you do come to Cambridge, I shall be most happy to help you over difficulties and give you some advice. Had I double my present strength, I should also enjoy giving you some instruction free of all duties and taxes, but I don't dare to propose any such thing, with as much work as I have, and so little ability to do it. Believe in my sincere regret for this action of our authorities. Can't you get to Worcester almost as easily as to Cambridge? Stanley Hall's Psychological department ought to be the best in the world.[6]

Josiah Royce to Calkins, May 27, 1890

I understand that the President [Eliot] is unwilling to have the arrangement made for your attendance of Phil 20a & b.[7] Prof. James will probably have notified you of this fact already. I need not add that I regard this official view as one of the mysteries into which no one may hope to penetrate who is not himself accustomed to the executive point of outlook. I suppose that you will understand my regret in the case for I had sincerely hoped that we could be of service to you, and I am still anxious to offer you all the aid in my power. This at any rate I may still suggest, that in case you appear in the annex[8] next year, it will cause me no small pleasure to give you such time as I can for advice in the pursuit of advanced work, to direct in a measure your reading, should you desire such aid, and to read a thesis or two of yours should you prepare such papers . . . I need not point out that my present offer would be quite independent of official approval, which I would not need to ask.

William James to Calkins, May 29, 1890

I have been attacking the President again on the subject you know of. He tells me that the overseers are so sensitive on the subject that he dares take no liberties. He received such a "tremendous wigging" from them a few years ago for

5   James's seminar in psychology.
6   Referring to Clark University where G. Stanley Hall was President and Edmund Sanford was in charge of the psychology laboratory.
7   Royce's course.
8   The Harvard Annex was where Harvard professors offered classes to women students for extra money; however, the courses did not carry official Harvard credit.

winking at just this thing, that he is forced now to be strict. They are at present in hot water about it at the medical school he himself being for the admission of women. I think that in justice to him you should know these facts.

Note: On July 1, 1890 Wolcott Calkins sent a letter to the Harvard Corporation, the over-seers, to ask that his daughter be admitted for study in Philosophy 20a and 20b. The letter was accompanied by another letter from the president of Wellesley College indicating the importance of the study at Harvard for the new subject Calkins was to teach at Welles-ley. They argued that this case was special because it involved postgraduate education for someone who was already a college faculty member. Likely Calkins notified James and Royce of the appeal to the Harvard Corporation which prompted the next two letters.

Josiah Royce to Calkins, July 21, 1890

I am glad to know that you will be with us next year, and I shall be glad to aid in the opening to you of Phil 20, as well as in the ways that I previously prom-ised. If we do not succeed as to Phil 20, there is still, I hope, much that can be done for you.

William James to Calkins, July 30, 1890

I am heartily glad to hear what you say about the Corporation etc. It is flagi-tious that you should be kept out. Enough to make dynamiters of you and all women. I hope and trust that your application will break the barrier. I will do what I can.

Note: The Harvard Corporation authorized James and Royce to allow Calkins in their classes during the coming year, but it was to be understood that "by accepting this priv-ilege Miss Calkins does not become a student of the University entitled to registration" (Corporation Records, October 1, 1890, Harvard University Archives).

William James to Calkins, October 3, 1890

I was about to write you today anyhow to express my gladness. My students 4 in number seem of divergent tendencies and I don't know just what will come of the course. Having published my two rather fat tomes [the two volumes of his *Principles of Psychology*], I shan't lecture, but the thing will probably resolve itself into advice and possibly some experimentation. Our evening meetings have been provisionally fixed for Thursdays at 7:15. Will you please come if you can, next Thursday at seven so as to have a little talk in advance, or rather come at 1/2 past six and take tea.

William James to Calkins, August 12, 1891

. . . Your thesis [on the association of ideas] has been waiting for me all this time. I hope you don't need it before October. I can't *look* at anything psychological for a fortnight.[9] Then I shall *devour* it.

William James to Calkins, November 6, 1891

I read your thesis at last, a week ago, and have just found a moment in which to drop you a line about it . . . The thesis has given me exquisite delight. The middle portion, with its classification and criticism gives the subject a real hitch ahead, and is luminous. It certainly ought to go to Schurman's Journal of Philosophy, and if you are too modest I will "introduce" it to him.

William James to Calkins, December 20, 1891

I have just written to Schurman, in a way that will ensure his attention. I had already done so without saying who you were.[10]

Edmund C. Sanford to Calkins, February 16, 1892

Assuming then that you are going to study next year, should it be Cornell or Europe? I say Europe? Why? Because 1. a European PhD will do you more good I believe than an American one . . . 2. Because I doubt the kind of course you would get at Cornell, because the psychological dept there is newly organized . . .

Josiah Royce to Calkins, February 17, 1892

I am disposed to think, from the data furnished in your letter, that you will do well, in case you can get the fellowship at Cornell,[11] to take your next year there,

[9] William James's desire to avoid anything psychological was no doubt due to the fact that he was spending much of his time condensing his two-volume *Principles of Psychology* into a smaller one-volume work entitled *Psychology: A Briefer Course*, published in 1892.
[10] Her paper was not published in Schurman's journal. Instead, it appeared as "A suggested classification of cases of association" in the *Philosophical Review*, 1, 1892, 389–402.
[11] Clearly Calkins received mixed advice from Sanford and Royce about studying psychology at Cornell University. The psychology laboratory there had been founded in 1891 by Frank Angell, one of Wundt's doctoral students. But he left after the spring semester of 1892 to accept a similar position at Stanford University. He was replaced by Edward B. Titchener, another Wundt doctorate (see Chapter 10) who, although no strong supporter of women, did admit them to his program. In fact, his first doctoral student at Cornell was Margaret Floy Washburn (1871–1939).

as you seem inclined to do. I think it very obvious that your work will be aided by another year of study taken pretty early, after your experience as a teacher has made you alive to your most significant ideals and consequent needs, and, before you have been teaching long enough to get tolerant as a teacher is so likely to do, of the incompleteness of which at first your work makes you aware . . .

Edmund C. Sanford to Calkins, June 25, 1892

. . . I spoke in a guarded way and without names to Dr. Scripture[12] about the chance for lady students at Yale. He . . . wrote: "I am willing to offer special advantages for the sake of having women graduate students at the start. I am quite willing to give them the same lecture and demonstration course as the undergraduates (undergraduate courses are not open you know generally) or with even greater fullness on the day before the undergraduate lectures or on the morning before them . . . This I am willing to do whether women are admitted to the course (undergraduate) in physiological psychology or not. I think, however, there will be no objection in case they wish to attend with the class . . ."

Please let me know when you finally make up your mind, for in the mean time (which please do not mention) I want to use the fact that you would like to take a degree for moral effect here [Clark University].

I fear that it is for the present quite a hopeless thing to think of but I should like to have Clark give you a chance though at the same time I do not know whether it would not be pedagogically well for you to go elsewhere. You know what we are like here . . .

Epilogue

In 1902, more than a decade after completing her work at Harvard, Calkins received a letter from Radcliffe College, Harvard's recently established college for women. The letter was from Agnes Irwin, Dean of the College, who informed Calkins that she would be granted a PhD degree from Radcliffe. Calkins replied:

I have seldom received so just, discriminating and kind a letter as yours of May 19 . . . and I am sorrier than I can tell you not to reply to it in the way which would best please you. I hope that I may make quite clear to you my reasons for declining to accept the honor of the Radcliffe doctor's degree. I . . . think it highly probable that the Radcliffe degree will be regarded, generally, as the practical equivalent of the Harvard degree and, . . . I should be glad to hold the Ph.D. degree for I occasionally find the lack of it an inconvenience; and now that the Radcliffe Ph.D. is offered, I doubt whether the Harvard degree will ever be open to women. On the other hand, I still believe that the best ideals of education would be better served if Radcliffe College refused to confer the doctor's degree. You will be quick to see that, holding this conviction, I cannot rightly take the easier course of accepting the degree . . . (Calkins to Irwin, May 30, 1902)

Thus Calkins refused to accept the doctorate offered her. She rejected the Radcliffe PhD "because it acquiesced to Harvard's stubborn refusal to recognize the accomplishments of women, like herself, who from the 1890s on studied in its graduate departments" (Scarborough & Furumoto, 1987, p. 49). The idea of a Radcliffe PhD was indeed a sham, as noted by Scarborough and Furumoto (1987), who wrote: "Radcliffe never was in the business of graduate instruction . . . [It] offered no graduate courses or seminars, nor did it have any laboratories for advanced work. Any woman who undertook *graduate* study did so not within Radcliffe but by going across to work at Harvard" (p. 49). It would not be until 1963 that women were finally eligible to earn a doctoral degree from Harvard, where many had already completed their graduate studies.

Calkins wrote that she never felt that the lack of the doctoral degree hindered her in any significant way, although its absence was sometimes an "inconvenience." She went on to enjoy a life of considerable scholarly accomplishment, publishing four books and more than 100 articles, divided between philosophy and psychology. Her most important contributions to psychology were her system on the psychology of self (Furumoto, 1991; Wentworth, 1999) and her experimental work on short-term memory (Madigan & O'Hara, 1992).

Calkins's story, as revealed in these few letters, describes some of the barriers for women of her time in pursuing graduate education. And for Calkins, these letters tell of her remarkable persistence, ability, courage, and sense of honor.

Suggested Readings

Calkins, M. W. (1892). A suggested classification of cases of association. *Philosophical Review, 1*, 389–402.

This is the thesis that so impressed William James (see his letters of August 12 and November 6, 1891).

Calkins, M. W. (1892). Experimental psychology at Wellesley College. *American Journal of Psychology, 5*, 260–271.

A detailed description of the experimental psychology course and laboratory that Calkins began at Wellesley.

Calkins, M. W. (1896). Association: An essay analytic and experimental. *Psychological Review Monograph Supplement Number 2*, pp. 1–56.

This classic article describes the series of experiments that originated the paired-associate technique which would become a major tool for studying learning and memory in the twentieth century.

Calkins, M. W. (1901). *An introduction to psychology.* New York: Macmillan; (1909). *A first book in psychology.* New York: Macmillan.

Calkins's two textbooks on psychology which are the most complete statements of her self-psychology.

Calkins, M. W. (1930). Autobiography. In C. Murchison (Ed.), *A history of psychology in autobiography* (Vol. 1, pp. 31–62). Worcester, MA: Clark University Press.

Written shortly before her death, the first ten pages of this chapter are autobiographical. In the remainder Calkins devotes herself "first, to setting forth and, secondly, to arguing for the essentials of a personalistic psychology" (p. 41).

Furumoto, L. (1990). Mary Whiton Calkins (1863–1930). In A. N. O'Connell & N. F. Russo (Eds.) *Women in psychology: A bio-bibliographic sourcebook*, pp. 57–65. New York: Greenwood Press and Furumoto, L. (1991). From "paired associates" to a psychology of self: The intellectual odyssey of Mary Whiton Calkins. In G. A. Kimble, M. Wertheimer, & C. L. White (Eds.) *Portraits of pioneers in psychology*. Hillsdale, NJ: Lawrence Erlbaum.

Two excellent treatments of Calkins's life and career. The former includes a bibliography of many of Calkins's publications; the latter emphasizes her psychology of self.

Madigan, S., & O'Hara, R. (1992). Short-term memory at the turn of the century: Mary Whiton Calkins's memory research. *American Psychologist, 47*, 170–174.

A discussion of Calkins's research on short-term memory, focusing on its anticipation of contemporary work in the field. The contributions described are substantial.

Scarborough, E., & Furumoto, L. (1987). *Untold lives: The first generation of American women psychologists*. New York: Columbia University Press.

Chapter 1 deals with Calkins's quest for graduate education in psychology. This outstanding book describes the problems faced by the early women psychologists: access to graduate education, claims from family (e.g., elderly and infirm parents), marriage vs career, evaluation of scholarly worth independent of gender, and exclusion from academic networks limited solely to men.

Wentworth, P. A. (1999). The moral of her story: Exploring the philosophical and religious commitments in Mary Whiton Calkins' self psychology. *History of Psychology, 2*, 119–131.

An excellent treatment of Calkins's self-psychology, illustrating the importance of the system to her ideas about ethics and morality.

Meeting of Titchener's Experimentalists at Princeton University, 1916; Edward B. Titchener is second from the left on the first row (Archives of the History of American Psychology/University of Akron)

Christine Ladd-Franklin (Archives of the History of American Psychology/University of Akron)

Titchener's Experimentalists: No Women Allowed

Edward Bradford Titchener (1867–1927) was born in Chichester, England. After earning a master's degree at Oxford University, he went to Leipzig, where he earned his doctorate in psychology with Wilhelm Wundt, graduating in 1892. He arrived in the United States that year, assuming the psychology position at Cornell University recently vacated by another of Wundt's students, Frank Angell. Titchener built his laboratory in the Leipzig tradition and soon established himself as one of the foremost psychologists in the United States. In the thirty-five years of his professional career he wrote more than two hundred articles and books and trained more than fifty doctoral students in his brand of psychology. Many of those students would found laboratories of their own, for example, Margaret Floy Washburn at Vassar College and Walter B. Pillsbury at the University of Michigan.

Titchener named his system of psychology *structuralism* because of its emphasis on discovering the elemental structure of consciousness. Conceptually, that focus of his system was similar to one of the goals of Wundtian psychology, although Wundt never used the label structuralism to refer to his psychology (see Leahey, 1981). Titchener defined psychology in the narrowest of terms. He generally opposed child psychology, abnormal psychology, and any studies on animals. His experimental science was built largely on introspection, a technique that proved to be of little use in those areas of study. It was narrower still, in comparison to Wundt, because of Titchener's adherence to positivism. Whereas Wundt sought to explain consciousness by invoking some hypothetical mental processes, Titchener avoided the mentalistic dilemma by focusing his efforts on a purely descriptive science. Cornell became the stronghold for descriptive psychology, protecting its purity from the infidels that Titchener felt made up much of American psychology.

The scientific acumen of Titchener was manifested in several ways, but is nowhere more evident than in the four volumes of his *Experimental Psychology* (1901–1905). Two of the books were for the psychology instructor and two for the student. Two dealt with quantitative studies, whereas the other two focused on qualitative studies. Collectively they were known as the "Manuals" or "Titchener's Manuals." And they were used to train an entire generation of American psychology students, not just those at Cornell, in the methods of this new science. Oswald Külpe, another Wundt doctoral student who frequently battled Titchener on theoretical grounds, called Titchener's *Experimental Psychology* "the most erudite psychological work in the English language" (Boring, 1950, p. 413).

Titchener was an excellent scientist, albeit narrow in scope, who sought to define experimental psychology wholly in his own terms. As the American Psychological Association (APA), founded in 1892 grew, its membership became increasingly diverse and its program grew to contain aspects of psychology unacceptable by Titchener's definition of experimental psychology. So in 1904 he founded his own society of experimental psychologists. In January of that year he sent a letter to approximately 20 colleagues whose research he considered acceptable. The group included James Angell, James McKeen Cattell, Raymond Dodge, Joseph Jastrow, Charles Judd, Hugo Münsterberg, Howard Warren, and Lightner Witmer, among others. The proposed organization was to be rather exclusive in its membership, "confined to the men who are working in the field of experimental psychology" (as Titchener defined them).

Many of those invited were troubled that this new organization might remove experimental psychology from the domain of the American Psychological Association. Angell, Jastrow, Judd, Münsterberg, and others wrote to Titchener expressing their concerns over the potential conflict with the APA. Warren was so upset about the conflict that he declined to attend the meetings of Titchener's new group for the first three years of its existence. A few complained to Titchener about the exclusion of women from the group, although one individual, Witmer, echoed his agreement with such a policy.

Although Titchener did not receive unanimous support for his group, he received enough endorsements to found the group. Its initial meeting was held at Cornell University, hosted by Titchener, of course. In his original letter he had implied that the group might be called the American Society for the Advancement of Experimental Psychology. A psychologist at the University of Toronto, August Kirschmann, urged Titchener to drop the word "American" from the title. And in Titchener's second letter to the group that term was gone. But in fact, the group never got a formal name. Instead it was always referred to as "The Experimentalists" or "Titchener's Experimentalists." Edwin G. Boring, a historian of psychology and student of Titchener's wrote that

> Titchener really wanted to start an informal club of experimental psychologists, an annual meeting of the heads of laboratories, who would bring with them their most promising graduate students for stimulation. He wanted oral reports that could be interrupted, dissented from and criticized, in a smoke-filled room with no women present – for in 1904, when the Experimentalists was founded, women were considered too pure to smoke. He did not achieve his goal all at once, but he worked toward it over the years. (Boring, 1967, p. 315)

Indeed, Titchener did not achieve his goal all at once. He struggled annually to make his society what he wanted. In addition to regular complaints about competition with the older APA and the exclusion of women, objections were also raised about the elitism of the group, about the definition of what research qualified as "experimental psychology," about which students were to be invited, about how many people should be invited to the meetings, and about people reading their papers instead of discussing them informally. Apparently these issues were raised at many of the annual meetings and, on occasion, dominated the meeting such that the agenda of experimental psychology became secondary. John Watson became so disenchanted with the frequent discussions of these other issues that he stopped attending.

At an APA meeting in 1922, E. G. Boring, Karl Dallenbach (both former students of Titchener), and Samuel Fernberger discussed organizing a regular and informal discussion of experimental psychology at the annual meetings of the APA. They were worried about Titchener's reaction to the idea because he could obviously perceive it as a threat to his Experimentalists. In an effort to soften the blow, they asked Raymond Dodge to organize the first of the APA round tables. Dodge, a more senior psychologist, was a charter member of Titchener's group and a member of the APA Program Committee for 1923. Dodge wrote to

Titchener to describe the idea and his letter and Titchener's reply are included in this chapter. The APA Round Tables on Experimental Psychology did begin in 1923 and continued to be a part of the annual meetings through 1928. Attendance at the sessions was large and kept the meetings from accomplishing what the organizers had intended. Thus they disappeared after a few years (Goodwin, 1990).

In August of 1927, after the twenty-third annual meeting of the Experimentalists (there was no meeting in 1918 because of World War I), Titchener died of a brain tumor. His death provided an opportunity for his colleagues to reconsider the structure and content of the society.

The letters in this chapter tell the story of the founding of Titchener's Experimentalists. They are revealing of Titchener as psychologist and as person, and they illustrate the roles played by others important to the early development of American psychology and its organizations. They also tell of the importance of such an organization for the scientific development of its participants.

These letters also tell the story of Christine Ladd-Franklin's struggle to participate in the intellectual exchange that was enjoyed by her male colleagues. Ladd-Franklin (1847–1930), an early experimental psychologist who was well known for her work in vision and her theory of color vision, made repeated requests to be a part of the meetings, to no avail. In the previous chapter on Mary Whiton Calkins we saw that women faced overwhelming obstacles in seeking higher education at the turn of the twentieth century. There were many other barriers for women, including what Scarborough and Furumoto (1987) have labeled "collegial exclusion," which is part of the story of this chapter. The letters begin with Titchener's invitation to found a new psychological organization.

The Letters

E. B. Titchener to approximately 20 colleagues in psychology, January 15, 1904

I write to ask your assistance in the organization of an American society for the advancement of Experimental Psychology.

It is generally admitted that, in matters of Experimental Psychology, our own country stands second, if to any other, at most only to Germany. This honourable position has been won by the efforts of a relatively small body of men, working under all the disadvantages and discouragements that naturally accompany the establishment of a new method in science. There is, I hope, no serious danger that we shall ever derogate from it. But there is, I am sure, a serious need of organisation and consolidation of our present forces. Not only would the directors of laboratories benefit by interchange of ideas and discussion of programmes; but the younger men also – and this is a point upon which I desire to lay special weight – would realise, by association, the community of their interests, the common dangers to which their profession is exposed, and their responsibilities to the science.

In proposing to found a new society, I have no desire to interfere in any way with the existing American Psychological Association. This association has done admirable work for American psychology at large. It is, however, evident that the opportunities which it offers for scientific and social intercourse have not met the special requirements of Experimental Psychology. If the new society is successful, I see no reason why it should not ultimately affiliate to the elder association. For the time being, however, it will be wiser, I believe, that the experimentalists act independently.

My ideas with regard to the proposed society are as follows: (1) that its membership be confined to men who are working in the field of experimental psychology, (2) that its discussions be confined to subjects investigated by the experimental method, (3) that it meet, once a year or oftener, at one of the larger university laboratories; and (4) that place and date of meeting be so chosen as to avoid conflict with the meetings of other scientific societies. The intention underlying these proposals is, very simply, that the experimentalists shall come together for a couple of days every year, to talk, think and act nothing but Experimental Psychology.

I earnestly hope that I may count upon your assistance. If I am fortunate enough to secure your general approval of the scheme, I will, later on, submit to you some further propositions of more detail.

Titchener to Hugo Münsterberg, February 1, 1904

For many years I wanted an experimental club – no officers, the men moving about and handling [apparatus], the visited lab to do the work, no women, smoking allowed, plenty of perfectly frank criticism and discussions, the whole atmosphere experimental, the youngsters taken in on an equality with the men who have arrived. I have waited so as not to interfere with the progress of the regular Assn. [the American Psychological Association] – which when all is said, cannot fulfill these requirements with present membership and organisation. Now, I think, the Assn. is firmly established; I cannot hurt it if I wanted to – as emphatically I do not; and there are enough men like-minded with me to make the Society or Club of experimentalists a reality. We cannot reduce exp. psych. to papers; and the Assn. is organized on a paper basis. We can't be frank if we have too many members; or if we have outsiders drifting in. We don't want officers – in science, of all things in the world! I have received good promise of support, and I hope we [can go ahead] without bothering the Assn.

Edmund C. Sanford [Clark University] to Titchener, January 19, 1904

... The question with regard to women in the association is a poser. Several of them on scientific grounds have full right to be there and might feel hurt (in a general impersonal way) if women are not asked. On the other hand they would undoubtedly interfere with the smoking and to a certain extent with the general freedom of a purely masculine assembly. Would it be possible to give them also the chance to say whether they would like to come – assuring them by a personal note that transactions would not come off except in a partially smoke-charged atmosphere? . . .

Lightner Witmer [University of Pennsylvania] to Titchener, January 25, 1904

. . . I am quite positive in my objection to inviting women . . . I am sure from my experience, that you cannot run an informal meeting of men and women . . . We want a small vigorous association where we can speak our minds with perfect freedom . . . The larger and more heterogeneous the organization the more likely is vigorous discussion to be misinterpreted and to be taken as an offence by individuals who may happen to be attacked. I think that the presence of women in the organization adds greatly to this danger, owing to the personal attitude which they usually take even in scientific discussions. I favor a small association, no invited guests, and no women members.

Titchener to various colleagues, February 6, 1904

On January 15th I addressed a letter to a limited number of experimental psychologists, of whom you are one, asking them to cooperate with me in the formation of a society for the advancement of Experimental Psychology. The large proportion of favourable answers shows that the need of such an organization is keenly felt. There seems to be a pretty general agreement, among those whose assistance is promised, that the new society should present the following features:

(1)   no fees; no officers; organization as simple as possible;
(2)   membership small; meetings entirely informal;
(3)   for the present at least, membership confined to men;
(4)   for the present at least, no affiliation to any existing society;
(5)   meetings to be held at the larger university laboratories;
(6)   place and date of meetings to be so chosen as to avoid conflict with the meetings of other scientific societies;
(7)   special effort to be directed towards the encouragement of graduate students and the younger independent workers in Experimental Psychology;
(8)   papers, demonstrations, symposia, etc., to be strictly confined to subjects investigated by the experimental method.

All these points, however, are entirely open to discussion among those who accept membership in the society. In order that the society may have a positive starting-point, I venture to ask you to reply to the two questions printed overleaf. I earnestly hope that the society may have the benefit of your assistance.

(1) Are you willing to become an active member of such a society as has been described, – on the understanding that the points raised are one and all open to discussion within the society? and,
(2) Can you attend a meeting at Ithaca during the coming Easter vacation? If so, what date would best suit you? An early reply would be appreciated.

Note: *After Titchener hosted the initial meeting in 1904 at Cornell, subsequent meetings were held at Clark University in 1905 (E. C. Sanford), Yale University in 1906 (Charles H. Judd), the University of Pennsylvania in 1907 (Lightner Witmer), and at Harvard University in 1908 (Hugo Münsterberg). The Titchener letter that follows was intended to give Münsterberg advice on invitations and the conduct of the 1908 meeting.*

Titchener to Hugo Münsterberg, February 29, 1908

. . . Our original membership (apart from Harvard) is, I believe, as follows: Frank Angell, [Madison] Bentley, [Raymond] Dodge, [Charles] Judd, [Edward] Pace, [Walter] Pillsbury, [Edmund C.] Sanford, [Carl] Seashore, [Lightner] Witmer. The Chicago and Columbia people declined to come in. We invited [Howard] Warren and he came last year for the first time: I suppose that he and [J. W.] Baird should be counted members.

All of these men, therefore, are entitled to invitation . . . Any further invitations are left, I believe, entirely to the discretion of the individual members . . . You are absolutely free to invite anyone you like; and I suppose it would fall to you as chairman of the occasion, to notify [James McKeen] Cattell, [George] Stratton and James Angell, in case they cared to come or send any of their men.

I heard nothing last year of any objections to the size of the meetings: I do not think they ran over 15, and at times there were only a half dozen present. [James H.] Leuba sent in ome girls [from Bryn Mawr College], whom we promptly turned out; that was sheer misunderstanding . . .

Note: *The previous letter shows an attempted breach, intentional or not, of the "woman question." The question of women invitees would not go away as shown in the next several letters.*

Christine Ladd-Franklin to Titchener, 1912

. . . I am particularly anxious to bring my views up, once in a while, for hand-to-hand discussion before experts, and just now I have especially a paper which

I should like very much to read before your meeting of experimental psychologists. I hope you will not say nay!

Note: Titchener's reply does not exist but apparently he denied Ladd-Franklin's request to attend, which prompted the following letter.

Christine Ladd-Franklin to Titchener, 1912

I am shocked to know that you are still – at this year – excluding women from your meeting of experimental psychologists. It is such a very old-fashioned standpoint! [How illogical it is] that you should include in your invitation . . . the students of G. Stanley Hall, who are not in the least experimentalists and exclude the women who are doing particularly good work in the experimental laboratory of Prof. Baird . . . Have your smokers separated if you like (tho I for one always smoke when I am in fashionable society), but a scientific meeting (however personal) is a public affair, and it is not open to you to leave out a class of fellow workers without extreme discourtesy.

Mary Whiton Calkins [see Chapter 9] to Christine Ladd-Franklin,
August 14, 1912

. . . As to the experimental psychologists: I of course share your regret at their attitude toward women. In fact, I have . . . spoken of the matter in years past to Dr. Titchener and to Dr. Münsterberg (the latter, I think favors their entrance). I feel the freer to speak because I no longer count myself an experimenter: but you, Miss [Eleanor] Gamble, Miss [Margaret Floy] Washburn, Miss [Helen Dodd] Cook, and several others should of course be invited. At the same time I doubt the wisdom of a public protest on the part of those who are shut out. It seems to be sufficiently a side-issue to be left to time or to protestants from within.

Christine Ladd-Franklin to Titchener, March 21, 1914

. . . Is this then a good time, my dear Professor Titchener, for you to hold to the medaeval attitude of not admitting me to your coming psychological conference in New York – at my very door?[1] So unconscientious, so immoral, – worse than that – so unscientific!

---

[1]   Ladd-Franklin was living in New York City.

Titchener to Robert M. Yerkes [Harvard University], April 2, 1914

I am not sure that we had better not disintegrate! I have been pestered by abuse by Mrs. Ladd-Franklin for not having women at the meetings, and she threatens to make various scenes in person and in print. Possibly she will succeed in breaking us up, and forcing us to meet – like rabbits – in some dark place underground . . .

Note: Ladd-Franklin did attend one of the sessions of the 1914 Columbia meeting, perhaps at her own initiative, perhaps at the invitation of Cattell, certainly not at the invitation of Titchener. According to E. G. Boring (1938), it marked the only attendance of women at the meetings until after Titchener's death in 1927. John Watson objected to Titchener's experimentalists for different reasons, as the following letter shows.

John B. Watson to Howard C. Warren [Princeton University], April 14, 1916

I have received your circular and the mileage book. I wish to thank you sincerely for the book and for the cordial invitation to come. Your memorandum, however, and certain other letters which I have received, have decided me to decline the invitation. I am going to be quite frank because I believe the ends of science and of friendship too are best conserved in that way.

Were your organization called the Titchener Club you would be acting entirely within your rights in sending out the memorandum. But this organization has called itself variously Meeting of the Experimental Psychologists, the experimentalists, etc. In other words, it is and has been a scientific gathering. In my earlier days I was more or less willing to stand for exclusiveness in science. As I grow older I get further away from this kind of thing. Every time I attend one of these meetings I am embarrassed by having to talk about the nature of the meeting, and to tell certain people that they cannot come, and I was criticized very severely for allowing too many people to come to the Baltimore meeting [hosted by Watson in 1910].

This embarrassment that I always feel in regard to these meetings takes away any pleasure that I might get from the meeting, and while I do not represent anybody but myself I seriously question the justice and wisdom of your using the term Experimental Psychologists or experimentalists. To make this organization work without hurting feelings, it should be called the Titchener Club, and invitations should be issued to join it.

Assuring both you and Titchener of my regret at not being able to see you, I am sincerely yours.

Note: The following letters describe the emerging experimental round-table sessions that were being planned for the meetings of the American Psychological Association. Note the difference in Titchener's replies to Dodge and Boring.

Raymond Dodge to Titchener, April 14, 1923

Several of the younger men wrote to me sometime ago asking about the possibility of an informal session at the time of the winter meeting of the American Psychological Association. I have been talking it over with a number of others who might be interested and believe such a session would enormously increase the profit of the winter meeting. I wish you would be good enough to give me your frank reaction to the following proposals. (1) A session open to experimentalists for the discussion of experimentali and procedures by those who are responsible for them. (2) No papers to be read that belongs to the formal session of the Association. (3) Time of the session to parallel the meetings of the psychology in clinical psychology, applied psychology, probably the last session of the meeting running over into Friday morning if there is demand for it.

I am particularly interested in getting your opinion as to how such a meeting would affect the spring meeting of experimentalists in which we are both deeply interested. I am particularly interested to know if you would attend such a meeting and lend your support. It seems to me that you would be the natural person to preside. As member of the Program Committee I can get a place for it whenever you think it desirable and can probably arrange for such announcements as the situation would call for . . .

Titchener to Raymond Dodge, April 19, 1923

I had heard of an idea for the establishment of an Experimental Section of the Association, but your notion of informal sessions is new to me. I do not think that you need for a moment take into account the spring meeting of the Experimentalists. We have now stood up for twenty years, and so far as I can see we are good for many years more; I doubt if any action on the part of the Association will have any effect on us. If it does then we shall deserve what we get.

I cannot say, however, that I am hopeful about your plan. For one thing, the whole atmosphere of the Association is against informality and, as you yourself say, in favor of presiding and being presided over. For another thing, an informal session, if it is to be really successful, presupposes an immense amount of hard work and unselfish work on the part of one or two members of the group; and I don't know who could be persuaded to undertake that sort of job. For a third thing, the right place for an informal experimental session is the laboratory, and the laboratory thrown open for mauling and examining. You will understand that this is simply my individual opinion, which may very well be offset by the desires and opinions of other people. Personally I have decided to leave the Association owing to the $5.00 subscription which seems to me to be preposterous. Cattell was good enough to say that the raising of the subscription would rule out the welshers, and so I mean to make myself a nucleus for the welshing group . . .

Titchener to Edwin G. Boring, date unknown (quoted in Boring's letter to Karl Dallenbach, May 25, 1923)

There is a threatening complication about the Experimentalists. Dodge has decided to try to imitate us, by inaugurating a sort of round-table experimental informal conference, at the Assn. meetings. I think . . . that we shall presently be snuffed out. We are an arbitrary and one-sexed lot; and the Assn. will give room to anybody who is a member and wants to attend, and will let women in . . . All the people whom we have offended will therefore work hard for the success of the venture; and we have offended a good many.

Note: The 24th annual meeting of the experimentalists was to be held at Yale University in 1928. But Titchener's death[2] on August 3, 1927 caused the group to reconsider the original plan.

Roswell P. Angier [Yale University] to Raymond Dodge, November 28, 1927

The Experimentalists were, as you will remember, invited to meet at Yale next spring. Titchener's death, however, seems to several of us to have altered the situation to such an extent that it is desirable to secure the reactions of those who have longest been associated with the group to the problems of the best course to pursue in the future. Three possibilities have been suggested in informal exchange of views.

1. To hold the meeting next spring as scheduled.
2. To give up the meetings altogether.
3. To omit next spring's meeting out of respect to Titchener's memory, and then consider at leisure what to do in the future.

The various pros and cons need not be dealt with here, for they will readily occur to us who realize that Titchener not only started the meetings but was

---

[2] Ladd-Franklin wrote to Margaret Washburn in August, 1927 to ask her to write an obituary for Titchener. Washburn replied: "I never had any quarrel with him or personal grievance against him, but I have never either liked or admired him, and have had for years little agreement with his views. I have not seen him, I suppose, for twenty years, nor corresponded with him. I can think of few persons to whom I have felt less near than I have always felt to him" (cited in Scarborough & Furumoto, 1987, p. 128).

throughout their inspiration and their central figure. One suggested course may, however, be mentioned, namely, that next spring's meeting occur as contemplated and assume a character commemorative to Titchener. Some think that this would on the whole be inadvisable since eulogistic tribute would be something alien to anything that Titchener himself would have wished; and that it is too soon, on the other hand, for any of us to attempt an objective appraisal of the quality and extent of his contribution to the development of psychological thought.

Naturally Yale would be delighted to serve as host to next spring's meeting if it appears advisable on the whole to hold it; on this point, or any other phases of the matter we earnestly seek advice, and shall be grateful if you will indicate your views.

Howard C. Warren to 14 other psychologists invited to be an organizing committee for a new organization, April 11, 1928

The group of Experimental Psychologists organized by Professor Titchener held its final meeting at New Haven [Yale] last week. In view of Dr. Titchener's death, and because of the increasing attendance, it was agreed that these gatherings no longer fulfilled the purpose for which they were designed, namely, a conference of experimental investigators for intimate discussion of current laboratory problems . . . The [organizing] Committee will meet at Princeton next spring, at a date to be determined later. The business will include (1) a definite decision as to the character of the new organization; (2) election of members in accordance with the policy agreed upon; (3) determination of time and place of next meeting and any other matters requiring action. It is expected that in addition to the business sessions, the opportunity will be taken to discuss laboratory problems and methods. You are requested to write to the undersigned signifying your willingness to become a member of the Committee.

Epilogue

Thus the 1928 meeting at Yale University was considered the last meeting of Titchener's experimentalists. At that meeting a committee of five, chaired by Warren, was given the task of reorganization. That committee decided to add ten others to its membership and held its next meeting at Princeton University in 1929. It was at that meeting that the Society of Experimental Psychologists (SEP) was formally organized. The Committee of 15 asked 11 others to join them in the new society as charter members. Two of that number were women – June Etta Downey of the University of Wyoming and Margaret Floy Washburn (Titchener's first PhD student) of Vassar College – and they were invited, with the others, to the 1930 meeting. Ladd-Franklin did not receive an invitation, and she could not have attended anyway. She died at age 82 at her home in New York City on March 5,

1930, shortly before the SEP meeting. She had persisted into 1916 in her attempts to change Titchener's mind, with no success.

The new bylaws for the SEP indicated that membership would be limited to those "engaged in the advancement of experimental psychology." Further, the Society was not to exceed 50 members at any time. It still exists today as an invitation-only organization, consisting of some of the most prestigious psychologists in North America, and holding an annual meeting for the purposes of discussing experimental psychology. It was and is an important network in the discipline of psychology. The 50-member limit was changed some years ago and today's membership is around 200. The Society no longer denies membership to women, but they remain a small percentage of the membership.

In 2004, the Society of Experimental Psychologists held its centennial meeting on the campus of Cornell University. One of the faculty members at Cornell brought a guest to the meeting – well, sort of. Titchener's brain, per his wishes, is part of the brain collection at Cornell, and it was brought to the opening session of the 2004 SEP meeting. Although Titchener would not have approved of the women present in the room, he would perhaps have been gratified that his organization is still active after 100 years.

Suggested Readings

Benjamin, L. T., Jr. (1977). The Psychological Round Table: Revolution of 1936. *American Psychologist, 32,* 542–549.

This article is a historical account (as described in Chapter 1) of a secret society organized in 1936 by a group of younger psychologists who were dissatisfied with their exclusion from the membership of the Society of Experimental Psychologists. Filled with the vigor of youth, and believing that their elders really didn't do all that much experimental work anymore, they first decided to call their organization the Society of Experimenting Psychologists. One of their elders (E. G. Boring) suggested that was not a good idea, and so they changed it to the Psychological Round Table, or PRT. Participation in the PRT was by invitation only and psychologists were excluded when they reached the age of 40. Women were barred from participating until the early 1970s.

Boring, E. G. (1927). Edward Bradford Titchener: 1867–1927. *American Journal of Psychology, 38,* 489–506.

Boring's obituary of his doctoral mentor.

Boring, E. G. (1938). The Society of Experimental Psychologists, 1904–1938. *American Journal of Psychology, 51,* 410–423 and (1967). Titchener's Experimentalists. *Journal of the History of the Behavioral Sciences, 3,* 315–325.

Boring attended his first meeting of the experimentalists in 1911 (the eighth meeting). These two articles are his histories of the experimentalist meetings.

Furumoto, L. (1992). Joining separate spheres – Christine Ladd-Franklin, woman-scientist (1847–1930). *American Psychologist, 47,* 175–182.

An excellent account of the barriers and enabling forces that shaped Ladd-Franklin as woman and as scientist.

Goodwin, C. J. (1985). On the origins of Titchener's experimentalists. *Journal of the History of the Behavioral Sciences, 21,* 383–389.

Discusses Titchener's reasons for founding the experimentalists and describes an earlier attempt in 1898 by Lightner Witmer to establish a similar group, independent of the American Psychological Association.

Ladd-Franklin, C. (1929). *Colour and colour theories.* New York: Harcourt Brace.

The culmination of Ladd-Franklin's research and theories on color vision.

Leys, R., & Evans, R. B. (Eds.) (1990). *Defining American psychology: The correspondence between Adolf Meyer and Edward Bradford Titchener.* Baltimore: Johns Hopkins University Press.

A collection of letters between Titchener and Meyer, one of America's most famous psychiatrists, that focuses on their markedly different views of psychology.

Scarborough, E., & Furumoto, L. (1987). *Untold lives: The first generation of American women psychologists.* New York: Columbia University Press.

See Chapter 5 – "A Little Hard on Ladies: Christine Ladd-Franklin's Challenge to Collegial Exclusion," which deals specifically with the exclusion of women from Titchener's experimentalists and more broadly with the issues of collegial exclusion as a barrier for women in psychology.

Titchener, E. B. (1910). *A textbook of psychology.* New York: Macmillan.

This is Titchener's textbook for the beginning psychology student which describes his brand of psychology, known as structuralism.

CHAPTER

The psychoanalytic group at Clark University, 1909; *front row (left to right)* Sigmund Freud,
G. Stanley Hall, Carl Gustav Jung; *second row (left to right)* A.A. Brill, Ernest Jones, Sandor Ferenczi
(Archives of the History of American Psychology / University of Akron)

Coming to America: Freud and Jung

In 1908, G. Stanley Hall (1844–1924), psychologist and president of Clark University in Worcester, Massachusetts, was busy planning a celebration of the twentieth anniversary of Clark that would occur the following year. On December 15 he wrote to Wilhelm Wundt and Sigmund Freud (1856–1939), inviting them to speak at Clark in July. Wundt declined the invitation. He may even have wondered about such elaborate preparations at Clark, a university in its infancy, given that his own University of Leipzig was then planning to celebrate an anniversary – its 500th! Freud also declined the invitation but in February, 1909, he changed his mind when the dates of the planned Clark Conference were changed to September and the compensation offered him increased. Hall also promised him an honorary degree. It would be Freud's first and only trip to America.

139

In the next six months, Freud and his disciple, Carl Gustav Jung (1875–1961), often discussed America in their letters, especially after Freud learned in June that Jung had also been invited. Both viewed the invitation as important recognition for psychoanalysis, and saw the visit as a golden opportunity to spread the word of psychoanalysis in the New World. But their eagerness was also tempered by some pessimism about the puritanical nature of the Americans and their willingness to embrace a theory of behavior emphasizing sexuality. Freud was both excited and anxious regarding the trip, fretting about his lecture topics and whether he should deliver the lectures in German or make the attempt to give them in English.

Freud invited another disciple, Sandor Ferenczi (1873–1933), a Hungarian psychoanalyst, to accompany him on the trip. They joined Jung in Bremen and on August 21, 1909, sailed for America on the liner *George Washington*. They arrived in New York City on August 29. The following day Abraham A. Brill (1874–1948), an American disciple, took Freud and his companions on a tour of the city. They visited Central Park and Chinatown in the morning and spent the afternoon at Coney Island. The next morning they toured the Metropolitan Museum of Art, a visit that Freud had looked forward to with great anticipation, principally because of the Greek antiquities in the museum's collection. Freud was a serious collector of Greek, Egyptian, and Etruscan antiquities.

The next day Freud was taken to see his first movie. We do not know what he saw, but according to Freud it involved "plenty of wild chasing." Freud's reaction was described as "quietly amused" (Jones, 1955, p. 56). By this time the three Europeans were suffering from their American diet. Jung, in a letter to his wife, complained that they all had diarrhea and bad stomachaches. Freud even believed he might be having an attack of appendicitis. The three of them fasted for a day in an effort to alleviate some of the discomfort.

After touring New York City, Freud and Jung journeyed to Worcester, Massachusetts, arriving on September 5, where they were invited to stay in Hall's home. Freud's first lecture was scheduled two days later.

The lineup of speakers for the conference was impressive, notwithstanding the presence of Freud and Jung. It included William Stern, Adolph Meyer, Franz Boas, Herbert Spencer Jennings, and Edward Bradford Titchener. Those in attendance were a *Who's Who* of American psychology and related disciplines, including William James and James McKeen Cattell.

Freud gave five lectures on successive days, at 11:00 each morning. The lectures covered his system of psychoanalysis and were delivered in German. He did not write out his lectures in advance. Instead, they were formed in the course of half-hour walks that he took with Ferenczi. No notes were used in delivering the lectures, and Freud's later published versions were derived wholly from his memory of those talks. Jung gave three lectures, also delivered in German, describing work with his word-association method.

Freud (age 53) was surely impressed with the attention and adulation he received. That feeling had begun on the trip over from Europe when he noticed one of the ship's stewards reading a copy of his book, *The Psychopathology of Every-day Life* (1901). At the ceremony when he received his honorary doctorate, Freud was visibly moved. He thanked Hall for what he termed the "first official recognition of our endeavors" (Jones, 1955, p. 57). Freud felt he received recognition in America that was denied him in Europe. He told his biographer: "As I stepped on to the platform at Worcester to deliver my *Five Lectures Upon Psycho-Analysis* [1910] it seemed like the recognition of some incredible daydream; psychoanalysis was no longer a product of delusion; it had become a valuable part of reality" (Jones, 1955, p. 59).

Jung (age 34), the youngest of the speakers, was also awarded an honorary doctoral degree from Clark University. It was a time of much rejoicing for the success of psychoanalysis and the friendship and close collaboration between Freud and Jung. In fact, at this time Freud viewed Jung as his successor in carrying forward the message of psychoanalysis, leading Freud to refer to himself as Moses and to Jung as Joshua, who would lead psychoanalysis to dominate the promised land of psychiatry. Others would refer to Jung as the "crown prince." But the friendship would last for only a few more years.

Although Freud and Jung relished the recognition for their work that the invitations represented, both had somewhat negative impressions of America and Americans. Some of those attitudes are revealed in the letters that follow. Nevertheless, their 1909 visit provided a substantial impetus to psychoanalytic theory in America, spreading both Freudian and Jungian ideas to American followers (see Hale, 1979; Hornstein, 1992). Today psychoanalysis is more prominent in America than any other country, something that Freud and Jung would surely not have predicted. The letters that follow tell some of the story of that historic visit.

The Letters

G. Stanley Hall to Sigmund Freud, December 15, 1908

Although I have not the honor of your personal acquaintance, I have for many years been profoundly interested in your work which I have studied with diligence, and also in that of your followers ...

The purpose of this letter is to ask if you can come to this country and to this university the first week in next July, and give perhaps four or six lectures, either in German or English, setting forth your own views, either the substance of those already printed or something new – whatever seems best to you.

The occasion is the twentieth Anniversary of the founding of this institution, and we hope to attract a select audience of the best American professors and students of psychology and psychiatry ...

We are able to attach to this proposition an honorarium of four hundred dollars, or sixteen hundred Marks, to cover expenses. You will, of course, be free, after the week's engagement here, to make any others in this country.

Freud to G. Stanley Hall, December 29, 1908

Your invitation to offer a series of lectures at your university in the first week of July is a great honor for me, but I do not know how the following difficulty can be overcome. I am a practicing physician and because of the summer habits of my countrymen I am obliged to discontinue work from July 15 to the end of September. If I were to lecture in America in the first week of July, I should have to suspend my medical work three weeks earlier than usual, which would mean a significant and irretrievable loss for me. This consideration makes it impossible for me to accept your proposal.

Freud to Carl Jung, December 30, 1908

Now finally I come to the news that I have been invited by Clark University, Worcester, Mass., Pres. Stanley Hall, to deliver four to six lectures in the first week of July. They expect my lectures to give a mighty impetus to the development of psychotherapy over there. The occasion: the twentieth (!) anniversary of the founding of the university.[1] I have declined without even consulting you or anyone else, the crucial reason being that I should have had to stop work 2 weeks sooner than usual, which would mean a loss of several thousand kronen. Naturally the Americans pay only $400 for travel expenses. I am not wealthy enough to spend five times that much to give the Americans an impetus. (That's boasting; two-and-a-half to three times as much!) But I am sorry to have it fall through on this account, because it would have been fun. I don't really believe that Clark University, a small but serious institution, can postpone its festivities for three weeks.

Jung to Freud, January 7, 1909

This is a real triumph and I congratulate you most heartily! Too bad it comes at such an inconvenient time. Perhaps you could arrange to go after the anniversary; even then your lectures would still be of interest to the Americans. Little by little your truth is percolating through to the public. If at all possible, you ought to speak in America if only because of the echo it would arouse in Europe, where things are beginning to stir too.

[1] Evidently Freud was amused at the sense of history in America, that Americans would celebrate something so short-lived as a twentieth anniversary.

Freud to Jung, January 17, 1909

There is a good deal to be said about America. Jones[2] and Brill write often. Jones's observations are shrewd and pessimistic, Brill sees everything through rose-coloured spectacles. I am inclined to agree with Jones. I also think that once they discover the sexual core of our psychological theories they will drop us. Their prudery and their material dependence on the public are too great. That is why I have no desire to risk the trip there in July. I can't expect anything of consultations. Anyway I have heard nothing more from Clark University . . .

We are certainly getting ahead; if I am Moses, then you are Joshua and will take possession of the promised land of psychiatry, which I shall only be able to glimpse from afar.

Jung to Freud, January 19, 1909

The Americans are a horse of a different colour. First I must point out with diabolical glee your slip of the pen: you wrote "your prudishness" instead of "their prudishness." We have noticed this prudishness, which used to be worse than it is now; now I can stomach it. I don't water down the sexuality any more.

You are probably right about the trip to America. I share Jones's pessimism absolutely. So far these people simply haven't a notion of what we're at. One of these days they will creep into a corner, prim and abashed. Nevertheless it will rub off on some of them and is doing so already, despite their audible silence. In any case the American medical material isn't up to much.

G. Stanley Hall to Freud, February 16, 1909

On December 15th I had the honor of conveying an invitation of our Board to you to be present at the celebration which we are planning for next June which, to our regret you were obliged to decline December 29th.

Our situation has changed here in two important respects. First, we have received an addition to our financial budget which enables us to increase our financial proposition to $750 (3000 Marks); and secondly, the date of the celebration has been changed from June to the week beginning September 6th.

In view of these two modifications of our programme, I venture to write you once more in the hope that you may be induced to spend a few days that week with us and give us a few informal lectures, and allow us to bestow upon you an honorary degree.

---

[2]   Ernest Jones (1879–1958) was an English psychoanalyst who was with Freud in America. An ardent disciple, Jones later wrote a three-volume biography of Freud.

Freud to G. Stanley Hall, February 28, 1909

Your letter of the 16th brought me a very happy surprise. The postponement of the celebration to the second week in September makes it possible for me to accept your invitation without substantial sacrifice to me . . . I shall therefore come and I also gratefully accept the increase for my travel expenses as well as the honor which you intend to confer on me.

Freud to Jung, March 9, 1909

You recall that last December I received an invitation from Clark University in Worcester, Mass., which I had to decline because the festivities during which my lectures were to be delivered were scheduled for the second week in July and I would have lost too much money by the transaction. At the time you yourself regretted that I was unable to manage it. Well, a week ago a second invitation came from Stanley Hall, the president of Clark University, who at the same time informed me that the festivities had been postponed to the week of September 6. Also the travel allowance has been increased not inconsiderably from $400 to $750. This time I have accepted, for at the end of August I shall be free and rested. On October 1 I hope to be back in Vienna. I must admit that this has thrilled me more than anything else that has happened in the last few years – except perhaps for the appearance of the *Jahrbuch*[3] – and that I have been thinking of nothing else. Practical considerations have joined forces with imagination and youthful enthusiasm to upset the composure on which you have complimented me. In 1886, when I started my practice, I was thinking only of a two-month trial period in Vienna; if it did not prove satisfactory, I was planning to go to America and found an existence that I would subsequently have asked my fiancée in Hamburg to share. You see, we both of us had nothing, or more precisely, I had a large and impoverished family and she a small inheritance of roughly 3000 fl. from her Uncle Jacob, who had been a professor of classical philology in Bonn. But unfortunately things went so well in Vienna that I decided to stay on, and we were married in the autumn of the same year. And now, twenty-three years later, I am to go to America after all, not, to be sure, to make money, but in response to an honourable call! We shall have a good deal to say about this trip and its various consequences for our cause.

Jung to Freud, March 11, 1909

I must congratulate you heartily on your American triumphs. I believe you will get an American practice in the end. My American has been behaving quite well so far. I am all agog for more news.

[3] The *Yearbook for Psychoanalysis and Research in Psychopathology*, the first journal on psychoanalysis, was planned by Freud and appeared in 1908 under Jung's editorship.

If you are going to America in September, I earnestly hope that you will put in a week with us here as a way-station. You will have all the holiday peace and quiet that could be wished for. We are boldly taking it for granted that you will come. After all, the road to America runs through Zürich too. (This piece of impudence was only half intentional, otherwise I would have deleted the sentence.)

Freud to Jung, June 3, 1909

I should like very much to talk with you about America and have your suggestions. Jones threatens me, not entirely without ulterior motive, with the absence of all leading psychiatrists. I expect nothing of the moguls. But I wonder if it might not be a good idea to concentrate on psychology since Stanley Hall is a psychologist, and perhaps to devote my 3–4 lectures entirely to dreams, from which excursions in various directions would be possible. Of course these questions have little practical interest in view of my inability to lecture in English.

Jung to Freud, June 12, 1909

Isn't it splendid about America? I have already booked a cabin on the *G. Washington* – unfortunately only a very expensive one was left. I shall sail with you from Bremen.[4] Now I am in for it – what am I to say? What *can* one say of all this in 3 lectures? I'd be grateful for advice.

Freud to Jung, June 18, 1909

Your being invited to America is the best thing that has happened to us since Salzburg;[5] it gives me enormous pleasure for the most selfish reasons, though also, to be sure, because it shows what prestige you have already gained at your age. Such a beginning will take you far, and a certain amount of favour on the part of men and fate is a very good thing for one who aspires to perform great deeds.

---

[4] Apparently Jung sent a telegram to Freud prior to this letter informing him that he too had received an invitation to speak at Clark University. Years later in his autobiography, Jung would say that he and Freud were invited at the same time. Certainly the Freud–Jung correspondence suggests that this was not the case. See *Memories, Dreams, Reflections* (1961), pp. 120–121. Jung's invitation evidently came about because Ernst Meumann (1862–1915), a German psychologist and disciple of Wundt, had declined Hall's offer to attend the Clark celebration (Rosenzweig, 1994).

[5] The reference is to the First Congress of Freudian Psychology, which was held in Salzburg, Austria in 1908.

Of course your joy is now beginning to be clouded by the same concerns as mine, culminating in the question: What am I to say to those people? On this score I have a saving idea, which I shall not keep secret from you. Here it is: we can think about it on shipboard, on our long walks round the deck. Otherwise I can only refer you to the astute observation with which you yourself recently allayed *my* misgivings: that the invitation is the main thing, that the audience is now at our mercy, under obligation to applaud whatever we bring them.

A most gratifying detail is that you too are sailing on the *G. Washington*. We shall both be very nice to Ferenczi.

Jung to Freud, July 10–13, 1909

I shall then start immediately on the American lectures. I really don't know what to say. I shall start nibbling away at some corner just to see what happens. I have a vague idea of speaking first on the family constellation, second on the diagnostic significance of associations, and third on the educational questions raised by psychoanalysis. Naturally I am not a little bothered by the fact that you will be present and know all this far better than I do. I shall go through with it all the same. Once the essentials are down on paper it won't worry me in the least, and I shall be able to give my whole attention to the impressions of the voyage.

Note: The Clark twentieth-anniversary celebration included speakers from many fields, including physics, chemistry, biology, mathematics, and astronomy, in addition to the eight speakers in psychology and pedagogy. Of that number, the only American psychologist invited to speak was Edward B. Titchener (1867–1927; see Chapter 10). The psychology conference was a success by all accounts. It was attended by most of the principal psychologists in the New England area as well as major figures from psychiatry, neurology, and anthropology.

On September 10, William James (see Chapter 7) was in town to hear Freud's fourth lecture, on the topic of dreams. James had arrived the day before and, like Freud and Jung, was staying with the Halls. Later that day Freud walked with a very ill James (suffering from heart failure) toward the Worcester train station, apparently the only opportunity they had to talk with one another. James suffered an attack of angina during the walk. He would live less than a year.

Jung wrote several letters to his wife from America, the first three from G. Stanley Hall's house. Excerpts follow.

Jung to his wife, Emma, September 6, 1909 (from Worcester, MA)

He [Hall] is a refined, distinguished old gentleman close on seventy who received us with the kindest hospitality. He has a plump, jolly, good-natured, and extremely ugly wife who, however, serves wonderful food. She promptly took over Freud and me as her "boys" and plied us with delicious nourishment and noble wine, so that we began visibly to recover.[6]

Jung to his wife, Emma, September 8, 1909 (from Worcester, MA)

The people here are all exceedingly amiable and on a decent cultural level. We are beautifully taken care of at the Halls' and daily recovering from the exertions of New York. My stomach is almost back to normal now; from time to time there is a little twitch, but aside from that, my general health is excellent. Yesterday Freud began the lectures and received great applause. We are gaining ground here, and our following is growing slowly but surely. Today I had a talk about psychoanalysis with two highly cultivated elderly ladies who proved to be very well informed and free-thinking. I was greatly surprised, since I had prepared myself for opposition. Recently we had a large garden party with fifty people present, in the course of which I surrounded myself with five ladies. I was even able to make jokes in English – though what English! Tomorrow comes my first lecture; all my dread of it has vanished, since the audience is harmless and merely eager to hear new things, which is certainly what we can supply them with. It is said that we shall be awarded honorary doctorates by the university next Saturday, with a great deal of pomp and circumstance. In the evening there will be a "formal reception." Today's letter has to be short, since the Halls have invited some people for five o'clock to meet us. We have also been interviewed by the *Boston Evening Transcript*. In fact, we are the men of the hour here. It is very good to be able to spread oneself in this way once in a while. I can feel that my libido is gulping it in with vast enjoyment . . .

Jung to his wife, Emma, September 11, 1909 (from Worcester, MA)

. . . Last night there was a tremendous amount of ceremony and fancy dress, with all sorts of red and black gowns and gold-tasseled square caps. In a grand and festive assemblage I was appointed Doctor of Laws *honoris causa* and Freud

---

[6] Hall's wife, Florence Smith Hall, was his second wife. His first wife and 8-year-old daughter died tragically in 1890 from asphyxiation in their home while Hall was away, recovering from diphtheria. Nine years later he married Florence Smith, a kindergarten schoolteacher he had met through his work in child study. Shortly after the Clark Conference of 1909, Hall and his wife separated. An escalating series of bizarre public incidents by his wife had produced many embarrassing moments for Hall. Eventually she was institutionalized with severe dementia (Ross, 1972). One of his biographers wrote: "Twice he lost a wife, once through death and once through madness, and in the end he had only work remaining to him as his passion and his pleasure" (Pruette, 1926, p. 104).

likewise. Now I may place an L.L.D. after my name. Impressive, what? . . . Today Prof. M. drove us by automobile out to lunch at a beautiful lake. The landscape was utterly lovely. This evening there is one more "private conference" in Hall's house on the "psychology of sex." Our time is dreadfully crammed. The Americans are really masters at that; they hardly leave one time to catch one's breath. Right now I am rather worn out from all the fabulous things we have been through, and am longing for the quiet of the mountains.[7] My head is spinning. Last night at the awarding of the doctorate I had to deliver an impromptu talk before some three hundred persons . . . Freud is in seventh heaven, and I am glad with all my heart to see him so . . .

I am looking forward enormously to getting back to the sea again, where the overstimulated psyche can recover in the presence of that infinite peace and spaciousness. Here one is in an almost constant whirlwind. But I have, thank God, completely regained my capacity for enjoyment, so that I can look forward to everything with zest. Now I am going to take everything that comes along by storm, and then I shall settle down again, satiated . . .

Note: Following the conference, Freud, Jung, and Ferenczi traveled by train to Buffalo and later Albany, New York. Freud wanted to see Niagara Falls, and did so. The group spent several days in the Adirondack mountains at the vacation home of James J. Putnam (1846–1918), a physician and friend of William James. Freud had expressed interest in seeing a porcupine, but alas, there were no sightings. After their holiday in the mountains, the trio set sail on September 21 for the eight-day sea voyage home on the Kaiser Wilhelm der Grosse.

Jung to his wife, Emma, September 18, 1909 (from Albany, NY)

. . . Two more days before departure! Everything is taking place in a whirl. Yesterday I stood upon a bare rocky peak nearly 5600 feet high, in the midst of tremendous virgin forests, looking far out into the blue infinities of America and shivering to the bone in the icy wind, and today I am in the midst of the metropolitan bustle of Albany, the capital of the State of New York! The hundred thousand enormously deep impressions I am taking back with me from this wonderland cannot be described with the pen. Everything is too big, too immeasurable. Something that has gradually been dawning upon me in the past few days is the recognition that here an ideal potentiality of life has become reality. Men are as well off here as the culture permits; women badly off. We have seen things here that inspire enthusiastic admiration, and things that make one ponder social evolution deeply. As far as technological culture is concerned, we lag miles behind America. But all that is frightfully costly and already carries the germ of the end

---

[7]   Refers to an upcoming trip to the Adirondacks in upper New York State.

in itself. I must tell you a great, great deal. I shall never forget the experiences of this journey. Now we are tired of America. Tomorrow morning we are off to New York, and on September 21 we sail! . . .

Jung to Freud, November 8, 1909

As a basis for the analysis of the American way of life I am now treating a young American (doctor). Here again the mother-complex looms large (cf. the *Mother-Mary cult*). In America the mother is decidedly the dominant member of the family. American culture really is a bottomless abyss; the men have become a flock of sheep and the women play the ravening wolves – within the family circle, of course. I ask myself whether such conditions have ever existed in the world before. I really don't think they have.

Freud to Jung, November 21, 1909

Stanley Hall wrote me recently: "I am a very unworthy exponent of your views and of course have too little clinical experience to be an authority in that field; but it seems to me that, whereas hitherto many, if not most pathologists have leaned upon the stock psychologists like Wundt, your own interpretations reverse the situation and make us normal psychologists look to this work in the abnormal or borderline field for our chief light." We are still very far from that in Germany. But coming from the old man such serious, thoughtful compliments are very nice.

Out of sheer gratitude I have already sent him three of the lectures and am working desperately on the last. I am making a few changes and additions, and also putting in a few defensive, or rather, aggressive, remarks. Deuticke wants to publish them in German, but I don't know if Hall would like that, and it troubles me that there is nothing new in them.

Freud to Jung, January 13, 1909

First a few words about the last post from America, which is very rich and might give one a feeling of triumph. Apart from Putnam's article, which you have already mentioned, I have received letters from St. Hall, Jones, Brill, and Putnam himself. Hall reports on the congress of psychologists at Harvard, which devoted a whole afternoon to ΨA [psychoanalysis], in the course of which he and Putnam gave the malignant Boris Sidis[8] a through trouncing. You have probably received the same

---

[8]   Boris Sidis (1867–1923) was a psychologist and director of a mental asylum in Portsmouth, New Hampshire. He was especially critical of psychoanalysis, calling it a "worship of Venus and Priapus which encouraged masturbation, perversion, and illegitimacy" (Gay, 1988, p. 196).

news; if not, it will give me pleasure to send you the letters. The old man [Hall], who is really a splendid fellow, writes that in April he is devoting a special number of the *American Journal of Psychology* to us; it is to contain your lectures, Ferenczi's paper on dream-work in translation, the shorter paper by Jones, and perhaps also my five lectures . . . My prophecy comes true! Our trip to America seems to have done some good, which compensates me for leaving a part of my health there.

Epilogue

The trip to America did do "good" for Freud's psychoanalytic theory, even if he had to suffer with stomachaches and diarrhea. Freud's ideas enjoyed incredible popularity, not only within the American medical community, but within the American public as well. Gail Hornstein (1992) wrote: "When psychoanalysis first arrived in the United States, most psychologists ignored it. By the 1920s, however, psychoanalysis had so captured the public imagination that it threatened to eclipse experimental psychology entirely" (p. 254). In 1911, the American Psychoanalytic Association was founded with Putnam as its first president. Two years later the journal, *Psychoanalytic Review*, was founded, the first American journal on psychoanalysis. In America, psychoanalysis was doing very well; the same could not be said of the Freud–Jung relationship.

The reasons for the breakup between Freud and Jung are as complex as the two men, and cannot be covered in this chapter in any detail. The suggested readings section lists two excellent books that treat the breakup in hundreds of pages (see Donn, 1988; Schultz, 1990). There were, of course, disagreements over their views of psychoanalytic theory, but the difficulties were also, perhaps even more so, at the level of personality. These were two very headstrong and intelligent individuals, the younger no longer willing to bend to the will of the elder, and the elder not willing to tolerate the differences expressed by the younger. Their correspondence, which had begun in 1906, ended in 1913. In December, 1912, Jung wrote to Freud:

> You go around sniffing out all the symptomatic actions in your vicinity, thus reducing everyone to the level of sons and daughters who blushingly admit the existence of their faults. Meanwhile you remain on top as the father, sitting pretty. For sheer obsequiousness nobody dares to pluck the prophet by the beard and inquire for once . . . *Who's* got the neurosis? (McGuire, 1974, p. 535)

Freud replied: "I propose that we abandon our personal relations entirely. I shall lose nothing by it, for my own emotional tie with you has long been a thin thread – the lingering effects of past disappointments. . . ." (McGuire, 1974, p. 539).

Suggested Readings

Cromer, W., & Anderson, P. (1970). Freud's visit to America: Newspaper coverage. *Journal of the History of the Behavioral Sciences, 6,* 349–353.

A summary of the newspaper coverage of Freud's Clark Conference lectures drawn from two Boston and two Worcester newspapers.

Donn, L. (1988). *Freud and Jung: Years of friendship, years of loss.* New York: Scribner's.
A very readable account of the Freud–Jung relationship.

Ellenberger, H. F. (1970). *The discovery of the unconscious.* New York: Basic Books.
This excellent book describes the "history and evolution of dynamic psychiatry" (its subtitle), focusing on Sigmund Freud and psychoanalysis in Chapter 7 and C. G. Jung and analytical psychology in Chapter 9.

Evans, R. B., & Koelsch, W. A. (1985). Psychoanalysis arrives in America: The 1909 psychology conference at Clark University. *American Psychologist, 40,* 942–948.
A historical account of the Clark Conference, drawing heavily on archival records.

Freud, S. (1910). The origin and development of psychoanalysis. *American Journal of Psychology, 21,* 181–218.
Freud's five lectures delivered at the 1909 Clark Conference, translated by Henry W. Chase, and published in G. Stanley Hall's journal.

Gay, P. (1988). *Freud: A life for our time.* New York: Norton.
There are more than 100 published biographies on Freud. This one is arguably one of the best. It covers both the life of Freud and the evolution of his creation (psychoanalysis) in their social and intellectual climates.

Hale, N. G., Jr. (Ed.) (1971). *James Jackson Putnam and psychoanalysis: Letters between Putnam and Sigmund Freud, Ernest Jones, William James, Sandor Ferenczi, and Morton Prince, 1877–1917.* Cambridge: Harvard University Press.
Putnam, a neurologist, has been called Freud's first American convert. As noted earlier, Putnam founded the American Psychoanalytic Association in 1911 and served as its first president. This book contains 89 letters between Putnam and Freud.

Hornstein, G. A. (1992). The return of the repressed: Psychology's problematic relations with psychoanalysis, 1909–1960. *American Psychologist, 47,* 254–263.
A history of the interface of American psychology and psychoanalysis that traces experimental psychology's strategies to discredit psychoanalysis.

Jones, E. (1953, 1955, 1957). *The life and work of Sigmund Freud* (3 vols.). New York: Basic Books.
Ernest Jones, a long-time disciple of Freud, authored this comprehensive work that stood for nearly 30 years as the most respected treatment of Freud's life and work. Some have referred to it as Freud's "autobiography," arguing that Jones wrote it as Freud would have dictated it. There are better biographies today (e.g., Gay and Sulloway) but this one bears reading by any serious scholar of Freud.

Jung, C. G. (1910). The association method. *American Journal of Psychology, 21,* 219–269.
Jung's lectures at the Clark Conference in 1909 (which were translated by A. A. Brill), describing his use of the word association method in the study of personality.

Jung, C. G. (1961). *Memories, dreams, reflections.* New York: Random House.
Jung's autobiography, edited by his secretary, Aniela Jaffe. It is supplemented by reliance on correspondence, some of which is published in appendixes.

Masson, J. M. (Ed.). (1985). *The complete letters of Sigmund Freud to Wilhelm Fliess, 1887–1904.* Cambridge: Belknap Press of Harvard University Press.
A collection of 301 letters important to the development of psychoanalysis. Fliess, Freud's closest friend, was a physician in Berlin. Fliess attended several of Freud's lectures in Vienna, after which their correspondence began. The breakup of their friendship com-

menced in 1900, following the publication of Freud's *Interpretation of dreams,* presumably because of Fliess's jealousy of Freud's success. The demise of their friendship was very painful for Freud.

McGuire, W. (Ed.) (1974). *The Freud/Jung letters: The correspondence between Sigmund Freud and C. G. Jung.* Princeton, NJ: Princeton University Press.

The complete collection of the correspondence between Freud and his crown prince, Jung, in the period 1906–13. All of the Freud–Jung letters in this chapter were taken from this book. The annotations are extensive, adding to the reader's understanding and pleasure.

Rosenzweig, S. (1994). *The historic expedition to America (1909): Freud, Jung, and Hall the kingmaker.* St. Louis: Rana House.

The author researched this book for nearly 50 years. It is the most thorough account of the Clark Conference and the events that surrounded it, and includes a new English translation of Freud's five lectures as well as the complete correspondence between Hall and Freud.

Ross, D. (1972). *G. Stanley Hall: The psychologist as prophet.* Chicago: University of Chicago Press.

An excellent biography of Hall, who introduced Freud and Jung to America. See pp. 381–413 for coverage of Hall's involvement in the Clark Conference and psychoanalysis.

Schultz, D. (1990). *Intimate friends, dangerous rivals: The turbulent relationship between Freud and Jung.* Los Angeles: Tarcher.

A fascinating account of the Freud–Jung relationship, that begins with an analysis of their childhoods. Drawing on those experiences, Schultz shows what drew them together and how they were destined to be driven apart. Although there are several books on this subject, none matches this one for its use of the scholarly record.

Sulloway, F. J. (1979). *Freud: Biologist of the mind.* New York: Basic Books.

The first major biography of Freud written by someone outside the Freudian community of family and followers. Sulloway, a historian of science, emphasizes the influence of Darwin on Freud as the latter constructed an evolutionary theory of the mind.

John B. Watson
(Archives of the History of American Psychology/University of Akron)

The Behaviorism of John B. Watson

John Broadus Watson was born in 1878 in the rural community of Travelers Rest, South Carolina. After graduation from nearby Furman University, he traveled to the University of Chicago, where he planned to study philosophy. He lost interest in the classes of John Dewey and turned instead to psychology, where he worked with James Rowland Angell (1869–1949), one of the chief founders of functional psychology (Angell, 1907; Dewsbury, 2003). Watson was also interested in biology and was much influenced at Chicago by courses he took with neurologist Henry H. Donaldson (1857–1938) and physiologist Jacques Loeb (1859–1924).

When Watson was a graduate student at Chicago, psychology was defined as the study of consciousness. The two dominant systems of psychology at that time were structuralism, associated with E. B. Titchener at Cornell University (see Chapter 10), and functionalism, as embodied in the work of William James at Harvard, G. Stanley Hall at Clark, Angell and others at Chicago, and Cattell and his colleagues at Columbia. Those espousing a structural psychology sought to identify the structure of consciousness, by breaking consciousness down into its elemental components of sensations, feelings, and images. The functionalists, as their name implies, were influenced particularly by the ideas of Charles Darwin and were thus more interested in identifying the functions of consciousness. They were more likely to study mental operations than mental contents. Although the functionalists were more eclectic in their research methods, both schools of psychology made use of the method of introspection; indeed, for the structuralists it was virtually their sole method of research. Introspection is, in essence, self-observation, or as Titchener (1910) called it, a "looking within" (p. 18). It was a form of self-report in which individuals were asked to describe in considerable detail their primary sensory and affective experiences.

Watson finished his doctorate in psychology at Chicago in 1903, with an experimental dissertation using rats, and stayed on the faculty for a few years before accepting a position at Johns Hopkins University in 1908. There he continued his animal work in the psychology laboratory that Hall had founded 25 years earlier, the first such laboratory in America. When James Mark Baldwin, the head of the Psychology Department at Johns Hopkins, was dismissed in 1909 (following a scandal caused by his being caught in a police raid on a Baltimore bordello), Watson found himself head of the department and editor of Baldwin's journal, *Psychological Review*.

Always somewhat of a counter-conformist, Watson was greatly dissatisfied with the psychology of his day, a dissatisfaction that had begun in 1904 when he was a fledgling animal researcher at Chicago. He was concerned about the objectivity of psychology and he particularly objected to psychology's reliance on the method of introspection. For Watson, introspection chained psychology to mentalism; it prevented psychology from being an objective science. His preference was for the controlled stimulus–response conditions of his laboratory studies with rats. In a long correspondence with fellow animal psychologist Robert M. Yerkes (1876–1956), Watson described his hopes for a science of psychology that would rightfully belong among the natural sciences.

After four years in his position as director of the Hopkins psychology laboratory, Watson apparently felt his position in psychology was secure enough to make his views known. In 1913 he published an article entitled "Psychology as the Behaviorist Views It." This article became known as the "behaviorist manifesto," and it marked the beginning of a revolution in psychology, although not an immediate rebellion (see Samelson, 1981). This brash analysis of the field of psychology began:

> Psychology as the behaviorist views it is a purely objective experimental branch of natural science. Its theoretical goal is the prediction and control of behavior. Introspection forms no essential part of its methods, nor is the scientific value of its data dependent upon the readiness with which they lend themselves to interpretation in terms of consciousness. (Watson, 1913, p. 158)

In this article he rebuked not only the structuralists, but also the functionalists with whom he had trained. He claimed that there was really no distinction between them. Both were mired in mentalism, in a mistaken belief that they were actually studying consciousness. In continuing his attack he wrote:

> I do not wish unduly to criticize psychology. It has failed signally, I believe, during the fifty-odd years of its existence as an experimental discipline to make its place in the world as an undisputed natural science . . . The time has come when psychology must discard all reference to consciousness; when it need no longer delude itself into thinking that it is making mental states the object of observation. (Watson, 1913, p. 163)

Certainly those were brash words from someone who had received his doctorate in psychology only a decade earlier.

Watson's behaviorism called for a psychology that studied those behaviors that could be objectively defined: discrete motor responses and glandular secretions. In his own work, Watson studied sensation and perception, learning, and emotions. His methods grew chiefly to depend on the conditioned reflex, as is indicated in the letters in this chapter. But he also advocated the use of observational methods, psychophysical methods, and psychological tests.

Watson was not alone in his dissatisfaction with the subjectivism of psychology, and his 1913 paper was by no means the initial appearance of such ideas (see O'Donnell, 1985). But behaviorism as a movement in psychology belongs to Watson. He crystallized the rumblings into a coherent whole that gained attention. The revolution started slowly, but by the 1930s American psychology and behaviorism were virtually synonymous.

When Watson assumed control of the psychology laboratories at Hopkins he was responsible for both the animal labs and the human labs. He had not worked with humans before and disliked such research, recalling that he "hated to serve as a subject" (Watson, 1936, p. 276). However, he began a series of experiments to study motor reflexes in human infants. Undoubtedly the most famous of those experiments was the fear conditioning study of Albert B. Indeed, this study may be the most frequently cited experiment in the history of American psychology (see Harris, 1979).

With a graduate student, Rosalie Rayner, Watson conditioned an 11-month-old infant, Albert B., who was initially unafraid of a white rat, to fear the rat when it was paired with a loud noise. In this study, Watson sought to demonstrate that fear could be acquired in humans as a result of conditioning, an idea he had proposed in a 1917 article (Watson & Morgan, 1917). The successful results provided support for Watson's environmentalistic theory of emotions in humans, and thus for his extremely environmentalistic view of all behavior. However, this experiment would be Watson's last at Hopkins. When his wife discovered his love affair with Rayner, their marriage ended in a scandalous divorce that occupied the pages of Baltimore newspapers and even the national press. Like Baldwin before him, Watson was forced to resign his academic position in 1920.

Watson and Rayner married on New Year's Eve in 1920, one week after his divorce became final. When no other university would hire him, he went to New York City to work for J. Walter Thompson Company, an advertising firm. He was extremely successful there, and was promoted to vice-president of the company after only four years. While learning the advertising business, Watson kept spreading the gospel of behaviorism through talks on radio shows and through a number of articles in popular magazines such as *Harper's*, *McCall's*, *Cosmopolitan*, and *Collier's*. He lectured regularly at the New School for Social Research in New York, and was a popular lecturer for a variety of groups, particularly women's organizations.

In 1923, Columbia University invited Watson to continue the promising infant research he had begun at Hopkins. Watson was unable to direct the research, but he offered to consult and to participate as much as his business schedule would allow him to do. Watson had been particularly interested in child psychology since the birth of his first child, and several of his popular articles were on this subject. The Columbia studies involved him to a greater degree in the applications of psychology to child rearing and was an impetus to his writing his most controversial book, *Psychological Care of Infant and Child* (1928). This book, which warned parents about displaying too much affection toward their children, became quite popular, and many parents sought to follow the child-rearing advice of this charismatic and distinguished authority on psychology. There were many other authorities and parents, however, who reacted quite negatively to the book (see Harris, 1984). Watson (1936) later expressed regret, saying that he did not know enough to write the book.

The letters that follow focus on Watson's determination to see that psychology shed its mentalistic baggage. They are especially critical of the method of introspection, arguing as he did in his 1913 article that the method had no place in a scientific psychology. In taking such a radical stance he excluded much of the work then being done by his peers and elders. The letters also describe Watson's conversion to human researcher and the studies that led up to the conditioning of little Albert.

All of the letters, except the final four, were written when Watson was a faculty member at Johns Hopkins. Most of the correspondence is with Robert Yerkes, a fellow animal researcher, two years older than Watson, who spent most of his career on the faculty at Harvard University and then Yale University. Yerkes studied a variety of animals but eventually settled on a plan for a grand set of investigations of the higher apes, especially chimpanzees. He struggled for more than 15 years to secure funding for a primate research station, which finally became a reality in 1930 as the Yale Laboratories of Primate Biology (later named the Yerkes Laboratories of Primate Biology) located in Orange Park, Florida (for an excellent history of these labs, of Yerkes, and of the growth of psychological science from 1930 to 1965, see Dewsbury, 2005).

Finally, note that the letters between Watson and Yerkes are often quite personal and provide insights about the personalities of both men. Watson was often described as brash or arrogant, and those qualities are well manifested in some of these letters.

The Letters

John B. Watson to Robert M. Yerkes, February 6, 1910

... You don't understand my position here [at Johns Hopkins University] or you wouldn't quarrel with the Harper's article [a 1910 magazine article entitled "The New Science of Animal Behavior"]. Suppose you were in charge of psychology and that all you got came about just to the extent to which you made the univ. community feel the importance of or take notice of psychology. This was the reason for the article. I am in a community which practically never heard of psychology ... I should be glad to get your criticisms though I don't believe we are as far apart as you seem to think. I am a physiologist and I go so far as to say that I would remodel psychology as we now have it (human) and reconstruct our attitude with reference to the whole matter of consciousness. I don't believe the psychologist is studying consciousness any more than we [animal researchers] are and I am willing to say that consciousness is merely a tool, a fundamental assumption with which the chemist works, the physiologist and every one else who observes. All of our sensory work, memory work, attention, etc. are part of definite modes of behavior. I have thought of writing ... just what I think of the work being done in human experimental psychology. It lacks an all embracing scheme in which all the smaller pieces may find their place. It has no big problems. Every little piece of work which comes out is an unrelated unit. This might all be changed if we would take a simpler, behavior view of life and make adjustment the keynote. But I fear to do it now because my place here is not ready for it. My thesis developed as I long to develop it would certainly separate me from the psychologists – Titchener would cast me off and I fear Angell would do likewise.

Watson to Robert M. Yerkes, December 12, 1912

... I think I wrote you that I have been made Non-Resident Lecturer at Columbia for the year and am to give eight lectures there. My second lecture takes up the actual problems in animal behavior. If you are in need of a general article during the year, I shall submit this[1] ... I am not anxious to have it published as it forms the second chapter of my book. All eight of the lectures will go in bodily as part of the book [*Behavior: An Introduction to Comparative Psychology*, 1914].

[1] Yerkes was editor of the *Journal of Animal Behavior*.

Watson to James McKeen Cattell, January 16, 1913

I have been working all fall upon my eight lectures for Columbia. The first lecture, "Psychology as the Behaviorist Views It," will be published in *The Psychological Review* for March. The second lecture is on "The Problems in Animal Behavior."

Note: As indicated in the brief excerpt above, by 1913 Watson could hold out no longer in expressing his concerns about a mentalistic psychology. He delivered his "behaviorist manifesto" as a lecture at Columbia University in February, 1913 and published it the following month in the journal he edited, Psychological Review.

Watson to Robert M. Yerkes, April 7, 1913

I am greatly obliged for your comments on the paper ["Psychology as the Behaviorist Views It"]. I think our main difference lies in this: you are willing to let psychology go its own gait, whereas I have probably an earlier and deeper interest in psychology than you have; consequently I am not willing to turn psychology over to Titchener and his school. The wise way would probably be to do as you suggest, – call behavior physiology or biology, and leave psychology to the introspectionists. But I have too sincere an attachment for psychology to do this way. I believe that it can be made a desirable field for work. I think it is probable that my second paper, which is now ready, will clear up some of the difficulties in the way and show you why I am not willing to turn psychology over to Titchener.

Watson to Robert M. Yerkes, October 27, 1915

... Yes, I suppose I am monkeying a bit with human behaviorism. Lashley[2] and I have been working now for nearly a year on the conditioned reflex, and it works [so] beautifully in place of introspection that I think it deserves to be driven home; we can work on the human being as we can on animals, and from the same point of view. Of course you disagree with me in this to a certain extent, anyway, but I hope to convince you before I die that I am right and you are wrong ...

[2]   Karl Spencer Lashley (1890–1958) was trained in zoology and biology, and remained a lifelong friend of Watson, with whom he worked at Johns Hopkins (Dewsbury, 1993). Lashley would become one of the premier behavioral neuroscientists in America in the twentieth century (see Bruce, 1986, 1991; Dewsbury, 2002). He was director of the Yale Laboratories of Primate Biology in a period that saw the labs produce their most outstanding research (see Dewsbury, 2005).

Robert M. Yerkes to Watson, October 30, 1915

. . . I appreciate what you say about training at Vineland [a New Jersey school for children with intellectual impairments], but I think your attitude toward my own work is based on a misconception, for after all it seems that I have quite as much right to work out objective methods with human subjects in the Hospital[3] as you have in your own laboratory or elsewhere.

This leads me to say once more that there is, so far as I can discover, only one point of disagreement between us with reference to psychology and its methods. You insist that introspection is useless as a scientific method and should be abandoned, while I maintain that there should be encouragement given those who are willing to make use of it. Neither of us is personally interested in the method. I consider myself quite as much an objectivist or behaviorist, if you eliminate our difference with respect to the value of introspection, as you are, and I am not only in hearty agreement with you in all objective work but my chief excuse for being at work in the Psychopathic Hospital is that I am there introducing objective or behavioristic methods. Were it simply a matter of introspection, someone else should and would have the job. You have absolutely nothing to convince me of with respect to the applicability or values of objective as contrasted with introspective work. I feel as though I had said precisely this to you several times before, but you and Holt[4] seem rather persistently to assume that for some reason, apparently because I believe in the value of introspection, I either disbelieve in the necessity of mixing the two sorts of methods, or combining them. I hope that I am not making myself disagreeable in putting the matter again in this way. For after all, I am extremely anxious that we should understand one another and should continue to work in as harmonious cooperation as we have during the past ten years or more . . .

Watson to Robert M. Yerkes, November 1, 1915

. . . I am mulling over your statements about introspection. There doesn't seem to be as much disagreement as I had supposed. I think the disagreement is rather on the subject of consciousness. I don't believe consciousness is any more a scientific concept than soul; and you can't agree with this or else you would not be willing to admit that introspection was a possible method. This is pretty radical I know, but it expresses my present views. I don't see that this need affect our feelings in regard to the comparative work. It would seem to me that both of

[3]   Yerkes, from his faculty position at Harvard University, had established a research program at the Boston Psychopathic Hospital.
[4]   Edwin Bissell Holt (1873–1946), like Yerkes, earned his PhD in psychology under Hugo Münsterberg at Harvard University.

us are interested in furthering objective methods, and the one as well as the other . . .

Watson to Robert M. Yerkes, March 31, 1916

. . . I have been so wretchedly busy and disturbed the last month or two I have not had time to write a really decent letter. It has not been because I have not wanted to, nor has it been because of any differences that we may feel exist between our points of view. Friendship to me is a far more precious thing than agreement about psychological positions. I have felt this keenly about Titchener and I have felt it even more so with respect to you. My feeling for you has nothing whatsoever to do with the question whether you think a certain amount of intro- spection is justifiable. If I dropped all my friends who think that a certain amount of introspection is justifiable, I would be living in a land of the friendless! I do not see why our mutual helpfulness should not go on as it has been going on during the past few years. I have gained a lot from my association with you and your interest has sustained me in a good many trying situations. Besides, I have got to have somebody to read my stuff, and you have got to have somebody to read yours! If we were to break off this relationship I am sure neither of us would have one person who understood his writings . . .

Watson to Robert M. Yerkes, October 12, 1916

. . . I shall await your publication on behaviorism and genetic psychology[5] with a great deal of impatience; please send me a galley proof at your earliest conven- ience. If I get sore at you, I shall probably tell you so with the same degree of frankness which we have always used in our relations . . .

I am starting in over at Phipps.[6] Naturally it is a devil of a job to get the labo- ratory going, but the Hospital has been exceedingly kind to me and I am getting everything I need. I shall really have a wonderfully complete laboratory, but no facilities for animal work . . . We're planning to carry forward the work this year on the emotions, speech movements, and on secretions . . . I am undertaking with Dr. J. J. B. Morgan,[7] a man Cattell sent me this year, to begin a rather comprehen-

---

[5] Yerkes, R. M. (1917), "Behaviorism and genetic psychology," *Journal of Philosophy*, 14, 154–160.
[6] The Phipps Clinic at Johns Hopkins University was headed by one of America's most famous psychiatrists, Adolf Meyer (1866–1950). Meyer invited Watson to set up a laboratory to study humans and offered him considerable space in the clinic and a promise to leave him alone to do what work he desired (see Buckley, 1989, pp. 88–94).
[7] John J. B. Morgan (1888–1945), who received his doctorate in psychology at Columbia Uni- versity in 1916, worked with Watson on conditioning studies in human infants, work that led eventually to the conditioning of fear in little Albert.

sive study of the order of appearance and development of reflexes and instincts in the human child. I am next door to the obstetrical ward here and I get about forty babies a month. These babies are sent over to the laboratory on demand and we can make the observations right here. We are including in this study the genesis of the early habits of infants and the extent to which they can be taught. Ultimately I hope to be able to use this material for the diagnosis of defectiveness somewhere within the first three years. I imagine this job will take most of my time; until I get my animal laboratory reestablished, I can see no better place for me to turn my meagre talents. It won't hurt me to work up the human infant and it seems to me a badly needed piece of work.

Please find time to write me a decent letter soon; we seem to have degenerated in our letter writing somewhat. I hope this is due only to pressure of circumstances and not to any strains which may have been present on one or two occasions. My expurgation has been complete.

Robert M. Yerkes to Watson, October 16, 1916

Your letter of the 12th gives me much satisfaction. I have been somewhat depressed by your attitude toward my primate work and have not felt as much like writing as usual. Yet I am confident as ever that our scientific conceptions and aims are at bottom the same and our disagreements fairly superficial . . .

I am tremendously pleased, John, that you have hit the primate trail [working with human infants] squarely and at full speed. I believe that it is the proper trail for both of us and that as soon as I can get the anthropoid work well under way and you get well established in your hospital laboratories, we shall begin to do what will be most useful to the world. It is my prediction that you will never escape from the interest you are now entering upon, and I have no desire to escape from the work with higher primates, if I once get adequate opportunities.

The work which you propose to do with babies is of fundamental importance, and I most heartily wish you success in it. It is the sort of thing which I should be happy to undertake myself, but I am equally happy to have you do it, for I know that it will be done well and that genetic [developmental] psychology will be enriched thereby . . .

Watson to Robert M. Yerkes, October 24, 1916

I have received your article [a draft of "Behaviorism and genetic psychology"; see footnote 5] . . . In regard to your paper I would say that I have nothing to kick at. But I have this to say to you and I am afraid it will make you mad, but I hope not. You were brought up in biology and in 1900 you were to all intents and purposes a biologist. If I must say it, you had never waked up to the glories of introspective psychology, nor did you the first few years. A good many people remarked on this to me, that you were not a psychologist and had never had enough interest in psychology to work out a satisfactory system in your own terms or any one else's. You began to get this interest I should guess somewhere around 1907 or 1908 . . . Now you are practically burning your bridges behind you for the introspective psychology, however much you may insist upon the fact that you ought to be called a behaviorist. My prediction is that by the time you have worked this end of it as long as I have had to, you will again revolt and come back with a refined behaviorism. I am hoping so. My own history was entirely different. I came up through philosophy into introspective psychology, ran the laboratory at Chicago for years, doing both my animal work and looking after the problems and teaching straight introspective psychology. I had to put away all outside thought and fight to make introspective psychology scientific, and I have had many rows and arguments with biologists and others trying to make my points. The first few years at Hopkins I had to do the same thing, running both the human laboratory and the animal. Finally my stomach would stand no more and I took the plunge I did in 1912. You have never had to teach the amount of introspective psychology that I have, and you have never had to emerse yourself in the systems the way I have; consequently it comes to you more or less as a satisfactory field. I am only praying that the next five years will show you the error of your ways . . .

Robert M. Yerkes to Watson, October 27, 1916

I happen to have time, this morning, to comment on your good letter of October 24, so I shall do so at once.

Happily, you are quite mistaken in your expectation that what you say will offend. Instead, I am pleased, first because you have a better grasp of the facts than I thought, and second because I agree almost wholly with your interpretation. It is difficult to say whether your experience or mine has been the more fortunate or the more unfortunate, but doubtless the future will indicate something about the matter. Let's try to make them both fortunate. And why should we not both "pray that the next five years may show you the error of your ways." Certainly I sympathize most heartily in that sentiment, and I have the feeling that I shall be willing and able to meet you half way. I believe that if you can limber up a little and take a more liberal attitude with respect to methods, we shall find ourselves on as good a cooperative basis, shortly, as of old.

And certainly I can assure you that I am not less of a biologist to-day than ten years ago. The chances are very great, since I have no professional interest in introspection, or skill in the use of it, that I should become more and more occupied with purely objecti[ve] work on behavior as the years pass and shall forget all about my subjective terminology. Nor can I resent your suggestion that I may sometime, like yourself, have a revulsion of feeling.

Watson to Robert M. Yerkes, November 16, 1916

... I am glad to hear that you are going into the conditioned reflex work. We are trying out the conditioned reflex on the babies and I hope to get some good work in on them through its use. We are delighted with the baby work. I have several hundred observations on the grasping reflex ... We are also finding it easy to record the movements of the newborn and older children so as to get an index as to whether the right or left hand is used more in [grasping] movements. We are also knocking out some stuff on the time that the eye learns to follow lights, the question of moving versus stationary light stimulus, etc. If we meet with any success on the conditioned reflex with these infants we ought to be able to find out more than we now know concerning the function of the senses, especially monochromatic light vision and hearing ...

Watson to Robert M. Yerkes, November 25, 1916

... I have been getting some bully results on the clinging reflex both on normals and abnormals ... Another rather interesting little reflex which we can work out is the defensive lid reflex to a threatened object. I have not had this develop under the first month and yet it is present from the beginning in the case of sounds – as a matter of fact, the closure of the lid is the clearest and most satisfactory index I can get to auditory sensitivity. In a child one hundred days of age the lid closure occurs to sudden shadows or threatened objects. It is rather interesting that you can have a reflex here which can be brought about by two such different stimuli as the approach of an object to the eye, and through sound; and yet the reflex cannot be touched off by eye threatening until some months have passed ...

Note: Watson's infant studies were interrupted by his military service in World War I. After the war Watson returned to Johns Hopkins. He began writing a beginning textbook for psychology touting his behavioral approach: Psychology from the Standpoint of a Behaviorist (1919). He also began his famous conditioned fear studies with the infant Albert B. Sadly we have no correspondence from this time. Watson's divorce from Mary Ickes in 1920, a woman from a very prominent family of wealth and political connections, cost him his job at Johns Hopkins. Evidently no other university was interested in hiring him. He left academe to join one of New York City's most prestigious advertising firms, the J. Walter Thompson Company. The following letter was sent to English philosopher and Nobel laureate Bertrand Russell (1872–1970), shortly after Watson began his new career in the business world. The letter was prompted by the receipt of Russell's latest book, The Analysis of Mind (1921).

Watson to Bertrand Russell, October 11, 1921

... Since my last letter to you I have left university work. You have suffered at the hands of the public, I know, so you will understand the necessity of my getting out of university work due to the publicity attached to my divorce.[8]

I am happily at work here, and have, I think, really a wider scope for my work than I had in university circles. I am carefully putting aside my scientific impulses until I have learned the technique of business. After I have qualified as a practical man and lived down the stigma in business circles of being an academician I hope to be able to bring all my scientific interests to bear in studying some of the psychological problems underlying the industries, especially those connected with markets, salesmanship, public resistances, types of appeals, etc.

I am with a very progressive firm that feels the need of such work and gives me considerable liberty . . .

You certainly were more than generous to me in the book [*The Analysis of Mind*]. I had not at all expected the honor of being mentioned in your preface because due to my disturbed state of mind in the spring when I was deepest in my troubles I had little spirit left to give your manuscript the reading it deserved . . .

Watson to Bertrand Russell, September 18, 1923

. . . Teachers College, Columbia University, has succeeded in getting together approximately $20,000 to continue the work I began on infants.[9] Because of business pressure I am not able to undertake the active work but I have secured a very competent person to carry out the daily routine of experiments.[10] Each week I shall spend one afternoon at the little laboratory generally supervising the conduct of the experiments.

The laboratory is really an apartment situated next to a day nursery. There we have quite a bit of material which I think can be worked up in this way. I am sending you a copy of a letter I wrote about this work, giving a summary of what we plan to do.

[8]   Russell was a controversial figure throughout his long life, expressing his often radical beliefs on religion, sexuality, marriage, politics, and education. His pacifism during World War I resulted in his imprisonment in his native England.

[9]   Columbia University received funding from the Laura Spelman Rockefeller Fund, which was a strong supporter of applied research in psychology. Watson agreed to supervise the research on preschool children so long as the experiments were applicable to child rearing. Buckley (1989) has written that Watson wanted to develop procedures "by which parents and teachers could control the behavior of children and shape the characteristics of their personalities" (p. 152).

[10]   The staff person selected to carry out the experiments at the nursery school was Mary Cover Jones (1896–1987). Jones knew of Watson through her Vassar classmate, Rosalie Rayner, and she had hoped to study with Watson at Johns Hopkins. However, his dismissal prevented that, so she enrolled in the graduate program at Columbia University instead. At the Manhattan Day Nursery School, Jones conducted her classic study of de-conditioning a child's fear of rabbits (Jones, 1924). The technique she used in removing the fear is quite similar to the modern-day therapeutic technique known as systematic desensitization, and consequently Jones is recognized as one of the early pioneers in behavior therapy (see Rutherford, in press).

Watson to Patty S. Hill [Professor, Teachers College, Columbia University],
August 1, 1923

First and foremost, I wish to tell you how delighted I am that there is a possibility that the work on infants can be continued under your general care.

A few reflections about the matter come to me which I should like to put down . . .

(a)   *Thumb sucking* is almost universally prevalent. Its dangers in the way of infection, in causing poor mouth and teeth formation, and other physical ills, has been considerably emphasized especially of late. Its dangers on the psychopathological side, while probably far more threatening, have received little attention. I admit I haven't all the facts to back me up, but from tests which I have made I am at least willing to venture the speculation that thumb sucking breeds introversion, dependent individuals, and possibly confirmed masturbators . . . I am sure methods for breaking this habit can easily be worked up. I have some vague ideas on getting control of this habit which I will be very glad to take up with the individual who is to take charge of the plant.

(b)   To my mind the *uncontrollable child* (and here I mean children from two to four) has been uncontrollable through bad handling – a series of negative conditioned reflexes have been set up which could be analyzed and, I believe, removed. While the child seems to be bad tempered and to fly into a rage at everything, I feel that daily analysis of the behavior of this infant with experimentation would soon locate the basal negative conditioning which has taken place. Once located, methods should be developed for removing such conditioned responses. Connected with this general problem is the *negative reactions* (sic) to certain foods. In view of the present convictions setting in against the theory of instincts and through my own work showing that practically all reactions of infants are positive, it is pretty evident that negative reactions in general have been built in and are not hereditary. Hence food aversions, or *aversions of any kind*, are due to bad handling . . .

(c)   *Fears*: It would not be a hard matter to sift over the children in the neighborhood and find many of them with very definite fear reactions to various types of objects. None of us, not even those who have worked most with children, has developed any method for removing them, or knows anything about the proper way of handling them. Two months' work on three children with very definite fears ought to be worth the whole cost of your equipment and expenditures for a year, because I am very sure that the problem would yield and yield quickly . . .

(h)   *Teaching the child to let objects alone* without saying "don't" a million times a day. Would it not be possible to arrange a table containing interesting but not to be touched objects with electric wires so that an electrical shock is given when the table to be avoided is touched – and to have other objects, the *child's own*, on another table which can be touched with impunity? . . . In closing may I say that I feel so hopeful about this work that I shall be only too delighted to co-operate in every way I can with the staff you select. I will gladly help plan, work out a more detailed program, help with ideas on apparatus and technique, spend time at the plant in the evening helping get things started, watching experiments and the like . . .

Note: In January of 1932, Robert Yerkes, perhaps feeling that Watson's talents were wasted in the business world, encouraged him to return to experimental research. Yerkes wrote: "Surely you can sufficiently forget your behavioristic philosophy to be happier in experimentation than in generalization" (as cited in Buckley, 1989, p. 177). A portion of Watson's reply appears below.

Watson to Robert M. Yerkes, January 22, 1932

. . . I am afraid there is too much water over the dam for me ever to be able to think of going back into observational work. In the first place all my habits and tastes are geared beyond the return I could hope for from any academic job,[11] even assuming that any university in the country were so misguided as to offer me a job. I would not mind this a bit but I doubt if my family would understand it.

In the second place, if I ever went back I would want a real infants laboratory . . . I should want a good staff and a lot of ground. Then I should want about fifteen years for work and never to have to publish a line or a note or to have anybody interview me on any subject whatsoever. Then if I got anything I would like to spend about five years writing it up. Then I would say to old Father Time that any time he was ready, I was.

I think I still have the guts to do this but it requires so much money that I am sure it will not come in my lifetime.

Epilogue

John Watson never returned to an academic job after his dismissal from Johns Hopkins. He and Rosalie Rayner had two sons who were raised the "behaviorist" way. Tragically, Rayner died at age 36, from a rare form of dysentery. She and Watson had been married for about 15 years. Watson's biographer, Kerry Buckley (1989), has described the aftermath of Rosalie's death:

Rosalie had been a "vibrant, sparky, fun-loving person" who loved the theater, parties, and an active social life. She had the ability to draw Watson out of his aloof, almost shy disposition. Watson distanced himself even more from the world after her death. He began drinking heavily and plunged into a routine of

[11] Meaning that he had become accustomed to the high salary of a vice-president in a prestigious New York advertising company and he couldn't see himself going back to the wages of a university professor.

work, at the office and on his estate. The social aspects of his life all but disappeared. He became much less inclined to experiment with new friends, or, for that matter, new ideas. (p. 180)

Watson retired from advertising in 1945 and lived virtually in seclusion on a farm in Connecticut for the last 13 years of his life. Before his death at age 80 he accomplished one more task.

Gathering up a lifetime of correspondence, research notes, and manuscripts, he carried them to the fireplace of his clapboard farmhouse and slowly burned them one by one. When his secretary protested the loss to posterity and to history, Watson only replied: "When you're dead, you're all dead." (Buckley, 1989, p. 182)

That act has prevented historians from learning more about Watson and his ideas. It has meant that the letters in this chapter had to come from other manuscript collections; for example, the bulk of the letters in this chapter are from the Yerkes Papers at Yale University, where Yerkes preserved the letters he received from Watson as well as copies of his own letters to Watson.

John Watson's impact on psychology was substantial, perhaps more so than any other figure in the history of American psychology. Yet the value of his legacy is debated today. In arguing for an objective science of behavior, he eliminated a number of topics that have only begun to reappear in American psychology in the last 35 years, for example, consciousness, thinking, and dreaming. Some psychologists believe that Watson's philosophy was too radical, that in throwing out what he saw as bad, he also contributed to the elimination of much that was good. They would argue that in the long run he inhibited psychology's progress.

Others would argue that psychology's progress as a science was largely because of Watson, that he was the one figure who demanded a complete break with philosophy and the mentalistic baggage attached to it. Watsonian behaviorism strengthened the role of physiological processes in psychological explanations, expanded psychological methods, and made apparent the ties between animal and human psychology. As a system of psychology, behaviorism dominated American psychology more than any other school of thought, and its tenets are still evident in most aspects of contemporary psychology, from research to practice.

Suggested Readings

Buckley, K. W. (1989). *Mechanical man: John Broadus Watson and the beginnings of behaviorism.* New York: Guilford Press.
A scholarly and very readable account of Watson's life and career that draws on his published work and unpublished materials from more than 30 archival collections.
Harris, B. (1979). Whatever happened to little Albert? *American Psychologist, 34*, 151–160.
A critical history of psychology's most famous experiment and the way it has been reported (and misreported) over the years.

Jones, M. C. (1924). A laboratory study of fear: The case of Peter. *Pedagogical Seminary, 31,* 308–315.
  Jones collaborated with Watson on the de-conditioning of Peter's fear of rabbits. For Jones's more personal account of this study see M. C. Jones (1974), Albert, Peter, and John B. Watson, *American Psychologist, 29,* 581–583.

Samelson, F. (1981). Struggle for scientific authority: The reception of Watson's behaviorism, 1913–1920. *Journal of the History of the Behavioral Sciences, 17,* 399–425.
  A search for the impact of Watson's ideas shows that behaviorism gained little acceptance in the decade following the publication of his manifesto.

Watson, J. B. (1913). Psychology as the behaviorist views it. *Psychological Review, 20,* 158–177.
  Watson's call to arms for a behavioral psychology.

Watson, J. B. (1919). *Psychology from the standpoint of a behaviorist.* Philadelphia: Lippincott.
  Watson's second book was a textbook for the beginning psychology course, emphasizing a behavioral approach to psychology. It was published shortly before he left academic life forever.

Watson, J. B. (1928). *Psychological care of the infant and child.* New York: Norton.
  Part of Watson's advice about children in this book was: "never hug and kiss them, never let them sit on your lap. If you must, kiss them once on the forehead when they say good night. Shake hands with them in the morning" (p. 81). The book represents behaviorism in its most radical form.

Watson, J. B. (1936). Autobiography. In C. Murchison (Ed.), *A history of psychology in autobiography* (vol. 3, pp. 271–281). Worcester, MA: Clark University Press.
  In reading this, one has the impression that Watson was not very serious about providing a meaningful account of his life. It is interesting but sketchy.

Watson, J. B., & Rayner, R. (1920). Conditioned emotional reactions. *Journal of Experimental Psychology, 3,* 1–4.
  The initial published account of the conditioning study of Albert B. A more popularized version appeared in *Scientific Monthly* (1921, *13,* 493–515).

13
CHAPTER

Clockwise from top left: Max Wertheimer, Kurt Koffka, Kurt Lewin, Wolfgang Köhler
(Archives of the History of American Psychology/University of Akron)

Nazi Germany and the Migration of Gestalt Psychology

In 1912, Max Wertheimer (1880–1943) published a monograph on the perception of movement that was to launch a new approach in experimental psychology – Gestalt psychology. That research on apparent movement (the Phi phenomenon) was carried out at the University of Frankfurt with two graduate students, Kurt Koffka (1886–1941) and Wolfgang Köhler (1887–1967). These three would become the triumvirate of Gestalt psychology, launching their opposition to the then current German psychology, whose atomistic approach was antithetical to their views of consciousness. Instead of beginning with elements and trying to syn-thesize from those the wholes of consciousness, the Gestalt psychologists started with a phenomenological analysis of the wholes of experience and sought to deter-mine the natural parts.

Wertheimer's (1912) Frankfurt experiments involved the stroboscopic presen-tation of two black lines – one vertical, the other horizontal – against a white background, so that if they were seen simultaneously they would form a right angle. The lines were presented successively with a small interval between the offset of the first line and the onset of the second. When that interval was optimal (around 60 msec), the observer would see a form of apparent movement in which a single line appeared to be sweeping across the 90-degree angle from vertical to horizontal and back and forth. Lengthening or shortening the time interval caused the movement to disappear and the observer would see either both lines appearing simultaneously or the two lines appearing succes-sively, with no movement. Wertheimer labeled this apparent movement "phi movement."

Phi movement was not new to science but Wertheimer's interpretation was. He saw the movement as an experience that was not reducible to its elements. That is, no amount of introspection could cause the apparent movement to be seen as its actual physical occurrence, which was two lines flashing on and off in succes-sion. There was something more to the experience that was not evident in just the flashes of the lines. That awareness is the basis of the Gestalt maxim that the whole is different from the sum of its parts. Motion pictures, like phi, are a form of stro-boscopic movement. The movement that you see in the movie theater is quite real, even though it is created by a series of still images projected onto the screen one at a time. This classic study by Wertheimer launched the Gestalt view, emphasiz-ing their belief in studying experience as it occurred, rather than breaking it down into elements that they viewed as artificial (King & Wertheimer, 2005; O'Neil & Landauer, 1966).

In their direct opposition to the prevailing German psychology, the Gestalt psy-chologists struggled to gain their place, and what began as a foothold eventually supplanted the psychology derived, in part, from the ideas of Wilhelm Wundt. Evidence of this metamorphosis in German psychology was the selection of Wolfgang Köhler to head the Psychological Institute at the University of Berlin in 1921, then arguably the most prestigious position in German psychology (Ash, 1995). At the University of Berlin a fourth principal figure emerged: Kurt Lewin (1890–1947), an exceptionally creative individual who would extend Gestalt ideas into the areas of motivation, personality, and social psychology.

Americans became aware of Gestalt psychology in the 1920s from an article published by Kurt Koffka in the journal *Psychological Bulletin* in 1922, and by a series of four articles published in the *American Journal of Psychology* in 1925 and 1926 by Harry Helson. By 1924, Koffka was lecturing in America as a visiting professor at Cornell University and the University of Wisconsin. In 1927 he settled at Smith College in Massachusetts, where he remained for the rest of his life. In the next decade he would observe with dismay and then horror the political changes in his native country as Adolf Hitler became chancellor of Germany in January of 1933. Two months later, Hitler had established his Nazi dictatorship.

Hitler's hatred for the Jews, a regular part of his political rhetoric, quickly became government policy. On April 1, 1933 the Nazi government called for a boycott of all Jewish businesses. The government banned Jews from holding a number of jobs such as farmer, teacher, or journalist, and from holding any public office. By 1935, the Nuremberg Laws had stripped all Jews of German citizenship and had left over half of them unemployed. Even for those with money it was difficult to buy things, as most shopowners would not sell to Jews. In some cities, Jews found it impossible to buy food or medicine.

As Hitler's Third Reich spread into Austria, many of the German and Austrian Jews sought refuge in other countries of eastern and western Europe, and later in North America (Cocks, 1988). Among that number were many of the Gestalt psychologists, including the founders of the movement. Wertheimer and Lewin, both of whom were Jewish, came to the United States in 1933. Köhler, who was not a Jew, joined them in 1935. These scholars left professorships in the best German universities to take lesser positions in the United States. The 1930s were hard times in the United States, the era of the Great Depression. Jobs were scarce for American doctorates, much less for the wave of European immigrants. But through American friends, the Gestalt leaders were able to find academic jobs: Wertheimer at the New School for Social Research in New York City, Köhler at Swarthmore College, and Lewin at Cornell University (in the Home Economics Department) and later at the University of Iowa. Adjustment was not easy. The culture was foreign, there was a new language to learn, and the dominant school of psychology – behaviorism – was inhospitable to the phenomenological approach of Gestalt psychology.

Although Gestalt psychology did not displace behaviorism, tenets of Gestalt theory became a part of the psychology of learning and perception. Moreover, Lewin's work would virtually define American social psychology for the next 40 years. The Gestaltists also played a significant role in the emergence of American cognitive psychology in the 1950s. Much of the contemporary work on thinking, problem solving, language, and information processing has direct antecedents in Gestalt psychology.

The letters in this chapter were selected to portray some of the human drama involved in the Gestalt migration necessitated by the Nazi regime. They tell of great human determination and courage. Obviously the migration represented a windfall of intellectual talent for the United States. And the enrichment of American psychology was part of that windfall.

The Letters

Kurt Koffka to Molly Harrower,[1] March 31, 1933

She writes that things are much better in Germany than they were before Hitler came to power. I can't understand that. I'm afraid it is the egotistic bourgeois point of view that judges merely on the ground of personal safety and order, unconcerned with the ideological forces behind it all, and ignorant of the actual suppression of liberty.

I wonder what her reaction will be to the boycott which is to begin tomorrow. People in Germany misunderstand foreign public opinion as always. They know that the atrocities reported in WWI were grossly exaggerated, largely invented. But they do not see that the physical violence is only a part of the causes which have stirred public opinion in the U.S. and in England. And that the fundamental causes are much deeper, and not done away with by a denial of atrocity stories. It is the discrimination against persons of other creeds and opinions which shocks the world rightly and against which it raises its voice.

Wolfgang Köhler to Ralph Barton Perry,[2] April 1, 1933

Nobody in Germany with any decency in his bones . . . knows very much about his near future. If nothing happens, I shall be in Chicago for the meeting of the American Association . . . As to myself, my patriotism expects the Germans to behave better than any other people. This seems to me a sound form of patriotism. Unfortunately it is very different from current nationalism which presupposes that [their] own people are right and do right whatever they are and do. However, there will still be some fight during the next weeks. Don't judge the Germans before it is over.

Note: Clearly Köhler was distressed at the changes he was witnessing in Germany, and he held out hopes that enough Germans would protest the Nazi policies that were disenfranchising so many loyal German citizens because they were Jewish. Even by April of 1933, Hitler's henchmen had given ample evidence that opposition would not be tolerated. To protest publicly meant risking your liberty, if not your life. Yet Köhler felt the need to act, to do something that would express his anger and dismay with the recent

---

[1]   Molly Harrower (1906–1999) earned her doctorate in psychology at Smith College with Koffka in 1934. She was spending a year as lecturer at the University of London when Koffka wrote her this letter. His remarks about Germany were prompted by a letter he received from a relative in Germany. The boycott to which he refers was the national boycott in Germany of all Jewish businesses, scheduled to begin on April 1, 1933.

[2]   Perry (1876–1957) was a professor of philosophy at Harvard University.

Nazi policies, and so he wrote an article for one of the Berlin newspapers, critical of the Nazi Party. Mary Henle (1978) has written that this was the last anti-Nazi article to be published openly under the Nazi regime. It was prompted by the dismissal of Nobel-prize-winning physicist James Franck from the University of Göttingen. Köhler knew the danger of writing this letter. He spent the night of April 28 playing chamber music at his home with friends, waiting for the Nazis to arrest him. But they never came. Portions of the newspaper article follow, followed by two letters prompted by the article, the first from Koffka to Molly Harrower, and the second from Lewin to Köhler.

Wolfgang Köhler to the Deutsche Allgemeine Zeitung, *April 28, 1933*

[The current rulers of Germany wonder why many valuable people have not joined the Nazi party?] Never have I seen finer patriotism than theirs.

[Regarding the dismissal of Jews from universities and other positions . . .]

During our conversation, one of my friends reached for the Psalms and read: "The Lord is my shepherd, I shall not want . . ." He read the 90th Psalm and said, "It is hard to think of a German who has been able to move human hearts more deeply and so to console those who suffer. And these words we have received from the Jews."

Another reminded me that never had a man struggled more nobly for a clarification of his vision of the world than the Jew Spinoza, whose wisdom Goethe admired. My friend did not hesitate to show respect, as Goethe did. Lessing, too, would not have written his *Nathan the Wise* unless human nobility existed among the Jews? . . . It seems that nobody can think of the great work of Heinrich Hertz without an almost affectionate admiration for him. And Hertz had Jewish blood.

One of my friends told me: "The greatest German experimental physicist of the present time is Franck; many believe that he is the greatest experimental physicist of our age. Franck[3] is a Jew, an unusually kind human being. Until a few days ago, he was professor at Göttingen, an honor to Germany and the envy of the international scientific community." [Perhaps the episode of Franck's dismissal] shows the deepest reason why all these people are not joining [the Party]: they feel a moral imposition. They believe that only the quality of a human being should determine his worth, that intellectual achievement, character, and

---

[3]   James Franck (1882–1964) was indeed one of the most important experimental physicists in the world at the time of his dismissal from Göttingen in 1933. Like many of Germany's best physicists, including Albert Einstein, he left Germany for America. There he would join the team of scientists who developed the atomic bomb. Franck opposed the dropping of the bomb on a Japanese city such as Hiroshima. In June, 1945, he authored what would become known as the "Franck Report." The document was signed by Franck and other scientists, urging the War Department to perform an open demonstration of the atomic bomb in an isolated site where the Japanese could be convinced of the bomb's destruction and encouraged to surrender and thus avoid it being dropped on Japanese cities.

obvious contributions to German culture retain their significance whether a person is Jewish or not.

Kurt Koffka to Molly Harrower, May 10, 1933

The article [Köhler's] is extremely well written, if anything could have any affect at all it would be this. Cautious, and yet brave appeal. What startled me is the introduction, in which he praises the achievement of the New [Nazi] Regime in rather glowing terms. I do not know whether this is just politics in order to give more weight to his defense of liberals, and Jews, or whether it represents his own opinion. [Fritz] Heider[4] showed us yesterday a clipping from a German newspaper with the names of those professors at a number of universities, who, till a final decision, have been given leave of absence. Wertheimer is of course among them. Frau Köhler wrote that Wertheimer is outside Germany at the moment.

Kurt Lewin to Wolfgang Köhler, May 20, 1933[5]

Many thanks for your article. Now, as I read through it quietly, its meaning and its nature have emerged much more clearly than the quick perusal on the trip. It is difficult to thank you adequately for this article, even face to face. But perhaps I should say how proud I am to be allowed to count among my friends one of those rare people who have demonstrated such conviction and have dared to do such a deed. Hopefully, even without words, it has become clear to you how deeply Gerti [Gertrud Weiss Lewin] and I appreciate what you and your dear wife have done.

I've been here a few days now. But I must admit that up to now nothing has happened to change my attitude. I was a little afraid that my attitude might appear exaggerated, or a little incomprehensible, or even somewhat ungrateful. This, and my wish that clarity should prevail, at least between us, almost obligates me to speak to you, although with some reluctance, about matters intimately connected to my personal future. Probably the fate of an individual Jew has never been only a personal fate. Surely it has been torn out of the sphere of the personal in our times . . .

---

[4]   Fritz Heider (1896–1988) earned his PhD at the University of Berlin, where he studied with Lewin and Wertheimer. He, too, was part of the Gestalt migration, taking a position with Koffka at Smith College. He would become one of the most important social psychologists of the twentieth century.

[5]   This letter was found among Kurt Lewin's papers by his daughter, Miriam Lewin. As she reports, evidently it was never mailed to Köhler. Mailing it would have been a risky act, dangerous for both writer and recipient. Lewin wrote the letter a few days after arriving back in Berlin after spending a year in the United States as a visiting professor at Stanford University.

If I now believe there is no other choice for me but to emigrate, you will understand that this thought certainly does not come easily to me. Considerations are involved that are far removed from feeling personally hurt or a temporarily wounded pride, be such feelings ever so justified. These considerations pertain to the simplest, most elementary necessities of life.

I have said it before and would like to repeat it now: When I think of leaving my parents and relatives, of giving up the house that we built, of going out into an uncertain future, of leaving a scientific structure that would take years to rebuild, at best, then surely at the root of such a decision is not a loathing of vulgarities of the fear of personal unpleasantness, but only an overwhelmingly decisive social reality.

I think it is practically impossible for a non-Jew to gauge what being a Jew has meant for a person, even in the liberal era of the last 40 years. There have probably been very few Jewish children of any generation who have not been singled out from the natural group of their peers between their 6th and 13th year. Quite suddenly and without any kind of predictable cause, they have been beaten up and treated with contempt. Whether instigated by teachers, by students, or simply by people on the street, these recurring experiences pull the ground out from under the feet of the young child, and cut off all possibility of objective discussion or unbiased evaluation. They throw the child totally back upon its own resources. They make all natural supports appear entirely deceptive and force the young person to exist in a conflicting world of appearance and reality right from the start. Very few children are capable of surviving such disrupting experiences without suffering serious damage to their natural growth. After all, these experiences are not just casual irritations, but instead involve the very foundations of life itself on which all important decisions are based. Thus the effects are ever present. At the same time, people have demanded absolute patriotism from Jewish children quite as a matter of course. One always had to reckon with the fact that evaluations of one's own achievements would be biased to an unpredictable degree. As a result, exaggerated personal qualities, whether aggressiveness or excessive softness, were scarcely avoidable . . .

The issue of German anti-Semitism is indeed a long chapter that would require an interpretation of the history of the Jews as well as of the Germans. I am quite aware that the foreign political pressures of the last 15 years have allowed primitive atavisms to surface in Germany as well as in every other people. The need for a scapegoat has become so strong that the battle cry "Kill the Jew," which we have been hearing daily for a decade, has led quite literally to a war of hundreds against one, the kind of war that used to be found only in Poland or Hungary. This is understandable, I think, only through the ancient and very deeply rooted anti-Semitic tradition in Germany, together with the political morality that Bismarck described as a lack of civil courage. That it is a basic characteristic of the German lifestyle – decidedly different from the political morality of, for example, the American or the Englishman – is something I myself learned to recognize only this year, although you have been telling me about it for a long time . . .

I cannot imagine how a Jew is supposed to live a life in Germany at the present time that does justice to even the most primitive demands of truthfulness. While I was in Tokyo at a dinner that the Japanese-German Cultural Institute gave for me, a speech was addressed to me as the representative of German science. I, in turn, answered as a representative of German science. I was able to respond to the Japanese with a good conscience. But two minutes later I got the terrible feeling that I had just done something impossible. I knew that here I was speaking in the name of German science and here I was recognized by the German embassy, while in Germany at the very moment they were knocking my feet out from under me.

Am I supposed to speak as a representative of Germany again on my next trip abroad and "to counter the reports of atrocities," as is tacitly expected of every Jew? Or as who am I supposed to step forward? As a person deprived of the basic rights of a citizen, and who nevertheless continues, for a salary, to provide the children of this people with knowledge and with preparation for positions from which his own children are excluded?

Perhaps, like many other Jews, a cruel destiny will not spare me this fate. Certainly I have no reason to voluntarily relinquish any rights and thereby to enlarge the enormous spiritual and material damage committed against us daily. But even though it will tear my life apart, I hope you will understand and approve of my attempt to find a place for me and my children where we can live an honorable life.

Note: In the fall of 1933 Lewin, his wife, and their children emigrated to the United States, where Lewin held a two-year position at Cornell University. Lewin's mother and sister, who fled to Holland, were captured by the Nazis and sent to the death camps, where they died.

The following letter was written by Köhler when he was out of Germany on a brief trip to Norway. The Nazis were exerting greater and greater control over the activities of the universities, and Köhler was finding it increasingly difficult to remain in such an environment. But he continued to hold out for the sake of his student assistants and his concern for the welfare of Gestalt psychology and the course of Germany.

Wolfgang Köhler to Ralph Barton Perry, March 1934

I am trying to build up a special position for myself in which I might stay with honour. As yet it seems to work, but the end may come [any] day. Quite exciting sometimes, not a life of leisure, occasionally great fun. The art is not to act in passion, but to make at once use of any occasion when the others make a mistake; then it is time to push a foot forward or to hit without serious danger to oneself. You will say that such is the method of cowards. But think of the difference in strength! . . .

Good work is being done in Berlin, as though we had to do what the emigrants are no longer able to do in Germany. Unfortunately my assistants have been in serious danger several times because of political denunciations – a denunciation a month is more or less our current rate; as yet, however, it has always been possible to save them.

Note: Köhler *wrote to Perry from Scotland, where he was lecturing. For several months* Köhler *had been writing to the rector of the University of Berlin, asking that commitments made to him regarding the Psychological Institute be honored. He indicated that without such action he would resign. In his final letter to the administration of the university he set a deadline for reply. When that date passed and* Köhler *had received no answer to his letter, he submitted his request for retirement.*

Wolfgang Köhler to Ralph Barton Perry, May 21, 1934

My resignation is most likely to be final. Since most of the serious workers in psychology had to leave before, and since my excellent assistants would not stay without me, this means the abolition of German psychology for many years. I do not regard myself as responsible. If only 20 professors had fought the same battle, it would never have come so far with regard to German universities.

Note: Koffka and Köhler *met in Cambridge, Massachusetts when* Köhler *came to deliver the William James Lectures at Harvard University. While at Harvard,* Köhler *received a letter from the deputy rector at the University of Berlin asking him to sign an oath of loyalty to Adolf Hitler. He refused. In the next letter,* Koffka *talks about his meeting with* Köhler.

Kurt Koffka to Molly Harrower, November 13, 1934

Now from here, Köhler's visit was absolutely magnificent. We had marvelous talks on psychology, physics and Germany. To begin with the last: I have changed my personal outlook a great deal after what he told me. I do not longer believe, as I did more or less, that a majority of Germans enjoy the Hitler regime. I see now utter chaos, the disunity, party strife, and chief and worst of all, the demoralizing influence which the regime exerts on the people. Köhler is furious with the slack attitude of American intellectuals – we had grand talks about tolerance in this connection. You may speak about this very freely provided you do not mention Köhler's name; as a matter of fact it would be good if you could influence public opinion in N.J.C. [New Jersey College for Women] in this direction. The present tolerance kills the efforts of all the decent people in Germany. They who want to be pro-German are really the worst enemies of the best German people. Köhler's own behavior is simply beyond praise. He does speak out to the man in power, and at the same time he does it diplomatically so that his actions have as much effect as they possibly can. I'll tell you more about it when we meet. To summarize: One cannot be sufficiently anti-Nazi! They are the enemies of all true morality, which they consider intellectualistic prejudice. Sneaking underhand creatures they are.

Wolfgang Köhler to Donald K. Adams,[6] 1935

I feel obliged to announce to all those who have taken a friendly interest in the Psychological Institute at Berlin that this institute does not exist any more – though the rooms and the apparatus and Mr. Rupp[7] are still there. The government has decided in May to dismiss all the assistants who were trained by me and in June, during the term, they were suddenly forbidden to continue their work and their teaching: Duncker, von Lauenstein and von Restorff.[8] Since, at my last visit in Berlin, I had expressly stated orally and in official documents that I could not possibly remain as director without the help of my young friends and since this is a clear case of their modern brutality (another man uses this method in order to push *me* out), the measure is morally equivalent to my own dismissal too. I shall have a last interview with the Nazi authorities in August. But there is not one chance in a hundred for my staying on in Germany . . . We were depressed for some days but have come back to the fighting spirit once more. Personally, I shall be glad when I have no contact with the official Germany of today, and I have so many good friends in this country, more indeed than over there. My deepest anxiety refers to the assistants. I am not yet sure whether I shall be able to place them somewhere.

Kurt Koffka to Molly Harrower, September 9, 1938[9]

So much has happened. The days in Berlin were painfully exciting. It is much worse on the spot than outside. The war situation was critical although I

[6] Adams (1902–1971), a professor of psychology at Duke University, was one of Köhler's closest American friends and had studied with Köhler in Berlin.

[7] Hans Rupp (1880–1954), a non-Jew, was an untenured psychologist in Köhler's institute. He is said to have embraced the Nazi party regulations for university professors, an action that caused him to be ostracized after the war.

[8] Karl Duncker (1903–1940), whose creative work on problem solving led him to discover the effect he labeled functional fixedness; Otto von Lauenstein (••–1943), known for his studies of time errors; and Hedwig von Restorff (1906–1962), discoverer of the serial position effect in recall, also known as the von Restorff effect, were indicative of the exceptional young talent that Köhler had gathered at Berlin as part of Gestalt psychology.

[9] As the situation worsened in Nazi Germany, Koffka felt compelled to visit his family and assess the political events first hand.

was assured on my second day in Berlin that nothing would happen before the Partietag [Nazi party conference]. The Jewish situation is unbearable beyond words.

You know, I presume, that all Jews have to assume the names of Israel and Sarah respectively on January the first. They have special licensed numbers on their cars; they have to use yellow benches in public parks. All Jewish shops have to bear the name of the owners in large white letters on plate glass. This is already in existence. But they are afraid, based on leading Nazi papers, that they will be driven out of their apartments since Jews must not defile houses owned by Germans.

Under these conditions I could only confirm my mother and my brother in their respective resolutions to emigrate to America. This means new responsibilities for me. I must give them affidavits, and must try to find some sort of employment for my brother . . .

The news after a few days' respite was most alarming this morning. It is not impossible that the world will be aflame by the time I arrive back in New York. Although I cannot really believe it yet. However, my reason tells me that a catastrophe is bound to come sooner or later. Things cannot continue to go as they are at the moment. A new holocaust, much more terrible even than the last, may be necessary, and it is the most depressing part of the situation that such a new wholesale slaughter would probably lead to a peace even worse than the last one, and therefore breed new wars. Berlin has thoroughly discouraged me. I can't help agreeing with Gloucester in Shakespeare's King Lear when he says something like this "what flies are to boys, we are to the Gods, they kill us for sport" you will know the quotation.[10]

Epilogue

Koffka, and Köhler, and no doubt many other Germans, could never have anticipated the horrific actions of their fellow-citizens in the name of German nationalism, anti-Semitism, and other deep-seated hatreds of all stripes. The letters suggest that both Koffka and Köhler held on to their belief that sanity would return to Germany shortly, that the good people of Germany would reject the fascist agenda. But they were wrong.

Köhler's action in writing an article critical of the Nazi party for a Berlin newspaper was quite a heroic act. And there are other stories of his heroism in his classroom and in his dealings with Nazi officials in an effort to protect his students. Those stories are told in two interesting articles, one by Mary Henle (1978), who studied with Köhler in America, and one by Clarke Crannell (1970), who was a student in Köhler's Berlin institute in 1933 and offers an eyewitness account of some of Köhler's actions.

[10] Shakespeare's *King Lear*, Act IV, Scene I. Gloucester says: "As flies to wanton boys are we to the gods, – They kill us for their sport."

The struggles faced by the Gestalt psychologists in the 1930s pale in comparison to the horrors of Nazi Germany that resulted in the death of six million in the Holocaust alone. Nevertheless, their story is one of the tragedies of the Nazi regime as citizens were forced to leave their homeland, their families, their possessions, and their livelihood to start anew in another country, another culture, another language. The Gestalt psychologists in Germany were forced to leave their major university positions, their psychological laboratories, and their talented graduate assistants to take up college and university positions in America that were nowhere nearly so prestigious.

These émigré psychologists arrived in America in the middle of the Great Depression, into a behaviorist psychology that discounted the value of a psychology that was phenomenological, wholistic, and nativistic. Of the four major figures, only Köhler, who served as president of the American Psychological Association in 1959 and who died in 1967, would live beyond the 1940s: Koffka died in 1941, Wertheimer in 1943, and Lewin in 1947. Mary Henle (1978), who studied with both Köhler and Lewin in America, has written: "The young generation of Gestalt psychologists was effectively wiped out" (p. 944). Duncker, long plagued by depression, committed suicide in 1940 at age 36, and von Lauenstein died in 1943. Others could not find positions in psychology outside of Germany. In America the Gestalt psychologists, with the exception of Lewin, were not in good places to attract graduate students and thus produce the next generation of Gestalt psychologists.

Despite such obstacles, Gestalt psychology has enjoyed considerable impact on American psychology. The migration, as noted by Sokal (1984), had begun before the Nazis came to power. Koffka was already in America, and by 1930 American psychologists were reasonably familiar with the tenets of Gestalt psychology. Thus, whereas the Nazis did not start the migration of Gestalt ideas, they did ensure the migration of Gestalt psychologists.

Initially Gestalt psychology had its greatest impact in the field of perception, especially through the work of Wertheimer on perceptual organization. Lewin's action research program shaped a generation of American social psychologists in such areas as prejudice, leadership, group dynamics, conflict, frustration, and personality. In contemporary psychology, Gestalt psychology has had, perhaps, its greatest influence in cognitive psychology, where researchers are rediscovering the innovative Gestalt work and theory on perception, learning, thinking, and problem solving (King & Wertheimer, 2005).

Sokal (1984) has nicely summarized the outcome of Gestalt psychology in America: "If Gestalt psychology has today lost its identity as a school of thought . . . it is not because the mainstream of American psychology has swamped their ideas. Rather, their work has done much to redirect this mainstream, which adopted many of their points of view. Few other migrating scientific schools have been as successful" (p. 1261).

Suggested Readings

Ash, M. G. (1985). Gestalt psychology: Origins in Germany and reception in the United States. In C. E. Buxton (Ed.), *Points of view in the modern history of psychology*. Orlando, FL: Academic Press.

Of several excellent accounts of the Gestalt migration, this one provides the best description of the evolution of Gestalt psychology in Germany.

Ash, M. G. (1992). Cultural contexts and scientific change in psychology: Kurt Lewin in Iowa. *American Psychologist, 47*, 198–207.

An analysis of the change in cultural context for Lewin from Berlin to Iowa and the impact of that change on his theory and research.

Ash, M. G. (1995). *Gestalt psychology in German culture, 1890–1967: Holism and the quest for objectivity*. New York: Cambridge University Press.

An excellent historical account of the birth and development of Gestalt psychology.

Harrower, M. (1983). *Kurt Koffka: An unwitting self-portrait*. Gainesville: University Presses of Florida.

This fascinating portrait of Koffka is largely based on excerpts from the more than 2,100 letters exchanged between Koffka and Harrower between 1930 and 1941. Some of the excerpts in this chapter are taken from this collection.

Henle, M. (1978). One man against the Nazis: Wolfgang Köhler. *American Psychologist, 33*, 939–944.

This is the dramatic account of the final days of the University of Berlin's Psychological Institute and Köhler's determined struggle to keep it going, independent of Nazi interference. Several letters in this chapter are taken from this article.

Henle, M. (1980). The influence of Gestalt psychology in America. In R. W. Rieber & K. Salzinger (Eds.), *Psychology: Theoretical–historical perspectives*. New York: Academic Press, pp. 177–190.

This article focuses on misunderstandings of Gestalt psychology as cause and effect of the "less than overwhelming" influence that Gestalt psychology had in America. It provides a concise summary of the contributions of Gestalt psychology to contemporary psychology.

King, D. B., & Wertheimer, M. (2005). *Max Wertheimer and Gestalt theory*. New Brunswick, NJ: Transaction Publishers.

An intimate and fascinating biography of Wertheimer written, in part, by one of his sons (Michael). The book is really a double biography as it covers the "life" of Gestalt psychology from its rise in Germany to its migration and subsequent development in America.

Köhler, W. (1947). *Gestalt psychology: An introduction to new concepts in modern psychology*. New York: Liveright.

The most readable account of Gestalt psychology.

Lewin, K. (1986). "Everything within me rebels": A letter from Kurt Lewin to Wolfgang Köhler, 1933. *Journal of Social Issues, 42* (4), 39–47.

This article is the complete text of the Lewin–Köhler letter excerpted in this chapter.

Mandler, J. M., & Mandler, G. (1969). The diaspora of experimental psychology: The Gestaltists and others. In D. Fleming & B. Bailyn (Eds.) *The intellectual migration: Europe and America, 1930–1960*. Cambridge, MA, pp. 371–419.

An account of the migration of refugee psychologists from Europe to America, focusing on the Gestalt psychologists.

Marrow, A. J. (1969). *The practical theorist: The life and work of Kurt Lewin*. New York: Basic Books.

This biography of Lewin describes his social research agenda as an outgrowth of his all-too-real exposure to frustration, prejudice, authoritarianism, and hatred.

Sokal, M. M. (1984). The Gestalt psychologists in behaviorist America. *American Historical Review, 89,* 1240–1263.

This article argues that the Gestalt psychologists were treated better in America than other historical accounts would lead us to believe, and that Gestalt psychology was quite successful in redirecting the mainstream of American psychology.

14
CHAPTER

David Krech (*left*) and Ross Stagner (*right*)
(Krech photo from the Archives of the History of American Psychology/University of Akron;
Stagner photo courtesy of Rhea Stagner Das)

A Social Agenda for American Psychology

By the beginning of the 1920s, much of the American public seemed convinced that the science of psychology held the keys to prosperity and happiness. Newspaper columnists urged the public to seek psychologists for advice about marriage, child rearing, and the selection of a career; businesses were urged to consult psychologists about employee selection; and educators were encouraged to use psychologists to improve educational methods. One columnist told his readers: "You cannot achieve these things [effectiveness and happiness] in the fullest measure without the new knowledge of your own mind and personality that the psychologists have given us" (Wiggam, 1928, p. 13). Public interest in psychology was strong, as is reflected in the publication of a number of popular psychology magazines, popular psychology books, and home-study courses intended to help people better their lives through psychology. Public demand for psychological services was high, and because there were not enough psychologists interested in applying their science, many individuals with little or no training in psychology emerged to fill the void.

The stock market crash in September, 1929 ended the public euphoria and ushered in a decade of economic and psychological depression, so much so that by literary convention it gets capitalized as the Great Depression. Although the United States has suffered a number of economic depressions in its approximately 230-year history, there is a reason that one of those has the adjective "Great." It is – especially in terms of longevity – the worst depression on record. Unemployment reached unbelievable levels of nearly 25 percent. Millions of people suddenly found themselves out of work, homeless, and hungry. It was a time of soup kitchens, apple carts, and "Brother Can You Spare a Dime?" "Riding the rails" was the phrase used for the hundreds of thousands who lived in the boxcars of trains, traveling from one community to another, looking for work, a meal, or trying to escape from the police. It was the time of the dustbowl, when drought and winds rendered the farmland in Oklahoma useless and sent thousands of "Okies" west to California, where they became exploited as part of migrant farm labor, the subject of John Steinbeck's *The Grapes of Wrath* (1939). It was a time of lawlessness and movie marquis criminals – John Dillinger, Charles "Pretty Boy" Floyd, George "Machine Gun" Kelly, and Bonnie Parker and Clyde Barrow.

Labor unions began to grow in influence in the 1930s, especially after Franklin D. Roosevelt was elected President of the United States. Soon there were major strikes across the country – in San Francisco; Flint, Michigan; Chicago – some of them quite violent. There were escalating racial tensions as activism grew in the African-American community, both in the cities of the North and amid the Jim Crow practices of the South. There were signs of a war brewing in Europe, with the rise of the fascist dictator, Adolf Hitler, in Germany. By 1938, the German army had taken Austria and Czechoslovakia, and by 1939, Poland.

It was in the midst of the Great Depression and the escalating European conflict that a new psychological organization was formed, one that had a clear public agenda (and perhaps a private one). It was an extremely controversial organization and its founding represented an act of courage, because there were many, no doubt, who saw the society as a communist or socialist organization – psychologists promoting pinkism, that is, leftist views (indeed, the FBI established a file on the organization in the 1930s; see Harris, 1980). The organization was named the Society for the Psychological Study of Social Issues (SPSSI) and it continues today as one of more than 50 divisions of the American Psychological Association.

The American Psychological Association (APA) was founded in 1892 and had always been dominated by psychologists in university settings. As opportunities for employment of psychologists outside of academic settings grew, there was pressure on the APA to broaden its mission to serve the interests of these applied psychologists. In response to that pressure an APA Division on Consulting Psychologists was founded in the 1920s, but it was never able to do much for the applied psychologists. The APA leadership actively resisted the centrifugal forces that sought to extend psychology beyond the campus, including those voices that sought an application of psychological science to social problems. And in the 1930s, as already noted, there were plenty of social problems facing Americans and the rest of the world: unemployment, hunger, racism, labor–management disputes, and impending war.

The beginnings of SPSSI can be traced to 1935, when psychologists Ross Stagner (1909–1997) and Isadore Krechevsky (later David Krech, 1909–1977), both about age 26 and at the beginning of their careers, talked about common frustrations such as the unemployment faced by new psychologists, the avoidance of political questions by psychologists, and the lack of opportunity for psychology to contribute solutions to the social ills of the day (Stagner, 1986). Their conversation led to a plan of action to organize psychologists with similar interests. In February of 1936, Krechevsky wrote to a small number of psychologists he felt might be kindred spirits. Sixteen, in addition to Stagner and Krechevsky, agreed to be part of an organizing committee. Acting as secretary, Krechevsky mailed a letter in March to several hundred members of the APA describing the plans for the new organization and asking for indications of interest.

The initial organizing meeting was held in September of that year in conjunction with the annual meeting of the APA at Dartmouth College. More than 100 psychologists attended a special meeting of the social issues group. Stagner chaired the meeting and Krechevsky served as secretary. Krechevsky announced that he had already received over 200 expressions of interest in the society from his earlier mailing and had collected $63.13 in advance dues and assessments. "Those present readily agreed that $63.13 in the depression year of 1936 was sufficient evidence of interest to justify formalizing an organization" (Krech & Cartwright, 1956, p. 471). Goodwin Watson was elected the first chairperson of the organization and Krechevsky the first Secretary-Treasurer. Ten others were elected to the first Council of Directors, which included several distinguished psychologists of that time: Edward C. Tolman, Gardner Murphy, and Gordon Allport.

Following the meeting, a letter was mailed to the entire APA membership offering charter membership of SPSSI to anyone who joined before the end of 1936.[1] The letter explained the two goals of the new society as follows:

> One is to encourage research upon those psychological problems most vitally related to modern social, economic and political policies. The second is to help the public and its representatives to understand and to use in the formation of social policies, contributions from the scientific investigation of human behavior. (Krech & Cartwright, 1956, p. 471)

That was the public agenda, and it was largely the motivation for the involvement of many early SPSSI members. The somewhat private agenda involved the

---

[1] As a result of the mailing, 333 of the APA's nearly 2,000 members joined the new organization. A year later SPSSI requested formal identification with APA and was granted affiliate status by APA's Council of Directors.

problem of unemployment of psychologists, a problem exacerbated by the influx of European psychologists fleeing the Nazi regime (see Chapter 13). Some of the SPSSI organizers hoped to manufacture jobs for psychologists by creating a social agenda for behavioral research (see Finison, 1976, 1979).

In the years that followed, SPSSI encouraged research on social issues and even established its own journal, the *Journal of Social Issues*, to publish such research. It supported the application of psychological knowledge to social problems as diverse as divorce and war. It also acted to help psychologists who might be persecuted for their political beliefs or social activism. And it also helped to organize psychological support, including the APA, for various social issues.

That SPSSI has been successful is evidenced in part by the fact that the APA has amended its bylaws to include, as one of its three goals, the promotion of human welfare. Today the APA is organized into four directorates, one of which is Public Interest. Such APA involvement is a direct result of the success of SPSSI in convincing the broader psychological community of the importance of a social agenda for psychology.

The letters that follow are taken from the SPSSI Papers, which are part of the Archives of the History of American Psychology at the University of Akron. The first three letters are in response to a February, 1936 letter from Krechevsky intended to recruit members for an organizing committee. Those are followed by the organizing letter mailed in March, 1936, followed by many responses to that letter. They illustrate a great diversity of responses to Krechevsky's call to social arms and tell part of the story of how this very important psychological society began.[2]

The Letters

Junius Flagg Brown[3] [University of Kansas] to Isadore Krechevsky,
February 26, 1936

I hasten to answer your letter of Feb. 24. You may count on me to support your society both with time and with somewhat paltry monetary donations . . . As an

---

[2]   Another psychological organization also formed in 1936: the American Association for Applied Psychology (AAAP). That group was concerned with improving the consulting and practice opportunities of psychologists, and not with the involvement of psychologists in social issues. When the American Psychological Association reorganized in 1945, AAAP and SPSSI merged with APA, becoming several of the APA's divisions (Benjamin, 1997).

[3]   J. F. Brown was a social psychologist and student of Lewin and, like most of the members of SPSSI, his politics leaned to the left. When he wrote this letter his book, *Psychology and the Social Order* (1936), had just been published. It has sometimes been characterized as a Marxist approach to social psychology. Brown said that he wrote the book because the other textbooks on social psychology were so inadequate: "They have little or nothing to say about the great social problems created by the economic and cultural crisis that all competent observers realize is now at hand" (p. v).

earnest [sic] of my good intent I am enclosing my check for $5.00 and will try to send you more later. Also I will be glad to serve on the organizational committee. My only suggestion is that we attempt to gain first support of the relatively few psychologists who are really politically literate rather than the wholesale support of the so called socially minded. Secondly I suggest that the organization is in no way officially to be affiliated with the A.P.A. as the embarrassment might be mutual. Thirdly that the cooperation and membership of scientists in closely related fields like sociology and philosophy be asked and allowed.

Gordon W. Allport[4] [Harvard University] to Krechevsky, March 6, 1936

I think I am willing to serve on your organizational committee. Certainly I am willing in principle. My only doubts come from the question of how pre-determined the policies are. Your letter is persuasive and for the most part unexceptionable. There is, however, a slightly over-emotional tone that might raise the question whether the committee itself is able to see issues clearly, and to pursue facts in an unbiased way.

In red I have made a few verbal suggestions for diminishing the excited tone of the letter. The passages in parentheses, might, for example, be deleted without loss of force and with a gain in dignity . . . It is necessary to postpone platforms, I think, until various regional meetings have been held. Most important of all it will be necessary to have answers to meet the coming ridicule and objections of the "pure" psychologists. Being a rather individualistic lot, I think the platform, to have any appeal, must be entirely unemotional, brief, and calculated to admit results and judgments that may in essence be neo-socialistic. We would discredit social planning, the profession, and ourselves, if we prejudged the outcome of our respective researches . . .

James Harlan Elder [Yale University] to Krechevsky, March 14, 1936

Considering my professional contacts your letter [of February 24] comes as a ray of promise that psychologists aren't all quite as hopeless as I have judged them. Several times I unhappily have concluded that no group of scientists could be as indifferent and provincial as psychologists . . . I still don't see quite why psychological training shouldn't serve as a somewhat better than average scientific background for thinking about the world we live in . . . I do not feel that my name on your committee would strengthen it much. It looks good as it stands. Furthermore,

---

[4]   Gordon Allport (1897–1967) was a professor at Harvard University, best known for his development of personality theory. He published a landmark book in 1954 that was particularly salient to SPSSI interests, entitled *The Nature of Prejudice*. His letter shows the political wisdom of someone a little more senior than Krechevsky and Stagner.

I haven't any funds to spare at this time. But you must not take this as the usual liberal attitude of approval but no participation. I am as earnest about the proposition as anyone and I will give my services and money as soon as possible . . .

Krechevsky and 17 Other Members of the Organizing Committee, including
J. F. Brown and Gordon Allport, and Ross Stagner to Members and Associates
of the American Psychological Association, ca. March 1936[5]

This letter is being sent to you by a group of associates and members of the A.P.A. which has organized itself as a temporary body to help express the attitudes of American psychologists on the important economic and political issues of today. We do not believe it at all necessary to belabor the fact that an economic depression exists in these United States and in the world around us. That other spheres than the purely economic have been affected is also obvious to most of us. Psychology and our other sciences are no less affected. We need but appeal to our own experiences to obtain instances of the senseless fate our present society has assigned to the many capable psychologists we have been turning out with so much hope. Most of us have probably tried to do some hard-headed thinking about this situation and all of its implications. It is becoming increasingly evident that such thinking is more than a "proper" mental exercise; it is, we believe absolutely essential *if we are to be allowed to continue as scientists at all.* Unfortunately, scientists in the past seemed to think that they had a very easy verbal way out of the necessity of thinking about these issues and of advising the rest of society on these important issues. All that was necessary was to repeat solemnly and gravely the magic phrase "pure science," and immediately, so it was believed, they had removed themselves from all environmental stimulation and influence! Certainly the psychologist should be the last scientist to rationalize his way out of the problem by postulating a sort of political-economic vacuum in which the scientist, *his theories and his work are supposed to exist.*

The group responsible for this letter was organized because its members believed that there are enough psychologists who are ready to translate some such "private feels" into behavior to justify an organized attempt to encourage this transformation. Last year, part of this same group was responsible for the circulation of a petition to the A.P.A. to recognize the existence of unemployed psychologists and to take active means to remedy such a socially undesirable situation. You may remember that the response was extremely gratifying and that the membership of the A.P.A. responded with a unanimity which betrayed a real social awareness on the part of the body of our membership. We are now ready to ask for your more active aid in organizing ourselves permanently.

[5]   This letter was also published in full in the journal, *Psychological Exchange* (4, 1936, 226–227), under the heading "Psychologists and Present-Day Activities."

The present committee has no completed and "closed" program in mind. We want and need your help in formulating such a program. In general, we wish to establish an organization of accredited psychologists to promote specific research projects on *contemporary* psychological problems; to collect, analyze and disseminate data on the psychological consequences of our present economic, political and cultural crisis; to encourage the participation of psychologists *as psychologists* in the activities of the day. Society very definitely needs our aid. Economists, politicians, physicists, editorialists, munitions manufacturers and "philosophers" have not hesitated to advise society on problems of social motivation, the inevitability of war as "inherent in human nature" and the like. What psychologists have come forth to substantiate or refute these psychological "laws"? These are important psychological questions *per se*; that their answers may have important social implications does not make them any less so and should not frighten us away from them. There is, we believe, a definite need for an organization to encourage, promote and support (both financially and "morally") such research.

Before we can go ahead with any program, however, we must know how many other psychologists we can count on. Specifically, will you write us telling us that you are willing to help organize an agency for some such purpose? Will you include in your letter any general or specific suggestions? Will you also include an estimate of the probable attitude of your colleagues toward this work?

Raleigh M. Drake [Wesleyan College, Georgia] to Krechevsky, March 20, 1936

I like your idea very much and see much value in it . . . The public does not have too much confidence in "psychology" now because psychologists have been so academic, impractical, theoritical [sic], and after all what have they contributed of an objective nature that the layman can observe? A committee, such as you suggest, might serve as a sieve to prevent unsound theories from reaching the public and thereby protect all psychologists, as well as to encourage the discovery and application of psychological laws which may be important for society . . .

Ralph R. Brown [United States Public Health Service] to Krechevsky,
March 20, 1936

I shall be very glad to cooperate in any possible way with your committee in its efforts to encourage, promote, and support psychological research on contemporary social problems . . . Naturally, I am quite partial to the psychologist's standpoint in these matters, but I cannot help but see that the medical man has several good reasons for his attitude. Above all, the physician takes a practical attitude toward research and is most anxious to solve those problems which are directly concerned with human welfare. Only too often, however, the psychologist – safe in the confines of a university – is engaged in what I would call "academic boondoggling" – research on insignificant problems . . . Let the efforts of your committee be directed toward the promoting of a research problem to be worked out in collaboration with a medical group. This will necessitate a problem having a definite significance for human welfare . . .

Ray Willoughby [Clark University] to Krechevsky, March 20, 1936

Sure, I'm with you "in principle"; but just to be ornery . . . I'm going to deny that you or anybody else, at least qua psychologists, can do a damned thing about it . . . And what research projects would you promote? Can you see anything in sight, in any direction, that you could do that would have any bearing on anything? I can't. The journals are crammed with tripe, in social as well as other fields, which no sensible person bothers to read. Suppose you "collected, analyzed and disseminated" data to your heart's content – to whom would it make the slightest difference? . . . "What psychologists have come forth to substantiate or refute these psychological 'laws'?" Well, I'll bite – what psychologists *could* substantiate or refute them? And how? By hollering louder than the propounders of the "laws"? Do you know anybody that knows anything at all (relevant and beyond common sense, I mean) about these alleged laws? I don't.

F. J. Adams (University of Texas) to Krechevsky, March 21, 1936

Because of the claims of pseudo-psychologists with respect to advice on "Health, Wealth and Happiness"[6] with their five free lectures, and such, it would seem quite unwise, particularly in this region, for the A.P.A. to come out with an attempt to solve the problems of the economists, sociologists, or those of any other group of specialists. In this area, the distinction, even among "educated" individuals, between scientific and pseudo-psychologists is not very clear; and between social reformers and individuals of "pink" or darker tendencies, even less clear. The combination of these would be distinctly harmful to those attempting to preserve the status of scientific psychology and to advance its influence, in my belief.

Calvin Hall [University of Oregon] to Krechevsky, March 23, 1936

Of course you can count on me for any inflation of the ego of homo psychologicus. Do we have to wave the red flag[7] or is this just a milksop, a parlor-pink

---

[6] This may have been a reference to a popular psychology magazine published monthly from 1923 to 1939, entitled *Psychology: Health, Happiness, Success.*

[7] A reference to communism, whereas the pink that follows in the sentence refers to a leftist view that is considered more moderate. The term "pinko" was a derogatory term for someone who had communist leanings or sympathies.

organization? . . . To be more serious however . . . Care must be taken . . . not to promise more than we can actually deliver. Just after the war some psychologists sold aptitude testing "short" and we are only now recovering from that period of exaggerated optomism [sic]. We ought to know, moreover, why some psychologists are unemployed. I am certainly in sympathy with the prospectus but I want to emphasis [sic] again that I hope this can all be done through the A.P.A. rather than through some independent organization.

Ralph White[8] [Wesleyan University] to Krechevsky, March 23, 1936

I was delighted to find that psychologists were at last beginning to wake up, and particularly to find that you were one of the wakers . . . Suggestions for what could be done? Plenty: 1. Get some non-A.P.A. members. Nearly all of the good social psychologists aren't in the A.P.A. . . . 3. Get a representative cross-section of the unemployed in the United States and make about a hundred careful case studies, stressing infantilizing effects, rationalizations, paranoid trends, conscious explanations of the depression, and ideas about what is to be done about it . . . 5. Collect case studies of strikers who are black-listed, and their families . . . 9. Catalogue the stereotypes of the American mind. Publicize the fact that the same stereotypes are utilized by both left and right . . .

Albert T. Poffenberger [Columbia University] to Krechevsky, March 23, 1936

I am heartily in favor of the ideas expressed in your circular letter. My views on the matters there discussed are expressed in my presidential address of last September before the American Psychological Association. It is my conviction that the A.P.A. should take the initiative in dealing with public questions either through a committee or through the machinery of a central office or preferably through a combination of these devices. I do not favor setting up a separate organization or an unattached or unofficial committee for purposes in mind. Such a move would, in my opinion, merely delay forcing the A.P.A. to become a more active public influence . . .

J. Stanley Gray (University of Pittsburgh) to Krechevsky, March 23, 1936

Indeed I am much interested in a proposal to form an organization to promote psychological interpretations and implications for our present economic and

---

[8]   Ralph K. White was an important social psychologist who made significant contributions to an understanding of the nature of war and conflict. He is considered one of the founders of the field known as peace psychology. One of his more important books is *Nobody Wanted War: Misperceptions in Vietnam and Other Wars* (1968).

political plight. I am greatly concerned with the enormous amount of "raw" data we psychologists are turning out and at the same time the poverty of interpretation of these data for use in American life. We are not making our science *useful* to any marked extent (except possibly in the field of education).

William E. Walton [University of Nebraska] to Krechevsky, March 26, 1936

I am in hearty accord with what your committee is trying to do to promote active research on contemporary psychological projects. I feel there should be several functions of such a group: 1. We should educate the public concerning the contributions which psychology can make to its immediate problems . . . 2. We should create a market for our students . . . 3. We must educate the public against psychological quackery. In order that we may do this we should campaign for legal recognition of the term psychologist and limit its use to those qualified . . .

John Mortimer Stephens [Johns Hopkins University] to Krechevsky, March 27, 1936

. . . I belong to that group who have considerable faith in "pure science" and whose position is so illogical that to state it (with an exclamation mark) is to refute it. I doubt if the psychological information with which I am most familiar is clearly enough understood even by psychologists to be of much practical value. Furthermore I am afraid that a pre-mature attempt to apply our hypotheses to practical affairs may discredit psychology as a science in somewhat the same way that some aspects of economic theory and political science have been discredited . . .

Ernest R. Hilgard [Stanford University] to Krechevsky, March 30, 1936

I wish to express my interest in the proposal of your committee that psychologists concern themselves in an organized way with regard to matters of public policy . . . I have been teaching industrial psychology for the first time this year, and I am amazed to find that our textbooks are almost unaware of the fact that labor unions exist. As though wage-incentives constitute motivational psychology, in complete disregard of the social realities which labor is facing! The trouble as I see it is that in our deference to physiology and physics we have not taken seriously the social sciences . . .

Merrill Roff [Indiana University] to Krechevsky, April 1, 1936

Your bulletins arrived and were properly dismissed. I have talked enough about the whole thing to become rather a nuisance to some of my associates, and since my status for next year is still indefinite, I am pulling in my horns. The thing works this way: any suggestion that psychologists take a look at the world is at once interpreted as an advocacy of "applied psychology," and dismissed summarily . . .

James McKeen Cattell[9] [Editorial Office, Science magazine] to Krechevsky, April 4, 1936

I have read your memorandum with interest and am in full sympathy with the objects of your committee. I am not convinced that psychology as a science is in a position to supply adequate guidance. There is consequently a danger that we may speak with the authority of science when the value of what we advocate depends not on expert knowledge but on general intelligence.

George H. Estabrooks[10] [Colgate University] to Krechevsky, April 10, 1936

With reference to your mimeographed sheets concerning the participation of psychologists in the contemporary political world, allow me to register my hearty dissent with approximately everything contained therein. If psychologists, as individuals, wish to make themselves politically vocal on any topic – white, red, or pink – it seems to me that is wholly up to them . . . It seems to me that, as psychologists, our duties are pretty clear cut. If any group of us wish to organize as a "Committee for the Propagation of Mild Pinkism", for goodness sakes let us organize ourselves as such and not in camouflage under the protecting skirts of the American Psychological Association.

Robert B. MacLeod [Swarthmore College] to Krechevsky, April 14, 1936

. . . I feel the same way as you do about the present impotence of psychology and psychologists in the contemporary social crisis and I feel very strongly that we ought to do something about it. You can count on me to cooperate in any way possible in the realization of your program. Just at present I feel myself somewhat restricted by the fact that I am not an American citizen and consequently would be chucked out of the country very quickly if I took part in any agitation. That would not interfere, however, with my contributing in any way possible to the organization of the group and to the research which it may undertake . . .

---

[9] Cattell (1860–1944) would have been, perhaps, the most distinguished of the senior psychologists at this time. See Chapter 5.
[10] Clearly George H. Estabrooks (1895–1973) did not lean to the left in his politics. He was an authority on hypnosis and in the 1940s had associations with the FBI involving the subject of mind control.

Epilogue

Although most of the letters received in response to the recruiting letter from Krechevsky and his organizing committee were positive, even among the supporters there were serious questions raised. Would the organization be in danger of promising more than it could deliver? Should the job of social action be the responsibility of the APA instead of some other organization? Would the public take psychology and the social sciences seriously? Is the science of psychology really adequate to the task of curing social ills? Will a focus on psychology in the service of social issues weaken the scientific standing of "pure" psychology? Should SPSSI seek affiliation with the APA or remain independent of it?

At the same time, the supporters felt that the time had come (or was overdue) when psychologists should use their science to speak to social and political concerns. Some believed that SPSSI should work to increase public awareness of psychology, and educate the public about scientific psychology versus the "quackery" of the pseudo-psychologies. One writer asked that SPSSI work to gain legal recognition of the term "psychologist," which would have meant certification (something that would have to happen by law in each of the states). Certification would restrict the use of the term "psychologist" to individuals with certain educational and training experiences as defined by each of the states.[11]

SPSSI proved largely true to its aims as set out in its initial bylaws. In a review of SPSSI's first 20 years, David Krech (formerly Krechevsky) and Dorwin Cartwright (1956) described the principal functions of the society:

(1) encouraging research on social issues; (2) encouraging the application in social practice of scientific knowledge in psychology and the social sciences; (3) giving moral and other support to individuals who take risks by undertaking or interpreting research on social issues; (4) acting as a kind of social conscience for psychologists, encouraging them in actions in which the entire psychological community is likely to be concerned. (p. 471)

They do not mention a focus on expanding the employment opportunities for psychologists. In truth, by 1956, there were few psychologists who had been able to find a job interpreting or applying psychological science to social problems. Thus it would have been difficult to tout that as a success, whereas SPSSI could point to important contributions in each of the four areas listed above. Nowhere would that have been more evident than the job that SPSSI did in assisting the National Association for the Advancement of Colored People's (NAACP) legal

---

[11] Certification (which defines a psychologist) and licensure laws (which define what psychologists can do) began in the 1940s, with Connecticut being the first state to license psychologists in 1945 and Missouri being the last of the 50 states to pass a psychology licensure law in 1977. These laws were achieved largely through the work of the state psychological associations rather than the work of SPSSI.

defense team, headed by Thurgood Marshall, in preparing what became known as the social science brief, filed in the Supreme Court case, *Brown v. Board of Education, Topeka, Kansas.* That historic document, prepared chiefly by three SPSSI members – Kenneth B. Clark,[12] Stuart Cook, and Isidor Chein – argued that psychological and sociological research showed that African-American children were psychologically damaged as a result of legally mandated segregation in the schools and other parts of society. In this case, the NAACP sought to overturn an earlier Supreme Court case, *Plessy v. Ferguson* (1896), which established the "separate but equal" doctrine that led to legal segregation in the schools in 17 states and the District of Columbia. On May 17, 1954, in a unanimous decision, the Supreme Court declared school segregation unconstitutional and, in a footnote to its decision, cited psychological and sociological research (much of it by SPSSI members) that had played an important role in influencing the Court's decision (see Jackson, 2001; Kluger, 1975). To cite psychological evidence in a Supreme Court decision, arguably the most important court decision in the twentieth century, was certainly validation for psychology as a science, and a great reward for an organization that was at the time less than 20 years old. The story of psychologists' involvement in the *Brown v. Board* decision is told in Chapter 16.

SPSSI continues today, seventy years old, as an organization still true to its original commitment to bring the science of psychology to bear on the social problems that confront the world. Divorce, child abuse, pornography, international conflict and war, racism, labor–management conflicts, legal justice, propaganda, social class, children's rights, and sexism are just some of the many subjects that SPSSI members have investigated. The contributions to an understanding of those topics have been substantial.

As for David Krech and Ross Stagner, the organizers of the 1936 meeting out of which SPSSI grew, they did well too. Krech spent most of his career at the University of California-Berkeley, first as a social psychologist and then working in the field of behavioral neuroscience, specifically on the chemistry of the brain important for learning. Ross Stagner, a long-time faculty member at Wayne State University, became a famous industrial-organizational psychologist, strongly identified with the concerns of labor in labor–management relations. Given his lifelong SPSSI membership, perhaps that was to be expected. Both lived long enough to see the many successes of the socially active organization they had founded.

---

[12] Kenneth Bancroft Clark (1914–2005) and his wife, Mamie Phipps Clark (1917–1983), conducted a series of studies in the late 1930s that were used in the segregation court cases in the 1950s, including *Brown v. Board*, to illustrate the negative impact of segregation on black children. Kenneth Clark is the only African American ever elected President of the APA, a post he held in 1971. For information about the Clarks, see Guthrie, 1990; Philogene, 2004; and Chapter 16 of this book.

Suggested Readings

Finison, L. J. (1976). Unemployment, politics, and the history of organized psychology. *American Psychologist, 31,* 747–755.

A history of the founding of two organizations, SPSSI and the Psychologist's League, both of which sought to force the APA to increase employment opportunities for psychologists.

Finison, L. J. (1979). An aspect of the early history of the Society for the Psychological Study of Social Issues: Psychologists and labor. *Journal of the History of the Behavioral Sciences, 15,* 29–37.

Focuses principally on SPSSI's involvement with labor and trade unions during the Great Depression.

Harris, B. (1980). The FBI's files on APA and SPSSI: Description and implications. *American Psychologist, 35,* 1141–1144.

A description of the FBI files on SPSSI, obtained by Harris in the late 1970s through the Freedom of Information Act.

Krech, D., & Cartwright, D. (1956). On SPSSI's first twenty years. *American Psychologist, 11,* 470–473.

A history of the founding and first twenty years of SPSSI whose senior author was the person most responsible for the establishment of the society.

Nicholson, I. (1997). The politics of scientific social reform, 1936–1960: Goodwin Watson and the Society for the Psychological Study of Social Issues. *Journal of the History of the Behavioral Sciences, 33,* 39–60.

Watson helped found SPSSI and was elected its first chair in 1937 after it was a formal organization. This fascinating article describes the transformation of Watson from his 1930s position of advocating that psychologists operate from a specific political framework (i.e., leftist) to calling for psychologists to provide expertise in a value-free way. The transforming event for Watson occurred in World War II when his activities caused him to be accused of affiliating with communists.

Sargent, S. S., & Harris, B. (1986). Academic freedom, civil liberties, and SPSSI. *Journal of Social Issues, 42* (1), 43–67.

A historical treatment of SPSSI's involvement in issues of academic and intellectual freedom from 1936 through 1970. Cases reviewed include those of David Krech, Goodwin Watson, and Gardner Murphy.

Stagner, R. (1986). Reminiscences about the founding of SPSSI. *Journal of Social Issues, 42* (1), 35–42.

A history of the founding of SPSSI by another of the two most significant principals.

Note: For further information on the history of SPSSI see two special issues of the Journal of Social Issues, *1986, 42 (3) and 42 (4).*

B. F. Skinner
(Archives of the History of American
Psychology/University of Akron)

Eve Skinner playing with daughter Deborah
in the baby tender, 1945
(B. F. Skinner Foundation)

B. F. Skinner's Heir Conditioner

B. F. Skinner (1904–1990) was perhaps the most important psychologist of the twentieth century and certainly one of the scientists best known to the American public (Rutherford, 2000). Among his many inventions was a chamber for studying operant behavior, principally in rats and pigeons. Research in those chambers led to a number of important discoveries, especially the ways that various schedules of reinforcement differentially affected behavior. The chamber, of course, became known as the Skinner box. Skinner built other boxes as well, including one he called the "baby tender" which he used for his younger daughter Deborah, born in 1944. Deborah Skinner (Buzan) would grow up known as the "baby reared in a box."

One can imagine the tragic consequences of such child rearing. Some reports said that Deborah was later committed for many years to a mental institution, where she died. Others said that she committed suicide. Still others reported that she brought a lawsuit against her famous father for child abuse. Alas, all of these horrible but interesting outcomes are false, although they are all part of the urban legends of "psychology experiments gone awry." Deborah Skinner Buzan is now in her sixties and has led a happy life and enjoyed success as an artist. But she did spend part of the first few years of her life in a device designed and built by her father. It was referred to by various names, including the baby tender, the heir conditioner, and the aircrib.

Early in his life, based on reading works of the English philosopher, Francis Bacon (1561–1626), Skinner adopted the technological ideal of science, that is, the belief that the aims of science are prediction and control (Smith, 1992). By the time of World War II, Skinner had published his first major book, *The Behavior of Organisms* (1938), a book that described a detailed system of behavioral science, based largely on the principles of operant conditioning. Skinner had always been interested in the application of behavioral principles. The experimental analysis of behavior, as he described his research program, sought to discover the contingencies governing behavior. Such an analysis maximized the prediction and control of behavior. And control of behavior offered a means to help individuals, companies, institutions, and even cultures (Rutherford, 2003; Smith, 1992).

During the war, Skinner carried out a classified program of research, known as Project Pigeon, to use pigeons, placed in the nosecone of a missile, to serve as a guidance system. The research program was a behavioral success but met much resistance from the military and was never employed (Capshew, 1993). Yet it served to show Skinner the practical value of his psychological system. In discussing his research on Project Pigeon, Skinner wrote: "The research that I described in *The Behavior of Organisms* appeared in a new light. It was no longer merely experimental analysis. It had given rise to a technology" (Skinner, 1979, p. 274). It was an epiphany; his system of psychology could be used as a behavioral technology for public good. It would set him on a path to use science in productive ways for practical solutions. In a little more than a decade Skinner developed a missile-guidance system for the US Department of Defense, a better baby crib, teaching machines that taught a variety of subjects (Benjamin, 1988), a new kind of textbook that enhanced learning, a method to teach writing, and an organizational design for a utopian society that used behavioral control based on reinforcement rather than punishment (see Skinner's novel, *Walden Two*, 1948).

B. F. Skinner's faith in his science of psychology led him to apply its principles to his own life as well. When he and his wife, Eve (also called Yvonne), were planning for the birth of their second child, he invented the baby tender, which was both a laborsaving device and an improved crib environment for an infant (Skinner, 1945). The baby tender was an enclosure with a large, safety-glass picture window, intended to replace the crib and bassinet. It offered a temperature- and humidity-controlled environment, and was partially soundproofed. The baby slept naked, except perhaps for a diaper, on a stretched-canvas mattress, covered by a 10-yard-long sheet that was on a roller. The baby tender was designed to reduce many of the laundry needs that are part of infant care. There were no pajamas, nor blankets. Diaper rash was reduced. The risk of infant suffocation in bedclothes was eliminated. In short, the baby tender was designed to provide Deborah with an optimum environment for growth and development. Skinner (1979) described it as follows:

When Debbie came home [from the hospital], she went directly into this comfortable space and began to enjoy its advantages. She wore only a diaper. Completely free to move about, she was soon pushing up, rolling over, and crawling. She breathed warm, moist, filtered air, and her skin was never waterlogged with sweat or urine. Loud noises were muffled (though we could hear her from any part of the house), and a curtain pulled over the window shielded her from bright light when she was sleeping. (p. 276)

The Skinners were most pleased with the success of the baby tender. Skinner decided to go public with his invention and so wrote an article describing it and their experience with Debbie. He sent the article to a popular magazine, *Ladies' Home Journal*. The magazine staff were intrigued by the idea but worried about potential problems with the device, and perhaps by the possibility of lawsuits from unhappy parents who might have bad experiences with the baby tender. Skinner was not only interested in sharing his invention with the public, but he also had some thoughts that it might become a commercially successful venture.

The letters that follow, which are housed in the B. F. Skinner Papers of the Harvard University Archives, tell the story of the baby tender, which became a commercial failure but a child-rearing success. It is a fascinating story that reveals some of the difficulties with behavioral technologies, especially when they are designed to change the age-old traditions of parenting.

Skinner sent his article describing the baby tender to the *Ladies' Home Journal* in April, 1945. He had entitled it "Baby Care Can Be Modernized." After a two-month delay he finally heard from the editors of the magazine.

The Letters

Mary Lea Page (Associate Editor, Ladies' Home Journal*) to B. F. Skinner,*
June 18, 1945

I would have written sooner, but your article on the "baby box" has aroused such controversial interest among the Journal editors, that we are still in the process of heated discussion. I am now writing to ask you first, to send me as quickly as possible, any and all snapshots you mentioned in your letter. We particularly want to see photographs of your child, in her compartments, and out. And second, to ask you to explain and enlarge on some of the questions raised by our staff members, after reading your article.

1. How can the mother hear her child cry in the "box" if she is in another part of the house, or asleep at night in a distant room? Have you installed some sort of wall microphone inside the compartment with an outside loud speaker?
2. Your 10-yard continuous roller sheet interested us, but brought up several protests. What prevents that soiled part of the sheet, waiting in the wire hamper,

from exuding an unpleasant odor into the outside room? Suppose due to illness, the child should vomit on his sheet, or having a bowel disorder, stain the sheet badly. (It happens with the best of diapers.) Must the washing of the roller sheet wait a *week* – mainly because of its ungainly size?

3.   Granted that the canvas "mattress" is always dry, or in a *process* of drying, what prevents it from all too quickly becoming strong smelling? Do you use rubber sheets at all?

4.   As I understand it, you have installed a small electric unit which produces air-conditioning, warmth, and enough moisture in the "box" to insure correct, healthy humidity. This unit, I assume, plugs into a room outlet. What would happen, therefore, if the electric current were to be cut off during the night (due to a storm). Wouldn't the child be exposed to rather severe suffering from lack of air, warmth, etc.? What precautions did you take to insure you and your wife's peace of mind should this event ever happen?

You also say that due to air-filtering, your baby only needs one "all-over" bath a week. Don't you believe that a baby's daily bath is necessary, not only for the normal hygienic reasons, but because the gentle soapings and washings, the towel pattings and powderings help to stimulate the child's skin and keep him firm and rosy? To say nothing of the fun for the mother and child?

Quick answers to the above – plus the snapshots – will add greatly to our final editorial decision, and I await both with tremendous enthusiasm. Don't keep me in suspense?

Skinner to Mary Lea Page, June 21, 1945

Herewith some photos of the baby-care apparatus. They are the best I have been able to get with limited equipment and in view of the film shortage.[1] They will give you a rough idea, at least, of the construction and appearance. I am sure that both models[2] would be quite "photogenic" in the hands of a good photographer with proper equipment . . .

As to the questions raised by your staff:

(1) *How can the mother hear her baby?* The apparatus is only partially sound-proofed. With the nursery door open we can hear the baby about as clearly as if she were in an ordinary crib with the nursery door closed. In our house, which is not small, we can hear her with the nursery door open in any part of the house well enough to feel perfectly comfortable about her. If it were desirable to hear very clearly, the window could be left partly open, with the opening covered by a cloth (say, if the baby were sick). There are microphone sets on the market, I understand,

---

[1]   Evidently one of the many kinds of shortages Americans experienced during World War II.
[2]   The Skinners had two baby tenders. The larger one was where Debbie slept; the smaller one Skinner referred to as portable and could be moved from room to room.

for the purpose of connecting distant nurseries with the parents' bedrooms. However, if the apparatus were to be redesigned to permit hearing the baby especially clearly, the simplest thing would be to have a panel of the soundproofing made removable, leaving only a thin sound-transmitting wall. The portable model, of which photos are enclosed, is not at all soundproof. The baby can be heard practically as clearly as in a crib. The soundproofing has enough advantages from the baby's point of view to make it worthwhile.

(2) *Doesn't the discharged sheet have an unpleasant odor?* Not in our experience. There is no noticeable odor in our nursery. Visitors frequently comment on the fact. The reason seems to be that dry urine does not give off a strong odor. Our practice has been to wipe up any traces of bowel movements before moving the sheet along. The only odor comes from our diaper storage can, and we have used a wick-evaporated deodorant from time to time for that. In case of bad soiling, the sheet could be moved out far enough to permit dipping the soiled section into a pan of water for sufficient cleaning, though we have never needed to do this. In a serious emergency the whole sheet could be changed. (We have three sheets to allow a spare for emergencies or delayed laundry.) . . .

(3) *Doesn't the canvas mattress acquire an odor?* Again, not in our experience. The canvas is constantly bathed in warm air, and there is little or no chance for the bacterial action which makes urine smell. The canvas is stretched on a removable frame, and we have a spare to permit cleaning when necessary (every two or more weeks). The canvas could, therefore, be changed in the case of vomiting. Or, if the child were known to be likely to vomit, a rubber sheet could be used. We have never used one, however, and have made rather a point of having no loose cloth in the apparatus, in which the baby might become entangled . . .

(4) *What happens if the current fails?* We have an alarm, operated on dry-cell batteries, which goes off if the temperature deviates more than two degrees from the proper setting. This is wholly independent of the power supply and would tell us of trouble long before the baby had experienced any extreme condition . . . As to the effect of only a weekly bath on the baby's skin, I think we can claim a considerable advantage. The baby suffers from having its own perspiration and urine bound against its skin by clothing. The skin may become pale and "water-logged." Moreover, clothing robs the skin of the normal stimulation which results from moving about the crib. Artificial stimulation at bath time may be necessary when the usual clothing and bedding are used, but not in our apparatus. From the very first the fine condition of our baby's skin attracted attention. The skin is soft, but not moist. It is rubbed gently and naturally throughout the day by the under sheet as she moves about. Much of the patting which is advised at bath time is to make up for the lack of normal exercise of the skin circulation, which is due to clothing . . .

I don't know what to do about your added remark about the bath: "To say nothing about the fun for the mother and child." Contrary to what one may expect from a psychologist, we have had a lot of fun with our baby, more perhaps than we could have had if we had been burdened down by unnecessary chores. We have always played with her when we felt like it, which was often. As for the baby, she certainly had more than her share of fun. The freedom from clothing and blankets has provided much of it. Her bath is fun, too, though probably not as much as the usual baby's because the contrast is not so great. The advice of the child-specialist to "allow the baby to exercise its legs for a few minutes at bath time" shows what I mean. Our baby exercises her legs all day long. (My wife insists that I tell you that we do bathe our baby twice a week, though once a week is enough.)

The fact that our baby is not only in perfect physical condition but keenly interested in life and blissfully happy is our final answer to the charge that we are somehow neglecting her . . .

I can see that my article has not been clear on these points, but it should not be difficult to anticipate these objections with slight changes in the text. Would you like to have me send suitable addenda? Or, if you like, have one of your staff make the changes . . .

The controversy among the members of the Journal staff is, I suspect, a fair sample of the reader reaction. It would not all be favorable, but it would be energetic. If our local experience is any guide, the discussion would go on for a long time.

Note: Apparently satisfied with Skinner's answers, the Ladies' Home Journal *decided to publish his article. They sent a photographer to shoot pictures for the article, which appeared in their October, 1945 issue. The questions that Page asked Skinner and his answers were included as an addendum to the article. The magazine did not use Skinner's title, which, as noted earlier, was "Baby Care Can Be Modernized." Instead, the* Journal *entitled it "Baby in a Box." Needless to say, Skinner was not pleased with that. But perhaps he should have seen it coming, given the frequent references to his baby tender as a "box" in Page's letter to him. The article certainly attracted widespread interest. Stories, based on the* Journal *article, were also published in the leading magazines of the day:* Time *magazine,* Life *magazine, and* The New Yorker. *Skinner received many letters resulting from the various articles, most of them positive, and many of them asking for the plans to build a baby tender. But not all reactions were positive.*

Anonymous to District Attorney, Bloomington, Indiana (copy was sent to Skinner, date unknown)

This professor who thinks he can rear his little child by depriving her of social life, sun and fresh air. Can't you people of the law do something about this? These crack-pot scientists. They say they will probably keep her caged in this box until she is three. If they want to rear her to be so healthy, come down to California. Little children are happy here, out in the sunshine, playing in yards with their dogs and other children and enjoying the flare for living. If I lived in the same town as these people I would be tempted to tell them what I thought of them. Caging this baby up like an animal just to relieve the Mother of a little more work. (Skinner, 1979, p. 305)

Marcelene Cox to Bruce Gould[3] *(Co-editor of* Ladies' Home Journal*),*
March 1946 issue, p. 14

Coming right on top of the atomic bomb, the artificial baby tender is almost too much for me to take.

The sense of touch is the most elemental form of communication. The satisfaction of loving arms around him and the consistent prompt response to a baby's needs do more for his emotional security than books, lectures, psychiatrists and preachers can do later on.

Of course the baby tender would be all right for that small minority who neglect their children anyway, or for use in the poorest homes where babies often suffer the affliction of vermin. But I doubt these homes could afford it.

I wonder to what advantage Mrs. Skinner placed the time she saved!

Note: Mrs. Skinner likely would have answered: "I use the time saved from laundry and *other chores to spend more time holding and playing with my baby!"*

From late 1945 after the article appeared in the Journal, *and through 1948 when a report of it had appeared in other popular magazines, Skinner received well over 100 inquiries from expectant parents wanting to buy or build a baby tender. Skinner sent each of them a set of plans and estimated that it could be built for around $50 worth of materials. He also got many letters from parents thanking him for the invention.*

Skinner to Bruce Gould, Ladies' Home Journal. *December, 1946, p. 15*

You may be interested to know that between 75 and 100 apparatuses ("Baby in a Box") are now in course of construction by your readers. I have been sending out mimeographed material giving details of the apparatus I built to those who asked for them. How many of these will be actually completed I cannot say, but the letters still coming in certainly indicate a desperate need for some such device.

Alice Saunders to Skinner, c.1948 (her husband had built their baby tender)

"Dr. Skinner, you certainly have taken the drudgery out of being a mama – to say nothing of making the baby's life so much healthier and pleasanter. It's really

---

[3]   Bruce Gould and his wife, Beatrice Gould, were co-editors of the *Ladies' Home Journal* from 1935 to 1967.

wonderful. Tommy is so well and happy and good. It is a real pleasure to care for him . . ."

Note: *Approximately two weeks after the article appeared in the* Journal, *Skinner received a letter from J. Weston Judd, a Cleveland businessman, asking about commercial possibilities for the baby tender.*

J. Weston Judd to Skinner, around the beginning of October, 1945

. . . I apologize for calling it a crib, which of course does not do it justice – may I suggest "Heir Conditioner."

Skinner to J. Weston Judd, October 15, 1945

Thank you for your enjoyable letter . . . My wife and I especially appreciated your suggestion of "Heir conditioning". We had tried to cook up something more interesting than Baby Tender, but with no better results than "Baby-nook" and "Kiddy Korner", which are pretty bad.

Your offer to make up a few to test the market appeals to me. Let me review quite frankly the history of that aspect of the problem. The idea has been inspected by two patent lawyers who are agreed in thinking that basic patents are out of the question. The tender is merely an air-conditioned room no matter what its special size. Some of the features (e.g., a continuous locking sheet) might be covered, but can be "designed around" by a competitor. Hence I have very little to see by way of rights and a manufacturer could hardly expect protection in return for developing the field.

However, patent protection is not the only thing. A registered trademark and an early appearance in the field could do a lot. Also new features and procedures are sure to appear in the course of further research, so that a given model could be kept out in front in public favor. My article did not cover all of the advantages nor all of my plans for the future.

I am interested in seeing a commercial model put on the market for several reasons: (1) I believe it is a very great advance in child care which not only emancipates the young wife but may prove to yield stronger and happier young citizens. (2) I want to get a number of such apparatuses for future research . . . I have had many offers from intelligent young couples to supply me with detailed records in return for the use of such an apparatus. (3) If there is any money to be made from the idea, I am not averse to getting a reasonable share of it.

I have had requests to sell stock and so on, but have not yet interested a reliable company in going into production. I am not a businessman and have no time to give to promotion, but there is definitely a big opportunity here for someone with initiative and vision. The response to the article has been almost unanimously favorable, and it has revealed not only a general acceptance of the scheme but a desperate need . . .

Would you please let me know about the action you propose. Have you an organization which could handle either the manufacture or distribution of such a device? . . .

What I have to offer a manufacturer is this. I would – 1. Assign whatever rights I have in connection with special features (now protected by "evidence of conception"). 2. Help to work out a good commercial model . . . 3. Supervise research and tests in actual homes, both for purposes of improving the product and establishing it in a position of prestige in the profession. 4. Turn over certain improvements and designs for related devices already worked out or to be worked out in the future. 5. Arrange a direct tie-in with the extensive publicity already obtained and to be obtained from future publications in this field.

In return for this I would hope to get support for research (mainly the use of a number of the apparatuses) and a reasonable share in the profits of the whole venture . . .

J. Weston Judd to Skinner, October 19, 1945

Thank you for your very welcome letter. Glad you liked "Heir Conditioner," a man who spends so much of his time dealing in conditioned reflexes should have thought of that right away. At any rate it seems to be a "natural" as a commercial name. I trust that it soon reaches the household word category.

I am very much interested in your offer. My associates and I have discussed it at some length and are unanimously agreed on the following rough plan for manufacturing and selling the "Heir Conditioner".

1. Form a company to be known as "The Heir Conditioner Company" which would be the sole proprietor of all copyrights, trade marks, patents, etc.

2. Make a royalty arrangement with you providing for quarterly payment to you of a percentage of the manufacturer's selling price on all units sold. The books would, of course, be open to your inspections at any time. Providing also for a fixed number of the first model to be delivered to you . . . and one of each succeeding model to be delivered to you prior to its release to the public . . .

Now about us – we have a small shop set up primarily to make displays and display fixtures. We have all the power woodworking tools, spraying and finishing room equipment necessary to produce the "Heir Conditioner" in lots of fifty at a time . . .

As a first step I would like to send out a mailing illustrating and describing our first model and quoting a price . . . If the price can be kept close to one hundred dollars f.o.b. Cleveland a sufficient number of orders to provide an encouraging beginning is to be expected . . .

If you find this outline reasonable, I would like to run down to Bloomington,[4] as soon as possible, to discuss it in detail. Or perhaps you would prefer to come here in order to see our shop etc. . .

My wife insists that we produce one, at least, immediately. I hope that there prove to be many more mothers of a like mind.

Skinner to J. Weston Judd, October 23, 1945

There are several points which I should like to talk over before setting any exact figure as to royalties or the number of Heir Conditioners to be supplied for research, but I am quite sure we can reach a satisfactory arrangement. Why don't you come down to Bloomington as soon as convenient? . . . We have only a davenport as a guest room, but you are welcome to it.

Note: *Evidently Judd went to Bloomington in November. Skinner signed an agreement with him and even put up $500 for starting production. But things did not go well in the dealings with Mr Judd.*

Skinner to J. Weston Judd, March 23, 1946

I have been thinking over the Heir Conditioner situation and have decided to send you a statement of my present feeling in the hope that we can then make better use of our time next Sunday in working out a satisfactory arrangement. Frankly I am quite disappointed with the way things have been going, and I think you are, too. I suspect that you may have been alibing yourself with the story of the shortage of supplies but that in reality there are other reasons why more progress has not been made. Perhaps the real reasons are obscure to yourself, although I feel that you have not been wholly fair in keeping me informed of the actual situation.

Skinner to J. Weston Judd, April 14, 1946

. . . I have lost a lot of sleep trying to see a way out of this mess. I can't see that any progress has been made during the past six months. On the contrary a lot of time, goodwill, and publicity have been lost . . .

---

[4] Skinner was on the faculty of the University of Minnesota when Debbie was born, but in the summer of 1945 the family moved to Bloomington, Indiana where Skinner was chair of the psychology department at Indiana University.

Note: As Skinner received inquiries from expectant parents wanting a baby tender, he forwarded their letters to Judd. Evidently Judd contacted them and, in at least some cases, got advance payments from them for their Heir Conditioners. Only a few of the devices were built, and they had significant engineering problems. Skinner was frustrated that he had not seen the design plans in advance. Skinner was receiving letters from angry parents-to-be, wondering where their Heir Conditioners were and indicating that they could not get a reply from Judd. Toward the end of April, 1946, Skinner received a call from one of Judd's associates indicating that Judd had disappeared. Skinner went to Cleveland immediately. He visited the shop that was so small no more than five Heir Conditioners could have been built at once, much less fifty. Many would-be customers were out the money they had already paid. Skinner was probably not legally responsible, but he had recommended many of the customers to Judd and thus felt responsible. He made restitution where possible. And, of course his partnership with Judd was ended.

Skinner to Thomas H. Vaughn, no date but likely May, 1946
(Vaughn had paid $125 in advance on an Heir Conditioner from Judd)

I have just returned from Cleveland where I found the affairs of the Heir Conditioner people unbelievably involved. Judd has proved to be completely incompetent and dishonest and has left his family for parts unknown . . . You can imagine the spot this leaves me in. I have got to start all over again to get a company interested in the device commercially, and I am morally bound to see that the people who advanced Judd money get it back or get an Heir Conditioner, since they undoubtedly relied on my recommendation . . .

Note: Skinner did not lose faith in the potential for his invention. He explored several other possible commercial manufacturers over the next ten years but with no success. Then in 1956 he was contacted by John Gray, an engineer who in 1947 had built a baby tender for his own son which was described in a brief article that year in Life magazine. Based on his own experience with his son, Gray was very optimistic about the device, and in 1957 he formed a corporation based on Long Island, entitled the Aircrib Corporation. The Heir Conditioner had a new name and a new life. Over the next ten years, Gray worked closely with Skinner on the design and marketing of the aircrib. They were costly units, about $335 to $385 over the decade that they were manufactured. It is not known how many aircribs were manufactured. Daniel Bjork (1993), one of Skinner's biographers, estimated the number at 1,000, but that number seems excessive, given other records. John Gray died in 1967, and apparently his company died with him. Another company also manufactured aircribs in the 1960s but that company seemed even less successful than the Aircrib Corporation.

Occasionally an article would appear in a newspaper or magazine about the aircrib, always describing the positive experiences of the parents and the seeming good health of their babies. But such testimonials did not stop the mail of those who felt outrage toward a device they did not understand and the man who invented it.

Senior English Class (Franklin High School, Pennsylvania)
to B. F. Skinner, March 5, 1966

What *in the world* do you think you are doing? We can not understand how you, as a psychologist, can eliminate the human aspects of raising a child by use of The Skinner Box. Objectively, we can understand how parents can be saved time, even needless backache, when a child is brought up in his loving "four walls." However, wouldn't it be better to sell a few more boxes of Ben-Gay[5] than to have a society made up of *Mother-less* citizens?

As long as you have gone this far, we wonder if you have ever considered inventing specialized baby boxes to make babies artistic, boxes for social climbing babies – just to name a few possibilities . . .

In closing, we must congratulate you. By creating this "revolutionary product," you have shown that you are ready to inaugurate a society composed of box-raised vegatables (sic) similar to the *Brave New World* of Aldous Huxley.

More power to you, Mustopha (sic)Mond![6]

Skinner to Franklin H.S. Senior English Class, March 11, 1966

You couldn't be farther from the facts. The so-called air-crib makes it so much easier for parents and siblings to love babies and display affection toward them. If you could see one in use, you would know what I mean. I am not interested in a Brave New World. If you want to see what I do believe, read my novel, Walden Two, which is available in paperback.

I am glad that you felt like writing as you did. I hope that when you find out the facts you will feel just as strongly about them in the other direction.

Epilogue

The baby tender, a.k.a. heir conditioner and aircrib, was never the success that Skinner hoped it would be, nor the success that John Gray hoped for when he said that he dreamed of a day when half of the babies in America would be raised in aircribs (Box-bred babies, 1963). There is no doubt that Skinner would have liked to have made some money from the baby tender, but that was not his principal motive. He was a scientist, and he enjoyed creating things that changed behavior for the better. Indeed, Skinner saw it as a moral imperative that scientists use their knowledge to improve the world (Skinner, 1983). In 1945 he had written to Charles A. Aldrich (1888–1949), a famous pediatrician at the Mayo Clinic:

---

[5]   *Ben-Gay* is an over-the-counter ointment sold for the treatment of muscle aches.
[6]   Mustapha Mond was a character in Huxley's 1932 novel, *Brave New World*. He was the world controller of western Europe and a scientist who advocated for behavioral conditioning and the lack of personal freedoms.

... I must confess also to an ulterior motive. If, as many people have claimed, the first year [of life] is extraordinarily important in the determination of character and personality, then by all means let us control the conditions of that year as far as possible in order to discover the important variables ... it should be possible to conduct experiments in private homes but with a minimum of interference from the household routine and to begin to accumulate some significant data from the subsequent history of the children involved. (Skinner to Aldrich, no date but early 1945)

Yet Skinner never conducted an experimental program of research that would have shown the advantages or disadvantages of the baby tender. Someone at the US Bureau of the Census offered to inform Skinner about the births of twins, assuming that the parents might be willing to raise one child in a standard crib and the other in a baby tender. Perhaps it was the ethics of such research that prevented him from carrying out those studies. He wrote:

Suppose a significant difference appeared in the health or well-being of one child? Suppose one twin was sleeping better, having fewer colds, growing faster, or simply being happier? How long could parents be asked not to give the other twin the same treatment? (Skinner, 1979, pp. 291–292)

Although Skinner never had anything more than anecdotal data to support his claims of the advantages of the baby tender over the standard crib, there were many hundreds of "personal experiments" adding to the anecdotal database and all seem to have had a favorable outcome.

Skinner's daughter Debbie spent part of the first two years of her life in a baby tender. Some friends of the Skinners built their own baby tenders, as did many parents who wrote to Skinner for the plans. Skinner's older daughter, Julie Skinner Vargas, whose doctoral degree was in educational research, used the baby tender for her two children. These devices were passed down from generation to generation and from friends to friends, creating a network of parents using Skinner's "baby box." Three separate surveys of such users, one unpublished in the Harvard Archives and two published ones (Benjamin & Nielsen-Gammon, 1999; Epstein & Bailey, 1995) contacted as many users as could be identified and every one of the respondents reported a positive experience with the device.

Deborah Skinner Buzan commented recently, at age 60, on a London newspaper article that had once more dredged up the rumors of her "horrible childhood" and subsequent insanity. She wrote:

My early childhood, it's true, was certainly unusual – but I was far from unloved. I was a much cuddled baby. Call it what you will, the "aircrib", "baby box", "heir conditioner" (not my father's term) was a wonderful alternative to the cage-like cot ... I was very happy, too, though I must report at this stage that I remember nothing of those first two and a half years. I am told that I never once objected to being put back inside . . . I loved my father dearly. He was fantastically devoted and affectionate . . . The effect on me? Who knows? I was a remarkably healthy child, and after the first few months of life only cried when injured or inoculated. I didn't have a cold until I was six. I've enjoyed good health since then, too, though that may be my genes. Frankly I'm surprised the contraption never took off. (Buzan, 2004, pp. 2–3)

Obviously the baby tender did not make it into half of American homes. And given the very high levels of satisfaction from parents who used the device, it seems reasonable to ask why. Why has it not replaced the traditional crib? Based on letters in the Skinner Papers at Harvard and some other records, it appears that the baby tender was perceived as a technology of displacement. It was viewed as a device that interfered with the usual modes of parental–infant contact. That is, the device was seen as displacing the parent from the child. That does not appear to be the reality at all for users of the baby tender, but it does seem to be the perception. Perhaps its worst feature was that it was an enclosure. The crib is as well, but with bars and lots of open spaces; somehow those are seen as less of a problem psychologically than the glass walls of the baby tender. It was seen as a box, and humans are not supposed to be put into boxes except at the end of life.

Whatever the reasons for the commercial failure of the baby tender, given the incredible advances in technology in the last decade, one wonders if the crib is really the best we can invent for babies. Maybe a better baby tender is just around the corner.

Suggested Readings

Benjamin, L. T., Jr., & Nielsen-Gammon, E. (1999). B. F. Skinner and psychotechnology: The case of the heir conditioner. *Review of General Psychology, 3*, 155–167.
   A history of the baby tender based largely on the B. F. Skinner Papers at the Harvard University Archives and the Cedric Larson Papers at the Archives of the History of American Psychology at the University of Akron, as well as survey data from aircrib users.
Bjork, D. W. (1993). *B. F. Skinner: A life.* New York: Basic Books.
   The most readable of several biographies of B. F. Skinner.
Capshew, J. H. (1993). Engineering behavior: Project Pigeon, World War II, and the conditioning of B. F. Skinner. *Technology and Culture, 34*, 835–857.
   A fascinating account of Skinner's work for the US government in training pigeons to guide a missile to its target.
Coleman, S. R. (1982). B. F. Skinner: Systematic iconoclast. *The Gamut,* Spring/Summer, pp. 53–75.
   An excellent treatment of the complexity of Skinner as a person and the place of his science in psychology.
Skinner, B. F. (1938). *The behavior of organisms.* New York: Appleton.
   Although pieces of his system of behavior had appeared in articles in the 1930s, this book marked the first comprehensive treatment of what would be the most radical of the various behaviorisms.

Skinner, B. F. (1945). Baby in a box. *Ladies' Home Journal*, October, pp. 30–31, 135–136, 138.
Skinner's original account of the rearing of daughter Debbie in the famous baby box. Also see his article in the March 1979 issue of *Psychology Today* (pp. 28–40), entitled "My experience with the baby-tender."

Skinner, B. F. (1948). *Walden two*. New York: Macmillan.
Skinner's novel about a utopian community founded on behavioral principles.

Skinner, B. F. (1971). *Beyond freedom and dignity*. New York: Alfred A. Knopf.
This book topped the *New York Times* bestseller list for a while. It argues that freedom is an illusion, that control (mostly haphazard) is a fact of life, and that cultures should structure contingencies (use control) to create desirable outcomes. Although many nonreaders of this book labeled Skinner a fascist, his humanitarian goals were recognized by the American Humanist Association which gave him its Humanist of the Year Award in 1972.

Skinner, B. F. (1976, 1979, 1983). [autobiography in 3 vols.]. *Particulars of my life* (part I), *The shaping of a behaviorist* (part II), *A matter of consequences* (part III). New York: Alfred A. Knopf.
A wonderfully readable autobiography that describes how Skinner shaped his behavioral theories and how they shaped him. The first volume, which covers Skinner's life through his undergraduate days at Hamilton College, is especially good reading.

CHAPTER

Mamie and Kenneth B. Clark
(Library of Congress)

Kenneth B. Clark and the *Brown v. Board* Decision

At the turn of the twentieth century, psychologists' views on African Americans evidenced the racial prejudice that was all too common in the dominant white population. Psychologist R. M. Bache (1895) had tested reaction times in white and African-American subjects, expecting to find that whites' reactions were faster. When his results showed the opposite pattern, he maintained his view of white superiority by arguing that reaction time was largely a reflexive response, and that one would expect the more "primitive brains" of African Americans to do better in such tasks, whereas whites, with brains that he argued were more contemplative and less reflexive, would perform better in more complex tasks. In an article in *Psychological Bulletin* reviewing the "findings" on African Americans, psychologist Frank Bruner (1912) wrote that

> the mental qualities of the Negro [may be summarized] as: lacking in filial affection; strong migratory instincts and tendencies; little sense of veneration, integrity, or honor; shiftless, indolent, untidy, improvident, extravagant, lazy, untruthful, lacking in persistence and initiative, and unwilling to work

continuously at details. Indeed, experience with the Negro in class rooms indicates that it is impossible to get the child to do anything with continued accuracy . . . (pp. 387–388)

With such prejudicial beliefs masquerading as facts, 17 states and the District of Columbia mandated segregated schools for the two races, that is, separate schools for blacks and for whites. School segregation had been challenged several times in the nineteenth century in the decades following the American Civil War, leading eventually to the "separate but equal" doctrine of the Supreme Court based on a case known as *Plessy v. Ferguson* (1896), a case challenging a Louisiana state law that required railroads to provide separate cars for white and black passengers. This ruling was interpreted more broadly by many states to argue that racially separate schools were permitted under the law, so long as the schools were equivalent in the educational opportunities they offered. Although the schools were separate, they were never equal, especially in terms of the quality of the physical facilities, teacher salaries, amount spent per pupil, and so forth. Almost 60 years would pass before the separate but equal doctrine would be declared unconstitutional.

Kenneth Bancroft Clark (1914–2005) was born in Panama Canal Zone. He attended Howard University, an African-American college in Washington, DC, as an undergraduate, where he studied under Francis Cecil Sumner (1895–1954), the first African American to earn a doctorate in psychology, receiving his degree from G. Stanley Hall at Clark University in 1920 (see Guthrie, 2000). Clark earned his bachelor's degree at Howard in psychology in 1935 and went to Columbia University to work with Otto Klineberg. Clark had met Klineberg when he came to Howard to give a talk. Clark was taken with his statements about racial differences and intelligence. Against a dominant belief in the intellectual inferiority of African Americans, Klineberg had published a book in 1935 entitled *Race Differences*, which concluded that "there is no adequate proof of fundamental race differences in mentality, and that those differences which are found are in all probability due to culture and the social environment" (p. vii). Clark finished his PhD with Klineberg in 1940 and took a faculty position at City College in New York City.

Kenneth Clark's early research involved a series of studies investigating self-esteem and racial attitudes in black children. The idea for the studies came from his wife, Mamie Phipps Clark (1917–1983), whom he had met at Howard. She was doing research on racial attitudes in young black children in segregated versus integrated schools using a series of judgment tasks involving dolls of differing skin colors. The Clarks teamed up to publish three studies in 1939 and 1940, suggesting detrimental effects of segregation on black children. Mamie Phipps Clark would also go to Columbia University, earning her PhD there in psychology in 1943. She would spend most of her professional life as director of the Northside Center for Child Development in Harlem, a center that provided a considerable array of psychological, medical, educational, and social services for African Americans (Guthrie, 1990; Lal, 2002; Markowitz & Rosner, 1996).

Kenneth Clark continued writing on the subject of racial prejudice, and in 1950 he prepared a paper for the Midcentury White House Conference on Children and Youth. The report was entitled "The effects of prejudice and discrimination on personality development." That paper and the earlier articles he published with his wife were about to garner a level of attention he never imagined. Lawyers for the National Association for the Advancement of Colored People (NAACP) were preparing a legal challenge to school desegregation when they discovered the work of the Clarks. Kenneth Clark has described his initial meeting with Robert Carter, a member of the NAACP legal team in February, 1951:

> So Bob Carter and I met for the first time. He told me the problem they faced; they had to prove to the Court that segregation, in itself, damaged the personality of the Negro child. They had come upon this question themselves. They had formulated their legal approach and the only thing they didn't know was whether they would get any support for it from the psychologists. They thought of Klineberg as the person who had done outstanding work in racial differences and he had worked with them before, giving testimony on the fact that there are no inherent racial differences. So they went back to Otto and he said your man is Kenneth Clark. I wasn't sure but I told Bob I would give him the manuscript to read [the 1950 White House Conference paper], and if he felt it did fit into their legal structure then psychologists could help him. He took the manuscript and read it and called me about a week later, all excited. I'll never forget his words. He said, "This couldn't be better if it had been done for us." (Clark, n.d., pp. 132–133)

So Clark began to work with the NAACP legal team, headed by Thurgood Marshall (1908–1983), later appointed to the Supreme Court by President Lyndon Johnson. Marshall and Carter asked for Clark's help immediately by testifying in a case in Clarendon County, South Carolina (*Briggs v. Elliott*) in May, 1951. Clark did so, taking to court his black and white dolls and explaining how they had been used in the studies that he and his wife had conducted. After South Carolina, he testified in school desegregation cases in Delaware and Virginia, thus participating in three of the four lower court cases that would be joined together at the Supreme Court as *Brown v. Board of Education*.

The NAACP wanted to submit a summary of social science research on the damaging effects of segregation as an appendix to the legal brief it had filed. The effort was coordinated through the Society for the Psychological Study of Social Issues (SPSSI; see Chapter 14). Three psychologists were selected to write the appendix: Kenneth Clark, Isidor Chein, and Stuart Cook. It was printed in late September, 1952, entitled "The effects of segregation and the consequences of desegregation – A social science statement," and was submitted to the Supreme Court as part of the NAACP's legal brief (see Appendix to Appellants' Briefs, 1975). Nearly two years after the Court first agreed to hear the cases, it finally rendered its decision on May 17, 1954. Chief Justice Earl Warren read aloud the unanimous decision, which concluded that

Segregation of White and colored children in public school has a detrimental effect upon the colored children. The impact is greater when it has the sanction of the law, for the policy of separating the race is usually interpreted as denoting the inferiority of the Negro group. A sense of inferiority affects the motivation of the child to learn. Segregation with the sanction of law, therefore, has a tendency to retard the educational and mental development of Negro children and to deprive them of some of the benefits they would receive in a racially integrated school system. Whatever may have been the extent of psychological knowledge at the time of *Plessy v. Ferguson*, this finding is amply supported by modern authority. Any language in *Plessy v. Ferguson* contrary to this finding is rejected. We conclude that in the field of public education, the doctrine of "separate but equal" has no place. Separate educational facilities are inherently unequal. Therefore, we hold that the plaintiffs and others similarly situated for whom the actions have been brought are, by reason of the segregation complained of, deprived of the equal protection of the laws guaranteed by the Fourteenth Amendment (quoted in Kluger, 1975, p. 782)

The "modern authority" of "psychological knowledge" was given in footnote 11 of the Court's decision. The footnote lists seven social science publications, including works by Isidor Chein and sociologist Gunnar Myrdal. But the initial reference, the first work cited in the list, was Kenneth Clark's 1950 White House Conference paper. Some sources have suggested that its place at the top of the list was the Court's way of acknowledging Clark's important role in the decision (see Kluger, 1975).

Thus research conducted by two graduate students, husband and wife, was discussed by the highest court in the land in what may be the most important legal case of the twentieth century, and the research proved to be important in shaping the Court's decision. What graduate student would ever dream that her or his master's thesis or doctoral dissertation would have that kind of impact? Were someone to admit to such a fantasy we would be dismayed by the bravado. But that is what happened to the Clarks. Their work would ultimately change the course of American history. That story is told, in part, in the letters that follow, which are part of the Kenneth B. Clark Papers in the Manuscripts Division of the Library of Congress, Washington, DC. The letters begin with Kenneth Clark answering some questions about the research that he and Mamie Clark had conducted.

The Letters

Kenneth B. Clark to William Delano [Yale Law Journal], *February 19, 1952*

It is not easy to answer your questions concerning the basic differences in personality adjustment found among Negro children in southern segregated schools, compared with Negro children in northern nonsegregated schools. Many problems arise which require not only an examination of the available results, but also an analysis of the social psychological significance of those results.

It is my personal belief that children in racially segregated schools are more seriously damaged in the area of self-esteem than are Negro children in racially mixed schools. I believe this in spite of the fact that northern children in unsegregated schools seem to be more overtly disturbed about racial status and self-identifications. My explanation for this seeming contradiction is stated below.

The comparison of behavior of the northern and southern children in reference to racial self-identification raises some interesting questions concerning the forms of adjustment which Negroes are able to make to their racial status. The investigation showed that only the northern children gave overt indications of personality disturbances when confronted with the conflict of identifying with a brown doll which they had previously stereotyped negatively. No southern child refused to continue the experiment at this stage or broke down in tears. Those southern children who gave any overt responses, either laughed or tried to appear casual about the whole question. Those few children who, when asked to identify themselves with one of the dolls and identified themselves with the brown doll with the remark "Well it is a nigger and I am a nigger", were southern children.

Superficially, this southern pattern of reaction to this conflict would seem to be less disturbing personally and an indication of a better adjustment to racial status than that found among northern children. This interpretation, however, is probably inaccurate. It may well be that the pattern among the southern children is an indication of their acceptance of their inferior status as a norm. The rigid patterns of segregation in all aspects of life, the fact of segregated schools characteristic of the South, may be responsible for the ability of southern children to accept their inferiority status as a matter of fact. Their apparent adjustment is an adjustment to a social pathology which in any fundamental approach to personality cannot be considered a basically healthy form of personality function.

Additional support to this interpretation is obtained by the more recent results from interviewing children between 12 and 17 in Clarendon County, South Carolina. All of these children were clearly aware of the fact that the Negro schools were woefully inferior to the white schools. They stated the fact of this inferiority in rather calm terms; almost invariably they interpreted this inferiority as an indication of things as they are. The impression which these young people give is that they passively and fatalistically accept their inferior status as practically an act of God . . .

Clark to William Delano, March 13, 1952

. . . As soon as I complete this book,[1] I would like to get down to the serious business of planning and directing the definitive study on this problem of the effects of prejudice and segregation on the personality of children. I hope that by then the

---

[1]   The book he refers to probably is *Prejudice and Your Child*, which was published in 1955 by Beacon Press.

Supreme Court would have handed down a decision in our favor so that I would be able to do this research without practical implications hanging over my head. If they hand down a decision against us, it will be even more important to do this work even if we cannot afford the luxury of complete freedom from a practical pleasure.

Robert L. Carter [Assistant Counsel, NAACP] to Clark, June 11, 1952

I thought you might be interested in reading this article. I don't think it does too good a job, but it does point up the basic weaknesses in available data concerning adverse effects of segregated education. It would be helpful to have proved data showing that segregated education as an isolated factor does specific harm to Negro children, and such a study may become essential dependent upon the outcome of the cases now in the Supreme Court.

As you undoubtedly know, the Supreme Court has decided to hear argument in both the Clarendon County, South Carolina and Topeka, Kansas cases. The cases will be set for argument after the court reconvenes in October. We will have to prepare the brief this summer and may have to call upon you for help . . .

Note: *The social science brief was prepared by Clark, Chein, and Cook, as noted above. In seeking signatures of endorsement for the brief, the following letter was mailed in September, 1952 to a number of prominent social scientists.*

Clark to M. Brewster Smith [Social Psychologist with the Social Science Research Council, New York], September 15, 1952

In line with the idea that social science knowledge should be made available wherever it can be of practical value, several of us have collaborated in preparing the enclosed statement summarizing the evidence on the effects of segregation and the consequences of desegregation. When we started to work on this summary, we had no clear idea as to how the statement might be used. We did know, however, that the problem was a pressing one and felt that there was relevant social science information that ought to be made available.

Shortly after we started this project, the attorneys for the National Association for the Advancement of Colored People learned about what we were doing and expressed considerable interest in it. They were working on the briefs in three cases now pending before the United States Supreme Court involving the validity of racial segregation in primary and secondary schools. They have now requested that the result of our work be filed as an Appendix to the briefs in these cases, for the purpose of bringing this information to the attention of the Supreme Court. We agreed, but in the light of the importance of this specific function, we felt that this statement should be reviewed by about twenty or twenty-five social scientists who have worked in this area. In order that this should not appear to be the private notion of the few of us who prepared the statements, we felt that it should bear the signatures of those of us who are in substantial agreement with its content. Unfortunately, the time available for this particular use of the statement does not permit revisions. It must be in the hands of the printers by the end of this week.

Enclosed you will find a blank on which you can indicate whether you do or do not give endorsement to the statement for the purpose indicated. Please return this immediately in the enclosed stamped, self-addressed envelope.

Note: Eventually the social science statement was signed by 32 social scientists, including Floyd and Gordon Allport, Hadley Cantril, Allison Davis, David Krech, Theodore Newcomb, Else Frenkel-Brunswik, Daniel Katz, Gardner Murphy, Nevitt Sanford, Otto Klineberg, Jerome Bruner, and Brewster Smith. Of the 32, 3 were still alive on the fiftieth anniversary of the Brown v. Board decision in May 2004: Jerome Bruner, Brewster Smith, and Kenneth Clark.

The following three letters are between Clark and NAACP chief counsel Thurgood Marshall, the last of which shows Clark's sense of humor.

Clark to Thurgood Marshall, December 5, 1952

Enclosed is the statement in reply to the questions raised by the attorneys for the State of South Carolina in their brief. As you can see, this statement concerns itself primarily with their attack on the validity of our conclusions concerning the detrimental effects of segregation on the personality of Negro children. I hope that you will find it useful . . .

[From the attached three-page statement] . . . In general, it is clear that the attorneys for the state of South Carolina have attempted to confuse the basic fact that there is now a consensus of social science knowledge which clearly indicates that segregation is detrimental to the personality of the individuals who are the victims. They have attempted to create this confusion by seeking to balance the weight of factual information which we have accumulated and presented with a host of out dated speculative opinions which they present as if they were equivalent to facts. It is clear from their own quotations that the opinions which they offer reflect more the racial biases of their authors than their knowledge of the most recent development in this field or their ability to think objectively about these problems.

Thurgood Marshall to Clark and 16 Attorneys, January 20, 1953

We are going to hold a small conference here in New York City among a selected group of our lawyers for the purpose of getting down on paper a program of legal action for the immediate future. We hope to agree upon areas of emphasis, procedures, and methods of cooperation among the lawyers and units of the N.A.A.C.P. in the proposed legal program.

In order to do this we need your cooperation and hope that you can so arrange your schedule as to be with us in New York from the night of February 26th to March 1st. . . . The subjects we expect to cover are as follows: Education, recreation, housing, transportation and places of public accommodation . . .

Clark to Thurgood Marshall, January 23, 1953

I accept with pleasure your invitation to participate in your small conference of "a select group of our lawyers." Your sudden decision to elevate me from the lowly status of a Ph.D. in psychology to that Olympian peak of a member of the legal profession leaves me stunned with happiness. Words almost fail me as I contemplate the implications of this promotion . . . I cannot understand how I could possibly deserve such a warm demonstration of your highest esteem. To be listed among such great minds as Reeves and Carter fills me with humility and awe. I thought to myself, look how far you have come Kenneth since those terrible days of the Clarendon case when you were being continuously told that a Ph.D. was lower than a worm and a Ph.D. in psychology lower than that. With one grand gesture Mr. Marshall, you have restored my self-esteem. You have freed me from the burdensome feelings of inferiority. In fact, you have undone, with one memorandum, what these many years of racial segregation and discrimination have done to my personality. You have made me a new man . . . P. S. I will be there. Just try to keep me away.

Note: *After listening to testimony and questioning attorneys on both sides of the arguments on the various school desegregation cases, the Supreme Court decided to put the cases on hold and call for rearguments in October 1953 (later changed to December). The court issued a set of five questions for which they wanted additional information at the next hearings. One of those – Question No. 4 – would involve Clark and his social science colleagues. The question was: "Assuming it is decided that segregation in public schools violates the Fourteenth Amendment, (a) would a decree necessarily follow providing that, within the limits set by normal geographic school districting, Negro children should forthwith be admitted to schools of their choice, or (b) may this Court, in the exercise of its equity powers, permit an effective gradual adjustment to be brought about from existing segregated systems to a system not based on color distinctions?" (Kluger, 1975, p. 615). In plain English, the Court asked, if we rule that segregation is unlawful, do we require schools to desegregate at once or gradually over time? Clark was asked by the NAACP to gather information to answer this question and he wrote to many of his social science colleagues for help.*

Isidor Chein [Social Psychologist, New York University] to Clark, August 5, 1953

. . . I think that the gradual adjustment idea might work if the decree not merely specifies effectiveness, but also specified a procedure which bears promise of being effective and of minimizing dangers . . . It should make clear that segregation per se is unconstitutional and that any delay in eliminating it should not be taken to imply any doubt on this point . . . The introduction of Negroes into white schools in the form of segregated classes will not be acceptable as a first step toward integration . . . A definite time limit should be set by which the adjustment must be completed . . . None of the above should be taken to imply that I favor the gradual change idea. There are too many ways in which the spirit of the above plan can be violated and, hence, its effects violated. I am merely saying that, if the gradual change plan is adopted, this is the only way it will work.

Theodore Newcomb [Social Psychologist, University of Michigan] to Clark,
August 10, 1953

. . . It seems to me very important (both scientifically and tactically) to make clear that we have no scientific evidence which would contravene the usual assumption that attempts to enforce a sudden and complete change not only might have very serious results but might be deleterious to good race relations in the long run. As I assume you agree, the policy should be that, "The only way to begin is to begin, but you don't begin and end at the same moment." . . . There are, of course, many studies of attitude change which show that those who take extreme positions are not only hard to change toward the opposite direction, but may become even more set in their attitudes by the influence attempt . . . Attempts to change attitudes which are recognized as such will be resisted by those strongly opposed, and individuals at each extreme will provide social reinforcement for each other, thus leading to increasing differentiation, or polarization.

Floyd Allport [Social Psychologist, Syracuse University] to Clark, August 18, 1953

. . . I do not know exactly what is involved in changing from Negro school segregation to non-segregation. Your letter implies that to make this change suddenly would be upsetting. It may be that there are institutional arrangements that would have to be worked out and would take some time. If, however, what is implied is a gradual series of steps toward non-segregation in which, for example, an increasing number of areas or schools would become non-segregated through time, I am wondering whether this is a wise procedure. From a purely theoretical standpoint it would seem to me better to make the shift all at once. When people understand that the legal structure has changed and there is no hesitancy about putting the rule into effect, I think they are more likely to go along with it than in a step-by-step procedure, which seems in a way apologetic.

Note: When the Court made its decision to overturn Plessy v. Ferguson, *it was followed by a second decision, often called* Brown II, *rendered on May 31, 1955. It addressed the time course, ordering that the desegregation of public schools should proceed "with all deliberate speed" (quoted in Kluger, 1975, p. 745). The wording was intended as a compromise between those who favored immediacy and those who argued for a gradual transition. The wording has been labeled oxymoronic (Tucker, 1994), and indeed, it allowed school districts to delay desegregation efforts for as much as 20 more years.*

The following exchange of letters is with Elizabeth Waring, the wife of federal judge Julius Waties Waring, who presided over the South Carolina case that would be part of the collection of school desegregation cases heard as Brown v. Board *(see Kluger, 1975, Chapter 13). Kenneth Clark had testified before Judge Waring in the South Carolina case. In his letter he reveals some of the anecdotal data that addresses the complexity of racism in the South and North.*

Elizabeth Avery Waring to Clark, August 16, 1953

...Judge Waring and I admired your contribution on the WEVD Radio program last Friday night. Your ATTACK was strong and you never let them put you on the defensive and always you were quiet and self assured with the basis and strength of your scientific knowledge and truth in the rightness of Negro RIGHTS. Your own innate self respect and dignity shone out over those unseen Radio wires and you made the White man look confused, sympathetic though he was and intended to be...

Negroes are not human beings to Southerners and to many other people. That idea infects the North and has been more or less the attitude of the Anglo-Saxon race... The Supreme Court has only this simple decision to make "Are Negroes people – are Negroes and all colored skinned people human beings – are they people?" If they are human beings like white skinned people the decision is simple and only justice need concern the Supreme Court not how it should be carried out ... Think this over wise doctor and make it your own wisdom. I know this is the core of the problem.

All good wishes and while this letter is my own idea and not the Judge's (who cannot enter into this discussion as he is involved in the Clarendon Segregation Case) still he joins me in best regards and congratulations on your superb Radio debate last week.

Clark to Elizabeth Avery Waring, September 4, 1953

It was most kind of you to write your comments concerning my contribution on the radio panel. I deeply appreciate your thoughtfulness and your keen analysis of the difficult problem which confronted us on that program . . .

My recent trip through the South has left me even more confused about America and its racial problem. My wife and I motored to Hot Springs [Arkansas, the family home of Mamie Clark] going the southern way through Virginia and Tennessee. We were treated with utmost respect, warmth and graciousness by all of the white tradesmen with whom we had occasion to deal. They seemed interested in us as human beings, concerned with our origin and destination and at times seemed particularly anxious to communicate to us that they were seeking desperately to show that they were decent human beings, and they wanted us to see them as such rather than as critical and unjust people. It could be that this was merely good business, but I believe that it was something more than that. I sincerely believe that many whites of the South as much as Negroes are straining to break the shackles of this artificial racial prejudice which binds them. They need help I agree with you. It is up to the forces of the federal courts and courageous individuals such as your Judge to help them and lead them through this darkness.

Paradoxically, we drove back the northern way through Illinois, Indiana, Ohio and Pennsylvania and met our only sign of barbaric racial prejudices in southern Pennsylvania. There it was impossible for us to get lodging for the night at any of the motels that we tried. We went to one after another that had vacancy signs and in spite of the fact that we had two children with us, no one would take us in. We saw the corrosive signs of racial ignorance on their faces. One man was kind enough in Washington, Pennsylvania to direct us to a Negro motel on a side road. By that time we were all fatigued with sleep and hurt. The next morning we were unable to get breakfast in the first place we tried because all of the tables "were reserved". Having slept, I had enough energy to tell the woman who told us this how childish she was being and how sorry I felt for her. The inconsistency of America was indicated by the fact that about a mile down the road we stopped into a finer place where the people were most gracious and had an excellent breakfast . . .

I am confused, but I still have hope. I shall continue to have hope as long as we continue to fight and as long as there are people like you and the Judge to continue to help us fight in this uncompromising way.

Note: Monday, May 17, 1954, afforded a flashbulb memory for many African Americans and perhaps anyone else, regardless of color, for whom the Supreme Court decision had special salience. Word spread quickly of the Court's unanimous decision that had declared school segregation illegal. And friends and colleagues wrote to congratulate Clark for his role in what is arguably the most important American court decision of the twentieth century. Most of the letters that follow are representative of the many letters that Clark received in the weeks following the Court's decision.

Otto Klineberg [United Nations Educational, Scientific, and Cultural Organization, Paris] to Clark, May 18, 1954

The great news has just reached me, and I am writing immediately because I know how you must be feeling, and because I want to take this occasion to congratulate you personally for the wonderful job that you have done. Although a number of social scientists did work with you, I have always felt that without your leadership and enthusiasm the task would not have been accomplished nearly so well. I noted with the very greatest interest that there were a few references in the Supreme Court decision which indicated that what we collectively had to say did not go entirely unnoticed.

Please tell our friends at the NAACP that I send my warmest congratulations and friendliest personal greetings on the occasion of what is really a very great victory.

Clark to Otto Klineberg, June 7, 1954

These three weeks since the Court's decision have been in many respects the most exciting period of my life. Starting from about 2:00 p.m. on May 17th, Mamie, Thurgood, Bob Carter and the entire staff of the Legal Defense and Educational Division of the NAACP and all of our friends have been celebrating. The first three or four days we were in the clouds and refused to be brought down to earth by a consideration of the really serious problems which we must now all face.

There are so many things which I wanted to enjoy with you during this period. My only regret is that you were not here to celebrate with us the victory of which you were so much a part. The Court left no doubt that it was basing its decision as much upon contemporary social science knowledge and theory as it was basing it upon law. Anyone who knows this field knows that you have been in the forefront of providing the basic facts upon which we could move from the ideas about racial differences which were prevalent at the time of the Plessy decision to those which we now hold and which made the present decision possible and tenable. It is difficult to write a letter such as this to a very dear friend and former teacher. It is probably easier to write than to tell you face to face what I have felt and what I feel about my academic and personal associations with you.

I considered it one of the most important events of my life that I was privileged to work with you so closely and so directly at Columbia University. I knew then as I know now, that something more than a purely academic problem for a Ph.D. was being incubated. Your work and your insistence that the problems of racial differences should be approached with the same scientific objectivity with which other problems in psychology were studied, changed the approach and atmosphere of this problem from one of flagrant and disguised expression of biases, and stimulated and inspired a number of us to continue to work in this direction. I do not think there is any doubt that you almost single handedly made this area of psychology respectable academically. The Supreme Court has put the final stamp of general world wide acceptance upon the validity of this work. You, Otto, can be justly proud. Your children and your academic children are most proud of you.

Gertrude Folks Zimand [General Secretary, National Child Labor Committee]
to Clark, May 18, 1954

I first learned of the Supreme Court decision as I was walking home from the office last night. I am so happy about it. I could not imagine any other decision, and yet I was very much afraid that "States' Rights" in the field of education might be used. And I had hardly dared for a unanimous verdict.

The social scientists played a large role in this and you are to be congratulated for your part in it. I know how much hard work and thought you have given to these cases. And I know also that this decision will not mean any rest from your labors but that the social scientists will be even more important than the lawyers in working out methods of effecting the change . . .

Gordon W. Allport [Social Psychologist, Harvard University]
to Clark, May 19, 1954

You are probably receiving congratulations on all sides. Let me add my word of admiration for your Herculean labors and adroit handling of social science evidence for proper presentation to the Supreme Court. The happy outcome marks an epoch in the development of social science, in the history of the Negro race, and in the improvement of American foreign relations. Since you had a large part to play in all these achievements I congratulate you with all my heart.

Clark to Gordon W. Allport, June 7, 1954

Your kind letter of congratulations was deeply appreciated. I cannot accept these congratulations, however, without expressing my gratitude to you and the other social scientists who helped us prepare and present the materials which the

Court relied on for so much of the basis of its decision. This decision, I believe, is a landmark in the development and practical significance of the social sciences.

Alberta C. J. Lewis [Secretary, Friends of the Northside Center for Child Development] to Clark, May 27, 1954

Each member of The Friends of the Northside Center has been vicariously basking in glory. Our pride knows no bounds . . . You have contributed in a major degree to the progress of democracy in America. You have been able to influence the decision of the most authoritative body in our land. And last, but not least, you have assisted in the future development of the education, cultural, and economic life of the Negro citizens of America.

Clark to Alberta C. J. Lewis, June 16, 1954

Of all the letters which I have received congratulating me on the small part which I played in obtaining the Supreme Court decision which outlawed segregated schools, the letter which you wrote for the Friends of the Northside Center was the most heart warming. The friendly, dignified sincerity affected me deeply . . .

As momentous as that decision was, it has not solved our basic social problems. It has only removed some of the obstacles in the path of the solution. Those of us who have been working toward making a better life for our children must continue to work with the same good will, clarity, intelligence and courage until that decision is translated into social reality.

Buell Gallagher [President, City College of New York] to Clark, May 30, 1954

This is literally the first ten minutes of my waking hours since *The Decision* which I have been able to wrest from a tyrannical schedule to write these lines.

With you, I am proud, deeply moved, and humbly grateful. That the real task is now before us is the sobering meaning of the hour.

But I cannot let the moment of rejoicing pass without entering in the record my profound appreciation of your part in setting straight the course of American history.

Clark to Buell Gallagher, June 7, 1954

It is with profound thanks that I accept your expression of congratulations on my small role in the recent Supreme Court decision on segregated schools. This decision is in fact a landmark in the struggle of man for the goals of democracy. It is a significant contribution of the American people in the making of a better and happier world for all men. We can all be justly proud that we are part of a nation in which such a demonstration of the meaning of democracy is possible. In a very real sense, we are all responsible for this historic decision.

Epilogue

Kenneth Clark, Thurgood Marshall, and all of the others who worked so diligently and so passionately to end the legalized racism of segregated schools were keenly aware that the problems of segregation would not be done away with overnight, even though the law of the land had changed. Yet it is unlikely that in their worst-case scenarios they ever imagined how gradual gradualness would be, how interminably slow "deliberate speed" would be. Many of the affected states dodged, delayed, stalled, and otherwise used every tactic – legal and illegal – to avoid compliance with the 1954 decision, such that many school districts maintained segregated schools into the 1970s.

The court decision was clearly monumentally important for those who opposed segregation, yet it was important for psychology as well. Indeed, it could be described as a watershed event in the history of psychology: the first time ever that the Supreme Court cited psychological research as a basis for changing federal law. If a science ever wanted evidence of its worth, what could be more validating? As Kenneth Clark wrote in his letter to Gordon Allport cited above, "This decision, I believe, is a landmark in the development and practical significance of the social sciences." Surely this incredible event – this affirmation of the value of psychology by the highest court in the land – was cause for celebration by psychologists.

Perhaps the American Psychological Association (APA) issued a press release to call attention to the role psychology played in the court case. No doubt the APA sent congratulatory telegrams to Clark, Chein, and Cook for their role in assembling the social science evidence for the Court. Perhaps the APA Board of Directors issued an official commendation for the psychologists who had used their science for such public good. In fact, none of these things happened. There were no press releases from the APA, no commendations from the APA Board, and no telegrams or letters from the APA to the psychologists involved. Although such actions would almost certainly occur today under similar circumstances, 1954 was a different time – America was different, the APA was different, psychologists were different. In brief, many Americans believed in the separation of the races, and psychologists too were divided in their beliefs about race. The APA would not have been able to take a stand in favor of the *Brown v. Board* decision without angering many of its members. And so the Association allowed what might be psychological science's greatest triumph to go officially unnoticed (Benjamin & Crouse, 2002).

Of course the *Brown* decision, although it brought about sweeping changes in the Jim Crow laws of the South that had hindered African Americans in so many ways, such as housing, employment, voting, public transportation, and access to many public places such as hotels, restaurants, and movie theaters, it did not eliminate prejudice and discrimination. Speaking at a conference on the thirtieth anniversary of *Brown*, Kenneth Clark (1986) said:

> Thirty years after *Brown*, I must accept the fact that my wife left this earth despondent at seeing that damage to children is being knowingly and silently accepted by a nation that claims to be democratic. Thirty years after *Brown*, I feel a sense of hopelessness, rather than optimism, because the underlying theme of *Plessy* and the explicit statements of *Dred Scott* persist. The majority of Americans still believe in and vote on the assumption that Blacks are not worthy of the respect, and the acceptance of their humanity, which our democracy provides to others. (p. 21)

Mamie Clark died of cancer in 1983, but not before she witnessed her husband elected president of the Society for the Psychological Study of Social Issues (SPSSI) and of the American Psychological Association. In fact, Kenneth Clark is the only African-American president of the APA in its more than 110-year history (see Pickren & Tomes, 2002 for a discussion of Clark's legacy for the APA). The fact that racism persists in the twenty-first century is a sad reality. Still, Kenneth and Mamie Clark did their part to move America toward a hoped-for equality. Their place in American history is an honored one, secured by the fact that their work as psychologists and social activists changed the course of history.

Suggested Readings

Benjamin, L. T., Jr., & Crouse, E. M. (2002). The American Psychological Association's response to *Brown v. Board of Education*: The case of Kenneth B. Clark. *American Psychologist, 57*, 38–50.
    This article describes the role of Kenneth Clark in the *Brown* decision and the response from the APA to scientific psychology's moment in a great spotlight.
Clark, K. B. (1953). Desegregation: An appraisal of the evidence. *Journal of Social Issues, 9* (4), 1–77.
    An extensive treatment of the data on desegregation efforts.
Clark, K. B. (1965). *Dark ghetto: Dilemmas of social power.* New York: Harper & Row.
    Clark's moving and insightful treatise on the ghetto and its importance to the maintenance of white power and black powerlessness.
Jackson, J. P., Jr. (2001). *Social scientists for social justice: Making the case against segregation.* New York: New York University Press.
    The most scholarly treatment of the scientific evidence and the work of the social scientists in the cases leading to *Brown* and the *Brown* decision itself.
Kluger, R. (1975). *Simple justice: The history of* Brown v. Board of Education *and Black America's struggle for equality.* New York: Random House.
    An extremely readable account of the history of the *Brown* decision, with rich biographical descriptions of the many individuals involved.

Markowitz, G., & Rosner, D. (1996). *Children, race, and power: Kenneth and Mamie Clark's Northside Center.* Charlottesville: University of Virginia Press.

A history of Harlem's Northside Center for Child Development, founded by the Clarks and administered by Mamie Clark until her death in 1983.

Phillips, L. (2000). Recontextualizing Kenneth B. Clark: An Afrocentric perspective on the paradoxical legacy of a model psychologist–activist. *History of Psychology, 3,* 142–167.

This article describes the lifelong social activism of Kenneth Clark and the controversy it created in both white and black communities.

Philogene, G. (Ed.). (2004). *Racial identity in context: The legacy of Kenneth B. Clark.* Washington, DC: American Psychological Association.

An edited book whose chapters explore current racial topics as extensions of the influence of Kenneth Clark.

Williams, J. (1998). *Thurgood Marshall: American revolutionary.* New York: Times Books.

A fascinating study of one of America's most distinguished jurists.

References

Allport, G. W. (1954). *The nature of prejudice*. Cambridge, MA: Addison-Wesley.

Allport, G. W., et al. (1936). Psychologists and present-day activities. *Psychological Exchange*, 4, 226–227. [Publication of the SPSSI organizing letter from the 18-member committee.]

Angell, J. R. (1907). The province of functional psychology. *Psychological Review*, 14, 61–91.

Appendix to Appellants' Briefs. (1975). The effects of segregation and the consequences of desegregation: A social science statement. In P. B. Kurland & G. Casper (Eds.), *Landmark briefs and arguments of the Supreme Court of the United States: Constitutional law* (Vol. 49, pp. 43–61). Arlington, VA: University Publications of America.

Ash, M. G. (1995). *Gestalt psychology in German culture, 1890–1967: Holism and the quest for objectivity*. New York: Cambridge University Press.

August, E. (1975). *John Stuart Mill: A mind at large*. London: Vision Press.

Bache, R. M. (1895). Reaction time with reference to race. *Psychological Review*, 2, 475–486.

Benjamin, L. T., Jr. (1977). The Psychological Round Table: Revolution of 1936. *American Psychologist*, 32, 542–549.

Benjamin, L. T., Jr. (1988). A history of teaching machines. *American Psychologist*, 43, 703–712.

Benjamin, L. T., Jr. (1991). *Harry Kirke Wolfe: Pioneer in psychology*. Lincoln, NE: University of Nebraska Press.

Benjamin, L. T., Jr. (1997). The origin of psychological species: A history of the beginnings of the divisions of the American Psychological Association. *American Psychologist*, 52, 725–732.

Benjamin, L. T., Jr. (Ed.) (1997). *A history of psychology: Original sources and contemporary research* (2nd edn.). New York: McGraw-Hill.

Benjamin, L. T., Jr. (2000). The psychology laboratory at the turn of the century. *American Psychologist*, 55, 318–321.

Benjamin, L. T., Jr., & Crouse, E. M. (2002). The American Psychological Association's response to *Brown v. Board of Education*: The case of Kenneth B. Clark. *American Psychologist*, 57, 38–50.

Benjamin, L. T., Jr., Durkin, M., Link, M., Vestal, M., & Acord, J. (1992). Wundt's American doctoral students. *American Psychologist*, 47, 123–131.

Benjamin, L. T., Jr., & Nielsen-Gammon, E. (1999). B. F. Skinner and psychotechnology: The case of the heir conditioner. *Review of General Psychology*, 3, 155–167.

Benschop, R., & Draaisma, D. (2000). In pursuit of precision: The calibration of minds and machines in late nineteenth-century psychology. *Annals of Science*, 57, 1–25.

Boring, E. G. (1938). The Society of Experimental Psychologists, 1904–1938. *American Journal of Psychology, 51*, 410–423.

Boring, E. G. (1950). *A history of experimental psychology* (2nd edn.). New York: Appleton-Century-Crofts.

Boring, E. G. (1967). Titchener's Experimentalists. *Journal of the History of the Behavioral Sciences, 3*, 315–325.

Box-bred babies. (1963). *Time*, February 15, p. 72.

Brown, J. F. (1936). *Psychology and the social order: An introduction to the dynamic study of social fields*. New York: McGraw-Hill.

Bruce, D. B. (1986). Lashley's shift from bacteriology to neuropsychology, 1910–1917, and the influence of Jennings, Watson, and Franz. *Journal of the History of the Behavioral Sciences, 22*, 27–44.

Bruce, D. B. (1991). Integrations of Lashley. In G. A. Kimble, M. Wertheimer, & C. L. White (Eds.), *Portraits of pioneers in psychology* (pp. 306–323). Washington, DC: American Psychological Association.

Bruner, F. G. (1912). The primitive races in America. *Psychological Bulletin, 9*, 380–390.

Buckley, K. W. (1989). *Mechanical man: John Broadus Watson and the beginnings of behaviorism*. New York: Guilford Press.

Bunn, G. C. (1997). The lie detector, Wonder Woman, and liberty: The life and work of William Moulton Marston. *History of the Human Sciences, 10*, 91–119.

Burkhardt, F., Smith, S., Browne, J., & Richmond, M. (Eds.) (1991). *The correspondence of Charles Darwin, Volume 7, 1858–1859*. New York: Cambridge University Press.

Burkhardt, F., Smith, S., Kohn, D., & Montgomery, W. (Eds.) (1985). *The correspondence of Charles Darwin, Volume 1, 1826–1831*. New York: Cambridge University Press.

Buss, D. M. (2003). *Evolutionary psychology: The new science of the mind* (2nd edn.). New York: Allyn & Bacon.

Butterfield, H. (1931). *The Whig interpretation of history*. London: G. Bell & Sons.

Buzan, D. S. (2004). I was not a lab rat. *The Guardian*, March 12. Story from the World Wide Web.

Cadwallader, T., & Cadwallader, J. (1990). Christine Ladd-Franklin. In A. N. O'Connell & N. F. Russo (Eds.), *Women in psychology: A bio-bibliographic sourcebook* (pp. 220–229). Westport, CT: Greenwood Press.

Calkins, M. W. (1892). A suggested classification of cases of association. *Philosophical Review, 1*, 389–402.

Calkins, M. W. (1930). Autobiography. In C. Murchison (Ed.), *A history of psychology in autobiography* (Vol. 1, pp. 31–62). Worcester, MA: Clark University Press.

Capshew, J. H. (1992). Psychologists on site: A reconnaissance of the historiography of the laboratory. *American Psychologist, 47*, 132–142.

Capshew, J. H. (1993). Engineering behavior: Project Pigeon, World War II, and the conditioning of B. F. Skinner. *Technology and Culture, 34*, 835–857.

Carr, E. H. (1961). *What is history?* New York: Random House.

Cattell, J. McK. (1885). The inertia of the eye and brain. *Brain, 8*, 295–312.

Cattell, J. McK. (1886). The time taken up by cerebral operations. *Mind, 11*, 220–242.

Christison, J. S. (1897). *Crime and criminals*. Chicago: W. T. Keener.

Christison, J. S. (1906). *The tragedy of Chicago: A study in hypnotism*. Author.

Clark, K. B. (n.d.). Untitled manuscript. Kenneth Bancroft Clark Papers. Library of Congress. Washington, DC.

Clark, K. B. (1950). *The effects of prejudice and discrimination on personality development* (Mid-century White House Conference on Children and Youth). Washington, DC: Federal Security Agency, Children's Bureau.

Clark, K. B. (1986). A personal view of the background and developments since the *Brown* decision. In L. P. Miller (Ed.), *Brown plus thirty: Perspectives on desegregation* (pp. 18–21). New York: Metropolitan Center for Educational Research, Development, and Training, New York University.

Cocks, G. (1988). *Psychotherapy in the Third Reich: The Goring Institute*. New York: Oxford University Press.

Collingwood, R. G. (1946). *The idea of history*. London: Oxford University Press.

Commager, H. S. (1965). *The nature and study of history*. Columbus, OH: Charles Merrill.

Coon, D. J. (1992). Testing the limits of sense and science: American experimental psychologists combat spiritualism, 1880–1920. *American Psychologist, 47,* 143–151.

Cox, C. M. (1926). *Genetic studies of genius: Vol. II. The early mental traits of three hundred geniuses*. Stanford, CA: Stanford University Press.

Crannell, C. W. (1970). Wolfgang Köhler. *Journal of the History of the Behavioral Sciences, 6,* 267–268.

Cranston, M. (1957). *John Locke: A biography*. Boston: Longmans, Green.

Daniels, R. V. (1981). *Studying history: How and why* (3rd edn.). Englewood Cliffs, NJ: Prentice-Hall.

Danziger, K. (1990). *Constructing the subject: Historical origins of psychological research*. Cambridge: Cambridge University Press.

Darwin, C. (1838–1843). *The zoology of the voyage of H. M. S. Beagle under the command of Captain Fitzroy R. N., during the years 1832 to 1836*. London: Smith, Elder, & Co.

Darwin, C. R. (1859). *On the origin of species by means of natural selection, or the preservation of favored races in the struggle for life*. London: John Murray.

Dewsbury, D. A. (1993). The boys of summer at the end of summer: The Watson–Lashley correspondence of the 1950s. *Psychological Reports, 72,* 263–269.

Dewsbury, D. A. (2002). Constructing representations of Karl Spencer Lashley. *Journal of the History of the Behavioral Sciences, 38,* 225–245.

Dewsbury, D. A. (2003). James Rowland Angell: Born administrator. In G. A. Kimble & M. Wertheimer (Eds.), *Portraits of pioneers in psychology* (Vol. 5, pp. 57–71). Washington, DC: American Psychological Association.

Dewsbury, D. A. (2005). *Monkey farm: A history of the Yerkes Laboratories of Primate Biology, 1930–1965*. Lewisburg, PA: Bucknell University Press.

Donn, L. (1988). *Freud and Jung: Years of friendship, years of loss*. New York: Scribner's.

Epstein, R., & Bailey, M. (1995). Babies in boxes. *Psychology Today,* November/December, pp. 12–13.

Fernberger, S. W. (1921). Further statistics of the American Psychological Association. *Psychological Bulletin, 18,* 569–572.

Fernberger, S. W. (1928). Statistical analyses of the members and associates of the American Psychological Association. *Psychological Review, 35,* 447–465.

Finison, L. J. (1976). Unemployment, politics, and the history of organized psychology. *American Psychologist, 31,* 747–755.

Finison, L. J. (1979). An aspect of the early history of the Society for the Psychological Study of Social Issues: Psychologists and labor. *Journal of the History of the Behavioral Sciences, 15,* 29–37.

French, F. C. (1898). The place of experimental psychology in the undergraduate course. *Psychological Review, 5,* 510–512.

Freud, S. (1901). *The psychopathology of everyday life.* In *Standard Edition,* Vol. 6. London: Hogarth Press.

Freud, S. (1910). *Five lectures on psychoanalysis.* In *Standard Edition,* Vol. 11. London: Hogarth Press.

Fuchs, A. H. (2000). Contributions of American mental philosophers to psychology in the United States. *History of Psychology, 3,* 3–19.

Furumoto, L. (1989). The new history of psychology. In I. S. Cohen (Ed.), *The G. Stanley Hall Lecture Series* (Vol. 9, pp. 8–34). Washington, DC: American Psychological Association.

Furumoto, L. (1990). Mary Whiton Calkins (1863–1930). In A. N. O'Connell & N. F. Russo (Eds.), *Women in psychology: A bio-bibliographic sourcebook* (pp. 57–65). Westport, CT: Greenwood Press.

Furumoto, L. (1991). From "paired associates" to a psychology of self: The intellectual odyssey of Mary Whiton Calkins. In G. A. Kimble, M. Wertheimer, & C. L. White (Eds.), *Portraits of pioneers in psychology* (Vol. 1, pp. 56–72). Hillsdale, NJ: Lawrence Erlbaum.

Gay, P. (1988). *Freud: A life for our time.* New York: Norton.

Gilderhus, M. T. (1992). *History and historians: A historiographical introduction* (2nd edn.). Englewood Cliffs, NJ: Prentice-Hall.

Gilliams, E. L. (1907). Letter to Hugo Münsterberg, September 12. Münsterberg Papers, Rare Books and Manuscripts Room, Boston Public Library.

Glassman, P. (1985). *J. S. Mill: The evolution of a genius.* Gainesville: University of Florida Press.

Goodwin, C. J. (1990). The Experimentalists and the APA: The Round Tables of the 1920s. Paper presented at the annual meeting of the American Psychological Association, Boston.

Guthrie, R. V. (1990). Mamie Phipps Clark: 1917–1983. In A. N. O'Connell & N. F. Russo (Eds.), *Women in psychology: A bio-bibliographic sourcebook* (pp. 66–74). New York: Greenwood Press.

Guthrie, R. V. (1998). *Even the rat was white: A historical view of psychology* (2nd edn.). Boston: Allyn & Bacon.

Guthrie, R. V. (2000). Francis Cecil Sumner: The first African American pioneer in psychology. In G. A. Kimble & M. Wertheimer (Eds.), *Portraits of pioneers in psychology* (Vol. 4, pp. 181–193). Washington, DC: American Psychological Association.

Hale, M., Jr. (1980). *Human science and social order: Hugo Münsterberg and the origins of applied psychology.* Philadelphia: Temple University Press.

Hale, N. G., Jr. (1979). Freud's Reich, the psychiatric establishment, and the founding of the American Psychoanalytic Association: Professional styles in conflict. *Journal of the History of the Behavioral Sciences, 15,* 135–141.

Hardcastle, G. (2000). The cult of the experiment: The Psychological Round Table, 1936–1941. *History of Psychology, 3,* 344–370.

Harris, B. (1979). Whatever happened to little Albert? *American Psychologist, 34,* 151–160.

Harris, B. (1980). The FBI's files on APA and SPSSI: Description and implications. *American Psychologist, 35,* 1141–1144.

Harris, B. (1984). 'Give me a dozen healthy infants . . .': John B. Watson's popular advice on childrearing, women, and the family. In M. Lewin (Ed.), *In the shadow of the past: Psychology portrays the sexes* (pp. 126–154). New York: Columbia University Press.

Hayek, F. A. (1951). *John Stuart Mill and Harriet Taylor: Their friendship and subsequent marriage.* Chicago: University of Chicago Press.

Heidbreder, E. (1933). *Seven psychologies.* New York: Appleton-Century.

Helson, H. (1925). The psychology of Gestalt, Parts I and II. *American Journal of Psychology, 36,* 342–370, 494–526.

Helson, H. (1926). The psychology of Gestalt, Parts III and IV. *American Journal of Psychology, 37,* 25–62, 189–223.

Henle, M. (1978). One man against the Nazis: Wolfgang Köhler. *American Psychologist, 33,* 939–944.

Heyd, T. (1989). Mill and Comte on psychology. *Journal of the History of the Behavioral Sciences, 25,* 125–138.

Hilgard, E. R., Leary, D. E., & McGuire, G. R. (1991). The history of psychology: A survey and critical assessment. *Annual Review of Psychology, 42,* 79–107.

Hill, M. R. (1993). *Archival strategies and techniques.* Newbury Park, CA: Sage.

Hornstein, G. A. (1992). The return of the repressed: Psychology's problematic relations with psychoanalysis, 1909–1960. *American Psychologist, 47,* 254–263.

Hothersall, D. (2004). *History of psychology* (4th edn.). New York: McGraw Hill.

Huxley, A. (1932). *Brave new world.* New York: Harper & Brothers.

Jackson, J. P., Jr. (2001). *Social scientists for social justice: Making the case against segregation.* New York: New York University Press.

James, H. (Ed.) (1920). *The letters of William James* (2 vols.). Boston: Atlantic Monthly Press.

James, W. (1890). *The principles of psychology* (2 vols.). New York: Henry Holt.

James, W. (1892). *Psychology: A briefer course.* New York: Henry Holt.

James, W. (1909). The confidences of a "psychical researcher." *American Magazine, 68,* 580–589.

Jones, E. (1953, 1955, 1957). *The life and work of Sigmund Freud* (3 vols.). New York: Basic Books.

Jones, M. C. (1924). A laboratory study of fear: The case of Peter. *Pedagogical Seminary, 31,* 308–315.

Jung, C. G. (1906). On psychophysical relations of the association experiment. *Journal of Abnormal Psychology, 1,* 249–257.

Jung, C. G. (1910). The association method. *American Journal of Psychology, 21,* 219–269.

Jung, C. G. (1961). *Memories, dreams, reflections.* New York: Random House.

Keller, P. (1979). *States of belonging: German-American intellectuals and the First World War.* Cambridge, MA: Harvard University Press.

King, D. B., & Wertheimer, M. (2005). *Max Wertheimer & Gestalt theory.* New Brunswick, NJ: Transaction Publishers.

Klineberg, O. (1935). *Race differences.* New York: Harper & Row.

Kluger, R. (1975). *Simple justice: The history of Brown v. Board of Education and black America's struggle for equality.* New York: Random House.

Koffka, K. (1922). Perception: An introduction to Gestalt-theorie. *Psychological Bulletin, 19,* 531–585.

Krech, D., & Cartwright, D. (1956). On SPSSI's first twenty years. *American Psychologist, 11,* 470–473.

Lal, S. (2002). Giving children security: Mamie Phipps Clark and the racialization of child psychology. *American Psychologist, 57,* 20–28.

Leahey, T. H. (1981). The mistaken mirror: On Wundt and Titchener's psychologies. *Journal of the History of the Behavioral Sciences, 17*, 273–282.

Leahey, T. H. (2000). *A history of psychology: Main currents in psychological thought* (5th edn.). Englewood Cliffs, NJ: Prentice Hall.

Leahey, T. H., & Leahey, G. E. (1983). *Psychology's occult doubles: Psychology and the problem of pseudoscience.* Chicago: Nelson Hall.

Locke, J. (1689–1692). *Letters concerning toleration.* London: T. Longman, B. Law, & Son (1794 printing).

Locke, J. (1690). *Two treatises on government.* Cambridge: Cambridge University Press (1960 printing).

Locke, J. (1690). *An essay concerning human understanding.* Oxford: Clarendon Press (1975 printing).

Locke, J. (1693). *Some thoughts concerning education.* Woodbury: Barron's Educational Series (1964 printing).

Locke, J. (1695). *The reasonableness of Christianity: As delivered in the scriptures.* New York: Oxford University Press (2000 edn.).

Madigan, S., & O'Hara, R. (1992). Short-term memory at the turn of the century: Mary Whiton Calkins's memory research. *American Psychologist, 47*, 170–174.

Malthus, T. (1789/1914). *Essay on the principle of population.* New York: Dutton.

Markowitz, G., & Rosner, D. (1996). *Children, race, and power: Kenneth and Mamie Clark's Northside Center.* Charlottesville: University of Virginia Press.

McGuire, W. (Ed.) (1974). *The Freud/Jung letters: The correspondence between Sigmund Freud and C. G. Jung.* Princeton: Princeton University Press.

Mill, J. (1829). *Analysis of the phenomena of the human mind.* London: Baldwin and Cradock.

Mill, J. S. (1843). *A system of logic, ratiocinative and inductive.* London: Longmans, Green.

Mill, J. S. (1859). *On liberty.* New York: Henry Holt (1885 reprint).

Mill, J. S. (1869). *The subjection of women.* London: Longmans, Green.

Mill, J. S. (1873). *Autobiography.* Boston: Houghton Mifflin (1969 printing).

Miner, B. G. (1904). The changing attitude of American universities toward psychology. *Science, 20*, 299–307.

Moore, R. L. (1977). *In search of white crows: Spiritualism, parapsychology, and American culture.* New York: Oxford University Press.

Moore-Russell, M. E. (1978). The philosopher and society: John Locke and the English revolution. *Journal of the History of the Behavioral Sciences, 14*, 65–73.

Morawski, J. G. (Ed.) (1988). *The rise of experimentation in American psychology.* New Haven: Yale University Press.

Münsterberg, H. (1907). The third degree. *McClure's Magazine, 29*, 614–622.

Münsterberg, H. (1908a). *On the witness stand: Essays on psychology and crime.* New York: Doubleday, Page, & Co.

Münsterberg, H. (1908b). Hypnotism and crime. *McClure's Magazine, 30*, 317–322.

Münsterberg, H. (1909a). *Psychotherapy.* New York: Moffat, Yard, & Co.

Münsterberg, H. (1909b). *Psychology and the teacher.* New York: D. Appleton.

Münsterberg, H. (1913a). *Psychology and industrial efficiency.* Boston: Houghton Mifflin.

Münsterberg, H. (1913b). The mind of the juryman with a side-light on women as jurors. *Century Magazine, 86*, 711–716.

Münsterberg, H. (1915). *Business psychology.* Chicago: Lasalle Extension Service.

Münsterberg, H. (1916). *The photoplay: A psychological study.* New York: D. Appleton.

Münsterberg, M. (1922). *Hugo Münsterberg: His life and work.* New York: D. Appleton.

Murray, F. S., & Rowe, F. B. (1979). Psychology laboratories in the United States prior to 1900. *Teaching of Psychology, 6,* 19–21.

Napoli, D. S. (1981). *Architects of adjustment: The history of the psychological profession in the United States.* Port Washington, NY: Kennikat Press.

Nichols, H. (1893). The psychological laboratory at Harvard. *McClure's Magazine, 1,* October, 399–409.

Nichols, P. (2003). *Evolution's captain: The dark fate of the man who sailed Darwin around the world.* New York: HarperCollins.

O'Donnell, J. M. (1985). *The origins of behaviorism: American psychology, 1870–1920.* New York: New York University Press.

O'Neil, W. M., & Landauer, A. A. (1966). The phi-phenomenon: Turning point or rallying point. *Journal of the History of the Behavioral Sciences, 2,* 335–340.

On the Witness Stand. (1908). [Review of Münsterberg's book.] *The Nation, 86,* 472.

Packe, M. (1954). *The life of John Stuart Mill.* New York: Macmillan.

Pappe, H. O. (1960). *John Stuart Mill and the Harriet Taylor myth.* Melbourne: Melbourne University Press.

Perry, R. B. (1935). *The thought and character of William James* (2 vols.). Boston: Little, Brown.

Philogene, G. (2004). *Racial identity in context: The legacy of Kenneth B. Clark.* Washington, DC: American Psychological Association.

Pickren, W. E., & Tomes, H. (2002). The legacy of Kenneth B. Clark to the APA: The Board of Social and Ethical Responsibility for Psychology. *American Psychologist, 57,* 51–59.

Pruette, L. (1926). *G. Stanley Hall: A biography of a mind.* New York: D. Appleton.

Raby, P. (2001). *Alfred Russel Wallace: A life.* Princeton: Princeton University Press.

Richards, R. J. (1983). Why Darwin delayed, or interesting problems and models in the history of science. *Journal of the History of the Behavioral Sciences, 19,* 45–53.

Roesch, R. (2000). Forensic psychology. In A. Kazdin (Ed.), *Encyclopedia of psychology* (Vol. 3, pp. 383–386). Washington, DC and New York: American Psychological Association and Oxford University Press.

Rose, P. (1983). *Parallel lives: Five Victorian marriages.* New York: Alfred Knopf.

Rosenzweig, S. (1994). *The historic expedition to America (1909): Freud, Jung, and Hall the kingmaker.* St. Louis: Rana House.

Ross, D. (1972). *G. Stanley Hall: The psychologist as prophet.* Chicago: University of Chicago Press.

Russell, B. (1921). *The analysis of mind.* London: Allen & Unwin.

Rutherford, A. (2000). Radical behaviorism and psychology's public image: B. F. Skinner in the popular press, 1934–1990. *History of Psychology, 3,* 371–395.

Rutherford, A. (2003). B. F. Skinner's technology of behavior in American life: From culture to counterculture. *Journal of the History of the Behavioral Sciences, 39,* 1–23.

Rutherford, A. (In press.) Mother of behavior therapy and beyond: Mary Cover Jones and the study of the "whole child." In D. A. Dewsbury, L. T. Benjamin, Jr., & M. Wertheimer (Eds.), *Portraits of pioneers in psychology* (Vol. 6). Washington, DC & Mahwah, NJ: American Psychological Association and Lawrence Erlbaum.

Samelson, F. (1981). Struggle for scientific authority: The reception of Watson's behaviorism. *Journal of the History of the Behavioral Sciences, 17,* 399–425.

Scarborough, E., & Furumoto, L. (1987). *Untold lives: The first generation of American women psychologists.* New York: Columbia University Press.

Schlesinger, A., Jr. (1963). The historian as artist. *Atlantic Monthly, 12,* July, 35–41.

Schultz, D. (1990). *Intimate friends, dangerous rivals: The turbulent relationship between Freud and Jung.* Los Angeles: Jeremy Tarcher.

Shermer, M. (2002). *In Darwin's shadow: The life and science of Alfred Russel Wallace.* New York: Oxford.

Skinner, B. F. (1938). *The behavior of organisms.* New York: Appleton-Century.

Skinner, B. F. (1945). Baby in a box. *Ladies' Home Journal,* October, pp. 30–31, 135–136, 138.

Skinner, B. F. (1948). *Walden two.* New York: Macmillan.

Skinner, B. F. (1971). *Beyond freedom and dignity.* New York: Alfred A. Knopf.

Skinner, B. F. (1979). *The shaping of a behaviorist: Part two of an autobiography.* New York: Alfred A. Knopf.

Skinner, B. F. (1983). *A matter of consequences: Part three of an autobiography.* New York: Alfred A. Knopf.

Smith, L. D. (1992). On prediction and control: B. F. Skinner and the technological ideal. *American Psychologist, 47,* 216–223.

Sokal, M. M. (1981). *An education in psychology: James McKeen Cattell's journal and letters from Germany and England, 1880–1888.* Cambridge, MA: MIT Press.

Sokal, M. M. (1984). The Gestalt psychologists in behaviorist America. *American Historical Review, 89,* 1240–1263.

Sokal, M. M., Davis, A. B., & Merzbach, U. C. (1976). Laboratory instruments in the history of psychology. *Journal of the History of the Behavioral Sciences, 12,* 59–64.

Stagner, R. (1986). Reminiscences about the founding of SPSSI. *Journal of Social Issues, 42* (1), 35–42.

Stagner, R. (1988). *A history of psychological theories.* New York: Macmillan.

Steinbeck, J. (1939). *The grapes of wrath.* New York: Viking.

Stocking, G. W., Jr. (1965). On the limits of "presentism" and "historicism" in the historiography of the behavioral sciences. *Journal of the History of the Behavioral Sciences, 1,* 211–218.

Titchener, E. B. (1901–1905). *Experimental psychology* (4 vols.). New York: Macmillan.

Titchener, E. B. (1910). *A textbook of psychology.* New York: Macmillan.

Tucker, W. H. (1994). *The science and politics of racial research.* Urbana: University of Illinois Press.

Wallace, A. R. (1855). On the law which has regulated the introduction of new species. *Annals and Magazine of Natural History, 16,* September, 184–196.

Watson, J. B. (1910). The new science of animal behavior. *Harper's,* February, pp. 346–353.

Watson, J. B. (1913). Psychology as the behaviorist views it. *Psychological Review, 20,* 158–177.

Watson, J. B. (1914). *Behavior: An introduction to comparative psychology.* New York: Henry Holt.

Watson, J. B. (1919). *Psychology from the standpoint of a behaviorist.* Philadelphia: Lippincott.

Watson, J. B. (1928). *Psychological care of infant and child.* New York: Norton.

Watson, J. B. (1936). Autobiography. In C. Murchison, (Ed.), *A history of psychology in autobiography* (Vol. 3), pp. 271–281. Worcester, MA: Clark University Press.

Watson, J. B., & Morgan, J. J. B. (1917). Emotional reactions and psychological experimentation. *American Journal of Psychology, 28,* 163–174.

Wentworth, P. A. (1999). The moral of her story: Exploring the philosophical and religious commitments in Mary Whiton Calkins' self-psychology. *History of Psychology, 2,* 119–131.

Wertheimer, M. (1912). Experimentelle studien über das Sehen Bewegung, *Zeitschrift für Psychologie, 61*, 161–265. An English translation appears in T. Shipley (Ed.) (1961). *Classics in psychology*. New York: Philosophical Library.

White, R. K. (1968). *Nobody wanted war: Misperceptions in Vietnam and other wars*. New York: Doubleday.

Wiggam, A. E. (1928). *Exploring your mind with the psychologists*. New York: Bobbs-Merrill.

Wolfe, H. K. (1895). The new psychology in undergraduate work. *Psychological Review, 2*, 382–387.

Worcester, E. (1932). *Life's adventure: The story of a varied career*. New York: Scribner's.

Wright, R. (1994). *The moral animal – Why we are the way we are: The new science of evolutionary psychology*. New York: Pantheon Books.

Zenderland, L. (1998). *Measuring minds: Henry Herbert Goddard and the origins of American intelligence testing*. New York: Cambridge University Press.

Index

Adams, D. K., 178
Adams, F. J., 190
Aesop's Fables, 23
Ainsworth, M., 6
aircrib, 197–211
Albert, B., 155–6, 163
Aldrich, C. A., 208–9
Allport, F., 219, 221
Allport, G. W., 185, 187–8, 219, 225–7
American Association for Applied
    Psychology (AAAP), 186
American Philosophical Association, 113
American Psychological Association
    (APA), 71, 126, 133–5, 184, 186–8,
    190–1, 194, 227–8
Angell, F., 70, 115, 120, 125–7, 131
Angell, J. R., 131, 153
Angier, R. P., 135
Anthony, S. B., 5
archival research, 1–2
Archives of the History of American
    Psychology, 6–7, 186
archives, viii, 5–6

baby tender, *see* aircrib
Bache, R. M., 213
Bacon, F., 198
Bain, A., 49–50
Baird, J. W., 131
Baker, D. B., 7
Baldwin, J. M., 89, 154
Beagle, H.M.S., 28

Behavior of Organisms, The (1938), 198
behaviorism, 153–68, 171
Bell, A. G., 5, 55
Bentley, M., 71, 131
Berger, G. O., 58, 64
Berkeley, G., 15
Berlin Psychological Institute, 178
Bessey, C. E., 71, 75
Boas, F., 140
Bolton, T. L., 79
Boring, E. G., 127, 135
Brill, A., 139–40, 149
British Psychological Association, 113
Brown v. Board of Education (1954), 195,
    213–29
Brown, J. F., 186–8
Brown, R. R., 189
Bruner, F., 213
Bruner, J., 219
Butler, N. M., 66
Buzan, D. S., *see* Skinner, D.

Calkins, M. W., vii, 5, 12, 113–23, 128,
    132
    doctoral exam, 115
    offer of Radcliffe degree, 121–2
    study at Harvard University, 114–15,
    118–21
    at Wellesley College, 113–17, 122
Calkins, W., 119
Cantril, H., 219
Carr, E., 8

CPSIA information can be obtained at www.ICGtesting.com
Printed in the USA
LVOW102132180812

294927LV00004B/80/P